Life's Little Miseries

Helping Your Child with
the Disasters of Everyday Life

For parents and teachers
of children ages 3–12

Diane Lynch-Fraser

Lexington Books

An Imprint of Macmillan, Inc.
NEW YORK
Maxwell Macmillan Canada
TORONTO
Maxwell Macmillan International
NEW YORK • OXFORD • SINGAPORE • SYDNEY

Library of Congress Cataloging-in-Publication Data

Lynch-Fraser, Diane.
Life's little miseries : helping your child with the disasters of
everyday life : for parents and teachers of children ages 3–12 /
Diane Lynch-Fraser.
p. cm.
Includes bibliographical references and index.
ISBN 0–02–919323–0
1. Child rearing—United States.   2. Crisis management—United
States.   I. Title.
HQ769.L846   1992
649′.1—dc20
92–12816
CIP

Lexington Books
An Imprint of Macmillan, Inc.
866 Third Avenue, New York, N.Y. 10022

Maxwell Macmillan Canada, Inc.
1200 Eglinton Avenue East
Suite 200
Don Mills, Ontario M3C 3N1

Macmillan, Inc. is part of the Maxwell Communication
Group of Companies.

Printed in the United States of America

printing number
1   2   3   4   5   6   7   8   9   10

To Randy

Contents

Author's Note

The reader should remember two things when reading this book:

1. This book represents a bridge between research and casual parental advice. It is not a child development journal, nor is it a simple account of parents' experiences. It is intended to be a comprehensive guide written expressly for parents and teachers of children aged three to twelve. As I wanted this book to read like a story and at the same time to provide an authoritative view of the subject, I included all references in a bibliography at the end so that they would not interrupt the flow of the text. An appendix of family support groups is also included, to assist you in finding additional information on this subject and related issues.

2. Though I have tried consciously to avoid the use of sex-stereotyped language in my text, I have found that avoiding it completely can contribute to an awkward writing style. I have avoided the awkward phrase "he or she" and instead substituted gender-specific proper names where appropriate. As I have indicated in all of my previous books, I am anxiously waiting for English grammarians and linguists to develop a suitable nonsexist pronoun.

What Problem Solving Is and How It Can Help

Some time ago I was riding home from work on the bus with my eight-year-old daughter, Skye. On the surface the day had been uneventful. Skye stared blindly out the window at the passing traffic. Suddenly her hands pressed into fists. "I hate them. I hate them," she cried. "I want to smash their faces." She hid her face in her hands sobbing. Angry, sad, humiliated—Skye seemed all these things. And there I was, feeling useless, trying to think of just the right thing to say to make it all better!

But Skye wasn't two years old anymore. She wouldn't be happy with a cookie or the promise of a toy. Skye was a tankful of confused, conflicting emotions. True, she was still a child, but Skye's feelings were no less strong or real or frightening than any adult's. She didn't have the experience to rationalize or intellectualize feelings the way some adults can. But emotionally, Skye, had fully experienced one of Life's Little Miseries.

While I had spent the day riffling through headaches of papers in my office, Skye had been making a Trojan effort to play with two eleven-year-olds, the daughters of other staff members. People often mistook Skye for much older than she really was. Outside, she was tall and articulate, but inside, she was still only eight years old. The girls had purposely left Skye out and made her feel stupid and inadequate. Skye had been burying her feelings all day so that no one would see how embarrassed she was. Skye wanted very much to be like those big girls, but now she hated them for being so mean to her.

I handled the situation very badly. First, I became irate. I was going to call the mothers of those girls and give them a piece of my mind. How dare they! Second, I became pompous. Why would Skye want to play with those girls anyway? Skye was a much better person than either of them. Third, I became avoidant. Skye was likely never to see those girls again. We'd forget about the whole thing. In fact, I was so overwhelmed with my own feelings, I forgot that Skye had any. Well, Skye eventually did forget, and so did I. Until the same thing happened again, in a different place with different kids, and I still didn't know what to do. I realized that I would know more about what to do for Skye if she were an alcoholic or if I were an alcoholic: there were people to call and books to read. I didn't have a clue about what to do in ordinary, everyday situations. And I was a teacher, a writer. I had been involved in parent education for years. But when "life's little miseries" came my way, I was paralyzed.

I suspect that many parents and teachers in their efforts to help children with life's everyday problems feel that the only way to help is to have all the answers immediately. We look at problem solving as a kind of emotional band-aid. Simply take the right answer out of the tin, peel off the wrapper, and apply. When we take out all the answers we've used before and they don't work right away, we feel horrible. But the question is not always one of *selection;* sometimes it is one of *invention.* The right Band-Aid is not always in our tin. Sometimes we have to make a brand-new one.

I finally had the opportunity to deal directly with these issues when I was assigned by my university department chairman to teach a graduate course in human relations and problem solving for young children. Problem solving was the *hot* topic. Educators and psychologists had come to the realization that nobody really knew what was to be expected of our children in the twenty-first century. Information and technique useful today would be obsolete by then. Rather than teaching children *about* something, teach them *how* something is done. Rather than merely teaching *about* the Declaration of Independence, also teach children the process of negotiation and compromise that went into it. It is rare in life that one is asked to account for the exact contents of the Declaration of Independence, but negotiation and compromise are human relations concepts people use everyday. "Teach children *processes!*" became the battle cry of education—processes that can be applied to any subject, anywhere, any day, any year. No small order.

The terms *human relations* and *problem solving* evoked a number of negative images, which included "easy therapeutic gimmick." With the 1980s came a mighty wind of change in America away from such humanistic urges as "problem solving" or "processes." Our nation was at risk because foreign competitors had overtaken America in commerce, industry, science, and technology. Yet reformers who tried to raise standards with rigorous academic programs almost always met with failure. There is now, as there was in the early 1980s, continued dissatisfaction with education, evidenced by the ever-present dropout rates, vandalism, and discipline problems in the schools. The problem is not only one of motivating students to acquire academic content. It is also one of helping children develop healthy personal relationships and self-regard. In reality, no gimmick can do this.

The failure of the schools is similar to the failure of diets. Although every guru in creation comes out with an absolutely proven diet every other week, the only diet that works is one of lifelong sound nutritional habits. Children, parents, and teachers had to be sensitized to the very human problems of everyday living. No one can escape them. Not handling these ordinary everyday problems well leads to loss of self-esteem, poor academic performance, drugs, violence—everything we fear.

This is not to say that considering intellectual problems is not valid, yet most parents seem to be comfortable with them. For example, when Alex has difficulty choosing a topic for his social studies project, true, he may be up all night. Still most of us feel confident that he will find his topic sooner or later. On the other hand, when Alex hasn't been invited to Jason's birthday party when everyone else in the class has, it is an understatement to say we feel "less confident." Most of us feel highly inadequate and often guilty. These personal problems are emotionally charged in ways that intellectual problems are not. The stress that emotional tension promotes does make personal problem solving difficult. Yet most current research continues to indicate that solving everyday personal problems effectively helps to develop the strong self-concept children need to succeed on other fronts. When Kimberly learns to like herself regardless of what happens out there in the big bad world, she is more likely to reach her intellectual potential as well.

Experts have been researching problem-solving skills for years. There is a multitude of highly developed approaches in mathematics, political science, and psychotherapy. Yet none of these have been translated to address something as basic as losing the fifty dollars grandma gave you for your vacation money. These other approaches are concerned with the so-called bigger problems.

Life's Little Miseries is a careful blend of the work of experts in philosophy, psychology, economics, science, mathematics, and education. It is not magic but it can have magical results. No matter what the problem, the process is actually very simple. It involves the following steps.

Making Time

Whatever problem your child is having, you will have to be prepared to be constructively involved. If you are busy, you must shelve the problem for another time. Make an "appointment" with your child to address the problem fully—*later,* when you are physically and emotionally available.

There are simple tactics to apply that even a three- or four-year-old can accept temporarily. If the problem is crucial, you may have to reorder your priorities to address the problem immediately. The point here is that problem solving takes *time*—not necessarily a great deal of time, but *time* nonetheless. I wanted to solve Skye's problem on the bus before we got home, and that was one of the reasons I couldn't help her.

Active Time Making

Active time making involves opening your schedule enough to suit each of your children's needs. Is this possible? Well, not for every child at all times, but you can do a great deal to insure success. Active time making can occur only when you make it an integral part of your own planning. Time is never something you have; it's something you make.

Some problems can be solved immediately without much reflection. For example, your daughter has misplaced a favorite shirt she wants to wear tomorrow. You have a shirt you know she likes. She agrees to wear that. The two of you will search for the other shirt Saturday afternoon when you've made time. Perfect scenario. Problems that need concentrated attention do not evolve so neatly and require different strategies.

THE SEVEN GOLDEN TIME-MAKING RULES

1. *If at all possible, address the problem immediately.* This is not a realistic strategy all the time; however, in order for children to be trusting and to feel confident that they can depend on you, it is an essential one. No one can shelve everything for later and be an effective problem solver. Dealing with the problem when it occurs can be the most productive time maker of all. Holding problems may create unnecessary stress and make a simple problem complex and thus more difficult to resolve than it was originally. In addition, young children have a totally different perception of time from that of adults or older children. They may seem to forget the actual circumstances that surround a problem. What they do not forget are the feelings. Fresh anger or fear is almost always easier to handle than feelings bottled up for a week or two.

2. *Identify good and bad times in your weekly schedule.* Let your children know what the *good* times are to talk to you. Let them also know about the *bad* times. Even a three- or four-year-old can respond to the announcement, "OK, this is Mommy's *good time.*" Young children look for observable signs. After Daddy fixes dinner is a good time. After Mommy gets out of the shower is another good time. When daddy is holding his briefcase and walking to the door is a *very bad time.* In reality, most time is neutral. Difficulties arise when children cannot identify appropriate times to discuss concerns. The result is stressed-out, unfocused, unresponsive parents and further distressed children. Problems can never be effectively resolved in that atmosphere. Once children can identify your good and bad times, help them identify their good and bad times for you. In this way, families grow to respect each other's time, rather than constantly battle for it.

3. *Never attempt to solve an emotionally charged problem quickly or in an inappropriate place.* Your child begins to sob in

the middle of the shopping mall. He seems very upset about something. If his itchy sweater is the problem; obviously, it can be removed. Problem resolved. If his best friend socked him in the schoolyard that morning, the response must be much more complex. There is no way you can adequately deal with your child's feelings that very moment. Tell your child this. Let him know that the reason you are not addressing his needs immediately is *not* because you are not interested, but because you can't. Ask him if he can save his feelings for later. If he is too distraught to contain himself, this is no time to be in a shopping mall. Go home. To continue shopping now will be an exasperating experience for both of you. No one's needs will be satisfied. Most children will welcome being taken to a more comfortable place to discuss what's bothering them.

4. *Know when you need "just a few minutes" for yourself before addressing a problem.* Older children, if appropriately coached, can respond sensitively to your request to "wait a few minutes." Young children often demand immediate gratification. Waiting even a short time can be agony. If your son has broken a beloved toy and has been waiting hours for your arrival, he is going to want immediate attention the minute you walk through the door. No matter how much you care, you will not be listening at that moment. You will give him the perfunctory hug and nod, "Uh-huh, uh-huh." You need transition time, too! Make a "waiting place." Young children are concrete and respond well to concrete strategies. The waiting place can be a space or place in the house—a corner of his or your room, a special chair; or it can be constructed from an old cardboard refrigerator box or the like. Whatever or wherever the waiting place is, it should be attractive and equipped with some time-passing items: a few books, a puzzle.

The waiting place is where your child goes to wait for you. He can wait a short time, roughly one minute for each year of his life. If you do not respond by then, he will most likely come to look for you or fall asleep. Holding in the waiting place is temporary; it just gives you the minimal time required to put your briefcase down, to finish cutting the sandwich, or to turn the computer off. It does allow you to compose yourself and focus, to make you truly available to your child.

5. *Know when and how to pass the buck or tell your child that*

you absolutely, positively can't talk now. By definition, chaos contains distractions and highly charged feelings. We all have bad days—even bad weeks. Now even the usual good times are bad. These emotional fluctuations are part of being human and cannot be avoided. If you are particularly overwhelmed, you cannot be effective. This is the time to pass the buck, if you have someone to whom you can pass it. Carefully direct your child and her feelings to this person.

In case you're confused, this is *not* the "go talk to your mother" routine. Children often select one parent to solve their problems, or one parent sees the other as being more appropriate or effective in a particular area. Both parents should be committed to the development of their child's emotional life. Children should know this and feel comfortable in bringing issues to either parent. It may be that one parent is seen as having "more time" for the children. In reality, one parent has simply learned to *make* more time.

If there is no "other" in the family, take a deep breath and make another time to talk together. This tactic may be hard for your child to accept at first. But if you follow through on your newly made appointments, she will come to trust your judgment. She will also recognize that her needs are met more optimally when you are focused and attentive, not upset or distracted. Some children actually prefer making appointments to acting spontaneously.

6. *Know how to establish time-making priorities.* Your twelve-year-old has not done his science homework. It is 10:30 P.M., and he comes into your room to ask for your help. You are very tired and somewhat annoyed. He told you that this work had been finished hours ago. Tell him that you are annoyed. You will help him with the homework now because homework is important for him to complete. However, tomorrow, well after the priority of the homework has been addressed, you would like to know why he waited so long to finish his assignment.

Parents can lose time addressing the wrong issue. Ten thirty at night is no time for explanations when there may be an hour of homework to do. Or you may address the immediate problem of the homework without ever getting to the issue of why you were told work was finished when it wasn't. If you don't address all the relevant issues at some time, then don't be surprised if you have the same problem over and over again.

7. *Make time specific.* If your child is eight years or older, she has a sense of time approximating that of an adult. If you cannot address a problem immediately or within a few minutes, tell your child exactly *when* you will have time. "Later" or "tomorrow" is not specific enough. Setting a specific time implies commitment. Children do respond to genuine interest. After you've set the time, stick to it.

Keeping the lines of communication open concerning time is critical to effective problem solving. If you want your children to talk to you about their thoughts and feelings, they need to know when you will be available.

Perspective Taking

You must be prepared to share your child's point of view, at least until you are certain you understand the problem. This is not a book about discipline, judgment making, or imposing your point of view. If your child is having real behavior problems, there are other books to help you. You must see the problem the way your child sees it, not the way you see it. Resist the temptation to dismiss the problem as ridiculous, unworthy, or trivial. If you do, you encourage your child to create big problems just to get your attention. When Skye told me her problem, I became furious, pompous, and then avoidant. I never really knew what *Skye* was feeling.

Ways to See

Carl Rogers (1980), the eminent person-centered psychologist, felt that to understand someone you must accurately sense the "feelings and personal meanings" that that person is experiencing. Rogers also felt that it is impossible to truly understand another's inner world if you have already developed an evaluative opinion of that world. Most of us, unfortunately, have a bundle of stereotypes about children that we routinely use, not always wisely.

For example, watch a middle-class adult male encounter a three-year-old. A smile comes to the adult's face, a beaming condescending smile. A greeting—"How are you doing today?"—is delivered with the exaggerated intonation one would use with the hard-of-hearing, the elderly, or a pet. We may hear many more appropriate encounters as well, but my point is that few adults really stop to think about *how* they talk to children.

When questioned, many people view childhood as a pleasant and relatively carefree period of life. Is it? I don't want to sentimentalize how tough childhood can be, but consider the following. When asked in a recent study which they liked better, childhood or the present, 90 percent of adults responded that they preferred childhood. However, when they were asked if they would return to childhood if they could, less than 10 percent chose the option. In his book *I'm OK, You're OK* (1969), Thomas Harris argues that childhood is not at all euphoric. It is a time when everyone is bigger, stronger, and smarter than you are and you can't do much of anything for yourself.

Suppose someone invited you to dinner, then reminded you to wipe your feet before coming in the door, and then reminded you to wash your hands, and told you you must eat your Brussels sprouts. You would be appalled by this person's rudeness. But such behavior is not a problem if the people invited to dinner are children because it is assumed that it is in some way helpful for children to be reminded; after all, they don't know how to be adults yet.

Children are not small adults. Seeing their world may take us time. You may ask yourself, "What would it be like if I didn't understand a great deal of what people said or did? Or if I were afraid to be alone? Or if I were totally dependent and had to rely on only one or two other people?" Childhood can be very confusing, frightening, and downright upsetting. To adults, children's problems may seem pale in the overall scheme of things—a broken toy, a missed playmate. What kind of problem is that? Adults have *real* problems. But to the child, that toy may be the equivalent of your wedding ring; that playmate, an important business opportunity. The persons, places, and things are different. The feelings are very much the same. One final tip. To really understand the child's world, see some children's television. Don't just look at it; *see it.* For the longest time, I could not get the premise of Mr. Rogers' Neighborhood. Frankly, I thought the show made little sense, if any. Finally, the concept dawned. This is how very young children see their world. This was why my own two children absolutely adored this man and I sat there with a puzzled expression. Once I learned to see Mr. Rogers with my "child's eye," so to speak, I actually began to enjoy the show. I'll even confess to watching it alone. Whenever you watch your child's favorite show, ask yourself, "If I liked this show better than anything else on TV, what kind of person would I be?"

The ability to sit in your child's shoes for a while may be the most potent factor in bringing about change and learning. By working to see things the way your child sees them, you learn to prize your child as an individual. Your understanding of his feelings is more complete and less clouded by your own experiences, which, in fact, may be very different from his.

Listening

When children are upset, they often have difficulty expressing themselves. Very young children have difficulty expressing themselves, period. When they are upset, self-expression may be impossible. Your role is to help your child calm down sufficiently to be able to tell you what happened. Many of us never get to that point. We stand there repeating, "What's the matter? What's the matter?" when the child is too angry, sad, or frightened to say anything. When Skye got angry, she triggered my own anger and inadequacy. I never listened to her.

Empathic Listening

Walter Loban (cited in Erickson, 1985 p. 13) compares the four language modes in this way: "We listen a book a day, we speak a book a week, we read a book a month, and we write a book a year." Despite the importance of listening in our lives, listening has been called the neglected or orphan language art for thirty-five years or more (Anderson, 1949).

Listening is elusive because it occurs internally. It is complex because it involves converting spoken language into a meaningful thought. Listening is more than just hearing, even though adults often use the terms *hearing* and *listening* synonomously. Rather, hearing is an integral component, but still only one component, of the listening process. It is the thinking about or converting to meaning of what one hears that is the crucial part of listening.

There are many reasons for adults to listen to children and for children to listen to adults. People listen to *comprehend* and *evaluate* school assignments. They listen to *appreciate* music and storytelling. The kind of listening involved in problem solving, however, is *not* these. Problem solving requires therapeutic or empathic listening. Empathic listening, like all active listening, is a highly complex, sensitizing process. It means that you have agreed to put yourself aside for the moment and listen very carefully not only to what your children are saying, but to *how* they are saying what they are saying and *why*.

This is not to be confused with Freudian adventure. You are not attempting to uncover unconscious feelings, although surely these exist. What you will do is listen to your children and reflect your perceptions of their feelings back to them. They, in turn, have the opportunity to tell you whether or not these perceptions are accurate. Through continual clarification of feelings, you both come to understand the experience at hand.

Take the following dialogue, for example:

Billie: Everyone hates me!

Mom: You feel everyone hates you!

Billie: Yeah, yeah, everyone! (*crying*)

Mom: That's a horrible feeling. I feel like that sometimes. When I feel that way, it's usually one or two people that have made me feel awful!

Billie: Yeah, yeah, Timmie said so. Timmie said he hates me.

Mom: Timmie is a good friend. So when Timmie says he hates you, it *feels* as if everyone hates you? Is that right? Is that how you feel?

Billie: Yeah (*crying, even more*).

OK, now Mom hasn't even got to the point where any problem solving is taking place, but now she knows the problem—and the feeling attached to it. Watch what could happen without empathic listening:

Billie: Everyone hates me!

Mom: Oh, now Billie, that's ridiculous. No one hates you!

Billie: Yes, they do. Everyone, everyone hates me!

Mom: Now, Billie, that is the silliest thing. Everyone loves you, dear. I love you. Daddy loves you. Grandma loves . . .

Billie: (*crying*) No . . . No . . .

In the second scenario, Mom is telling her child that his feelings are incorrect. He should be feeling something else. Now, children may have very distorted, immature, and unenlightened views of the world, but for the most part, their feelings fit them. You have to decide, do you really want to understand your child and the way he feels? Then you must accept his feelings—no matter how strange, surreal, or threatening these feelings may sound to you. Just think about the last time someone really listened to you—didn't give unsolicited advice or admonishments, just listened and appreciated your feelings. Didn't it feel glorious! You probably talk to this person often because she is such a good listener. This is the kind of relationship you want to build with your child. You want her to feel comfortable talking with you about her thoughts and feelings. If your child feels she will be reprimanded or cajoled into feeling differently, she is not going to talk to you—at least not about important feelings.

The surest way of stopping the flow of communication between a parent and a child is for the parent to adopt the role of judge of what is right and wrong with all the child says and does. Children are not looking for a judge when they share their feelings with parents. They are looking for someone who says, "I care about you, and I will try to understand what you are feeling."

Parents who judge their child's feelings teach the child to keep her feelings to herself. The child quickly learns that there is something wrong with her as a person. The child's self-concept suffers because she believes there is something wrong with her for possessing feelings you have condemned.

Empathetic listening is *not* the same as *agreeing* with your child's point of view. It is not necessary or realistic to think that we will always agree with our children. What is necessary and helpful to your child is that you recognize and accept her *need to possess and express her feelings*. When you choose empathy above criticism, your child is given the opportunity to calm down and think more clearly about what has happened. When she is able to work through her feelings in this judgment-free environment, her self-worth is reinforced.

The way a parent listens and responds to a child's feeling greatly affects the child's self-concept. Parents who listen and respond with empathy, caring, and patience encourage the child to feel accepted and loved. These feelings nurture a positive self-concept, open parent–child communications, and a quality parent–child relationship.

Being Together

This might sound like a throwback to the 1960s' "being there," "coming together," and so on. It's not meant to be. If we want to help our children, we must let them know that we are there for them—even when there aren't any problems. This doesn't mean planning elaborate events or even eating dinner together every night, but it does mean planning a special time to be together each week. This means that for those few hours every week, neither of you has distractions. You can play a few computer games, bike-ride for an ice cream cone, and read a few stories together. If you have an older child, you can take her for that special haircut, walk through a few fleamarkets, and go to an exercise class. You don't even have to talk to each other if you don't feel like it. I've spent many hours with my children in silence, leafing through old magazines or doing small chores. The point is that you can help your children only if you really know them. To know them means being with them.

Solving

It is only after you've *made time, altered your perspective, listened,* and *been with your child* that the two of you can really begin to problem-solve together. Like everything else worthwhile, effective problem solving takes practice. True, there are a few of us who are naturally gifted in it. However, if we view problem solving as some great gift available to only a chosen few, we lose sight of the fact that problem solving can be learned by almost anyone.

Pointers for Problem Solvers

A problem is nothing more than the difference between what you have and what you want. That may seem simplistic, but how else would you define it? The ultimate resolution to any problem is not especially complex either. You generally do one of three things:

1. You accept the problem.
2. You change the problem.
3. You alter your perception of the problem so that you can then either accept it or change it.

These are the only three resolutions I know of. No one has ever told me otherwise, except the few that insist that there is a fourth resolution: Forget about the problem. My response to them is that I don't think we ever really forget.

Once, when I was six, one of the bullying boys in my neighborhood took a pliers and twisted my nose with it. He did this in front of a group of children. I was not hurt physically. I was humiliated. My mother handled the situation badly, as I would do later with Skye. She told me to stay away from that boy, but she never asked me how I felt, and so I never really knew what to do with those feelings. I'm not saying that this single experience damaged me for life. But out of all the childhood problems one can have, being teased or humiliated is the one I have the most difficulty with when it comes to my own children. We don't forget our childhood problems, and we don't forget how we felt. This is why these experiences are so emotionally charged for us. History repeats itself. We continue the patterns of our parents because we don't know what the alternatives are or could be.

Depending on the nature of the problem, each step in the problem-solving process is handled differently. For example, you are going to spend a great deal more time with the child whose closest friend has just moved out of the country than you ordinarily would with the child who has misplaced a favorite toy. Each chapter in this book also gives you alternatives to the same kind of problem. In some cases, accepting the situation is the best solution; in others, specific change or altering a perspective would be better. In no case are you given the sure-fire cure-all for all of life's little miseries. Remember, this is not a gimmick. It is a very carefully planned process whose rewards are long term, not short term like the diet of hard-boiled eggs and grapefruit.

In the beginning, you are expected to make mistakes. But instead of "beating yourself up" and feeling guilty, you will learn to learn from your errors. As you and your child work together solving everyday problems, both of you will reap many benefits. The care, trust, and mutual understanding that evolve are unmatched by any other interaction you are likely to have with your child in a lifetime.

First, a content chapter covers the characteristics and psychological implications of a certain childhood issue. Following this, a "methods" chapter on the same issue provides activities and strategies for addressing this topic with children of various ages and stages of development. Every chapter reviews the latest research as well as the most effective strategies for communicating with your children about day-to-day problems.

2

Loving and Losing

"I Had Something Special.
What Happened to It?"

He could have been any little boy riding the train with his grandma and his juice pack, asking endless questions. But he wasn't. He sat on the edge of his seat, eyes peering intently over the rim of the Plexiglas divider. Focused and searching, elated, distressed, his face registered a continuing cycle of intense emotions. This wasn't normal behavior for a three-year-old riding the train with his Girl Scout–cookie-bearing grandma.

Then it became evident. His cycle of facial expressions coincided with the passing of the conductor. His face rose as she entered the car and just as quickly collapsed when she left. This was his mom.

Our experience of loss is intrinsically bound to our experience of loving. One cannot truly experience the absence of something unless he has in some very real way "had" this thing. For example, the behavior of many autistic children may appear depressed, and for decades, this was the diagnosis. Sadly, in reality, these impaired children can never be depressed. They have never connected.

The greater our connectedness, if you will, the greater our capacity to experience loss. Psychiatrist Daniel Stern's (1985) concept of falling in love as the most primitive of all human bonds is the child's tie to her parents. This is, truly, the first love of any individual's existence; what we call the first discovery of adolescence isn't so much discovery as rediscovery of this intense passion, first experienced beyond our conscious reach and buried now in the distorted dreamlike memories of our infancy.

It was, of course, Freud (1962) who first drew our attention to the potency of this early love and how it is the very cornerstone of our personality. Yet, the work of Stern (1985), and earlier of Bowlby (1973), has led us away from the deeply psychoanalytical view of loving with its overemphasis on guilt and the mother. We can now ask ourselves these questions: Is this business of loving and losing preprogrammed? Is it one of our uniquely human survival behaviors—and not something shameful that our mothers have "done to us"?

My point here, in case you're wondering, is that the experience of loving and losing in childhood is a central human experience, perhaps *the* central human experience. Loving and losing is a necessary and productive part of the emotional banquet of being human. Parents should not try to protect children from these difficult feelings nor feel guilty that they have them. Our responsibility as parents is not to diminish loss, or to disguise it, but to help children express and resolve it.

We are all, during the process of growing, developing, and living our lives, engaged in the periodic forming and relinquishing of our love bonds, just like our little commuter friend with his conductor mom: loving and losing. A parent learns to love a child and then must know how to let go of her; the child's emotional task is the complementary one. A great part of the normal suffering of people has to do with this: the child, the adult, is being forced, in distress and sorrow, to part with familiar relationships and to move on to the strange and often frightening wider world. A new self, involved in new relationships, must be found—somehow, somewhere. Our entire lives are fraught with striking this delicate balance: what must be given to be gained.

The crisis issues involving loss—death, divorce, stepfamilies, and so on—have all been examined at length in several informative, supportive texts (see the appendix and reference sections). But crisis is not what we're about here. Each and every day, children cope with the smaller issues of loving and losing. How they piece these daily fragments together will determine their ability to cope when the big issues are presented.

There are, of course, many loving and losing issues that could be discussed here. Those presented in this chapter have been selected because of their frequency and overall impact on lifelong development: going to bed, starting school, losing things, losing friends, and sibling rivalry.

Some of these issues, such as going to bed, are more specific to younger children, ages three to five; others, like losing friends, affect older children more acutely. No matter what the particulars of the loss experience, children generally proceed through three stages:

1. The first stage is characterized by the most intense emotions: anger, rage, fear, or plain shock.
2. The second stage is marked by ambivalence, exploration, or observation. The child has worked through the intense emotions and is questioning and/or evaluating the experience.
3. In the last stage, the child accepts the loss or changes her perception of it and resolves to move forward, to "get on with it," so to speak.

The intensity and duration of each of these stages is determined by the age of the child, the significance of the experience, and the manner in which the child is helped to build effective coping strategies. This chapter is a discussion of the underlying causes of loving and losing. The next chapter provides specific coping strategies.

Before we examine each of the selected situations at length let's take a look at the most important issue involved in loving and losing, your child's *self-concept*.

Finding the Self

Your child's ability to attach to persons, things, and situations is directly related to the development of his self-concept. Here the old cliché "You must understand yourself before you can understand anything else" certainly applies. A child's self-concept consists of his own evaluation of all his personal characteristics and qualities. It is his overall/inside picture, how he feels about himself. This inside picture influences how he feels today and will influence what he becomes tomorrow.

Periodically, all people size themselves up, measuring their personal attributes and abilities against those presented by others. Children evaluate themselves on a great number of characteristics, including physical appearance, ability in sports, personality, special talents, ability in school, and social relationships. People often speak of "losing themselves" or "finding themselves" in terms of how much they feel a particular situation fits this personal evaluation. Your child's evaluation of his many personal characteristics makes up this overall self-concept.

Children, like all people, feel better about themselves in some areas than in others. The total of all the child's judgments represents his self-concept. If this overall picture is good, we say the child has a positive self-concept. If this overall picture is poor, we say the child has a negative self-concept. It should be noted that no child has an entirely positive or entirely negative picture of himself.

Children who have positive self-concepts see themselves very differently from children with negative self-concepts. A child who has a positive self-concept respects himself and feels worthy, competent, and lovable. A child with a negative self-concept lacks respect for himself and believes he is incapable, insignificant, unsuccessful, unworthy, and unlovable. It is absolutely necessary for a child, to be a happy, fully functioning individual, to possess a positive self-concept and a high degree of self-esteem. Dorothy Briggs (1975) said it well: "Self-esteem is the mainspring that slates every child for success or failure as a human being."

No one is born with a fully honed self-concept. Children acquire their self-concept through their interactions with life and people. Yet wanting your children to hold this positive regard for themselves and helping them achieve it can be two very different things. Almost all parents will agree that a positive self-image is vital to mental health, yet establishing a secure self-concept for children requires much effort and even wisdom.

Very simply, children learn who they are by how others react to them. During the first few years of life, parents are generally the key reflectors of self-concept for children. Later, teachers, neighbors, friends and relatives clarify and enhance or detract from that initial image.

Long before your child knows what you are saying to her, she can sense your feelings by the way she is touched, held, fed, played with, and bathed by you. Your positive physical communications during infancy provide the foundation for her developing self-esteem. Once your child can understand you, what you say and how you say it become vitally important. It is much easier to notice other parents making negative comments to their children and to be critical than it is to be objective about what we say to our own children. We think, "Underneath it all, my child knows I love her, so what I say is not important." This is not the case. What we say and what we don't say make a great deal of difference in how children feel about themselves and whether they truly feel loved.

How Parents Can Know If Their Children Have Positive or Negative Self-Concepts

No one test will give an accurate picture of how a child really feels about himself. Self-concept is extremely difficult to measure, even by professionals. Yet parents can gain information about their children's self-concepts by using *emphathic listening,* listening carefully to what their children are saying and how they are acting. Children usually do not openly say, "I'm not important. I feel insecure. I'm not worthwhile." Instead, they express their feelings in more covert ways.

> Karen has arrived home to find that Angela, her five-year-old, has destroyed three dolls in the prized collection of Mary Jean, her eight-year-old. When Karen confronts Angela, she cries and screams, "I don't have any dolls. I never have any dolls. Mary Jean is always playing with her friends, and I never have any dolls."

This kind of situation between siblings is common in many good homes where parents love their children very much. Karen is puzzled and frustrated by Angela's behavior. Karen and her husband, Tom, love both girls and feel they give them equal attention. Yet Angela continues to act as if she is being shortchanged.

These frustrations are real and painful for many parents. Surprising as it may seem, Angela *is telling* her parents why she is unhappy. She is sending messages through her behavior and through her conversations with others. If we listen empathically, we can hear what Angela is trying to tell Karen.

If we see through the child's eye, we begin to see why Angela may see herself as having the sticky end of the lollipop, as opposed to the sweet candy. Angela and Mary Jean are close in age. Their abilities and interests are similar, yet Tom and Karen feel a responsibility to Mary Jean because she is the oldest. They allow Mary Jean more responsible enthusiasms than Angela, like the doll collection. They have given Angela many dolls; yet no matter how many Angela has, she does not perceive them as equal to Mary Jean's collection. The question confronting Angela—unconscious, of course—is "Do Mommy and Daddy love Mary Jean better?" The doll collection is an expression of a special kind of love from Mommy and Daddy. Angela is not certain she warrants this love.

In addition to having this doll collection, Mary Jean also has a few special friends from school. She likes to play with these friends by herself on occasion, without Angela. Angela wants to play with Mary Jean whenever she has friends over and is angry when Karen insists that this is Mary Jean's special time. Angela has school friends, too. She often plays with them without any intrusion from Mary Jean. Very simply, no matter how rational Karen's, Tom's, or Mary Jean's behavior is, it will always be seen as exclusionary by Angela because she doesn't see what *she* does or what *she* has as special.

In attempting to treat their two children as the same yet different, Karen and Tom have made the common oversight of making one child feel just *too* different and, as a result, unworthy. It is true that if you give both children exactly the same thing, you discourage individuality; if you give children separate things, you encourage conflict. There doesn't seem to be any cozy solution when we view this situation with a parent's eye.

Yet when we see the same situation from Angela's point of view, Karen and Tom clearly prefer Mary Jean. Angela's dolls are just dolls; Mary Jean's are a *collection.* However erroneous Angela's interpretation is, she still needs *actions,* not explanations, to counter these negative impressions. Improving Angela's self-concept may involve planning a being-together tactic. Right now, Angela needs special time with either Karen or Tom, special time without Mary Jean.

Karen and Tom may need to find an equally coveted item for Angela, something she, just like Mary Jean, can care take of and value. When we give children time and special things to take care of, we are also telling them, "You are very special."

This does not mean that children who have problems can't have good self-concepts. They can. In fact, some children with very limited resources or ability can have extraordinary self-images:

Ten-year-old Kevin goes to resource room for math and writing three times a week. He has been in mainstream class since third grade, when he transferred from a special school. Even though national achievement test scores place Kevin in the lower third of his class in reading and math, Kevin has been able to maintain a C average. He is also part of a peer-tutoring program in which he works with another student on his math and writing difficulties after school. Of late, Kevin has shown an interest in music and has begun to study the piano. Although he attends piano lessons only once a week, he practices often on weekends and in the evening when his schoolwork is complete. Kevin's music teacher says he has "a good ear."

On the basis of Kevin's intellectual characteristics, we might expect him to have a poor self-concept. We might even predict that he will a difficult time with life, in general, because of his academic difficulties. Yet the child who is less than perfect academically is not doomed to a negative view of himself. Kevin has a realistic view of his strengths and weaknesses. With support from parents, teachers, and peers, Kevin has overreached his potential. As a result, he is very content. Effort and encouragement are powerful concept builders regardless of specific abilities.

In general, the following ten characteristics are indicative of a good self-concept. (The items presented here are most appropriate for children over the age of six. Before the age of six the child cannot be expected to have completely integrated the social skills listed. The very young child's self-concept is still very much in the process of being formed. Self-centered and dependent behavior is a normal and necessary part of early development and cannot be viewed as a poorly developing self-concept):

- Child seeks to be independent: "I can do that all by myself."
- Child handles failure well: "I didn't make the team but I'll try out again next year."
- Child is responsible and completes tasks: "Don't worry. I'll make Pete's lunch tomorrow."
- Child provides self with positive feedback on skills: "I did a great job today."

- Child takes pride in accomplishments: "I can swim all the way to the other side of the pool."
- Child relates well to others: "Why don't you sit with us; we have room."
- Child tries new experiences: "I've never gone skiing before, but I'd love to try."
- Child expresses own ideas: "I loved reading *Little Women*. I liked the character of Jo especially."
- Child is persistent: "I did poorly again on this social studies test, but I am going to study until I get it."
- Child expresses anger and sadness in constructive ways: "I was very angry when you pushed me. Next time, just ask me to move over."

This is not to say that children with good self-concepts have all of these characteristics, nor that they *consistently* have any one of them. A good rule of thumb is four out of five, or 80 percent. For example, Alyssa cannot be said to be entirely responsible or persistent in her daily life, yet in all of the other listed attributes she seems to shine. So eight of the ten, or 80 percent of these characteristics, do describe Alyssa. Jeff, on the other hand, seems to exhibit all of the previous characteristics but not all the time. For example, if given the opportunity to express his ideas, Jeff may be expected to do so four out of five times, or 80 percent of the time.

In contrast, a predominance of the following five characteristics implies a poorly developing self-concept:

- Child keeps to himself most of the time and seems overly critical of others: "I don't want to play with him. He thinks he is so smart."
- Child attacks others verbally and/or physically, makes fun of others: "You're stupid and ugly! I hate you!"
- Child has a negative attitude toward most things and feels that he usually gets shortchanged: "I don't want to go to that party. I never get the piece of cake with the flower."
- Child appears shy, daydreams excessively, and dislikes meeting new people: "No, I want to stay here. I don't want to see your friends."
- Child is unable to accept failure: "I didn't miss the ball. You're lying!"

All children, even those with highly developed self-concepts, exhibit negative behaviors occasionally, particularly when under stress. Extraordinary circumstances encourage negative behavior that is not normally seen. The presentation of depressed, angry, negative behavior in a situation that warrants these expressions does *not* indicate a negative self-concept. In fact, if Suzanne's beloved guinea pig dies, a lack of feeling would be more a cause for concern than would overt crying or tantrumming. If the child's behavior does not seem in concert with the happenings around him, this is cause for concern.

It is also important to look at children from the standpoint of stylistic differences. Shy children do not always have negative self-concepts. There are many perfectly wonderful quiet, reflective people in the world. Thank God there are! And just because a child appears outgoing and boisterous, it does not always mean he has a positive self-concept. Expressive bragging and bravado may reveal, in reality, a very negative self-concept.

Happily, positive self-concepts can be maintained, even enhanced, and negative self-concepts can be improved. This book is full of suggestions for accomplishing both goals.

For those parents who want a more official evaluation of their own and their child's self-concept, I include the About Me Scale.

About Me

ABOUT ME (PART ONE). The members of the family evaluate themselves on the characteristics listed below. Young children will need assistance from parents or older siblings. When all family members have finished, feelings about each item are shared.

Self-evaluations are done on a scale of 1 to 5. A "1" rating indicates that the person believes he has very little of this characteristic. A 5 rating indicates that the person believes this item is *very* characteristic of him.

Some children may not want to evaluate themselves openly on the listed characteristics in front of all family members. They may feel more comfortable sharing their evaluations with just one understanding and sensitive parent.

A parent may need to explain the meaning of some items to

younger children (i.e., "Confident means you think you are able to do many things").

Generally speaking on a scale from 1 to 5, I consider myself a person who is:

1.	1	2	3	4	5	Friendly
2.	1	2	3	4	5	Truthful
3.	1	2	3	4	5	Happy
4.	1	2	3	4	5	Good working with my hands
5.	1	2	3	4	5	Confident
6.	1	2	3	4	5	Physically attractive
7.	1	2	3	4	5	Organized
8.	1	2	3	4	5	Even-tempered
9.	1	2	3	4	5	Optimistic about the future
10.	1	2	3	4	5	Intelligent
11.	1	2	3	4	5	Kind
12.	1	2	3	4	5	Productive
13.	1	2	3	4	5	Well-liked by others
14.	1	2	3	4	5	A good student
15.	1	2	3	4	5	Enthusiastic about life
16.	1	2	3	4	5	Sensitive to others' feelings
17.	1	2	3	4	5	Athletically inclined
18.	1	2	3	4	5	Creative
19.	1	2	3	4	5	Musically inclined
20.	1	2	3	4	5	Thought well of by my father
21.	1	2	3	4	5	Thought well of by my mother
22.	1	2	3	4	5	Thought well of by my brothers and sisters
23.	1	2	3	4	5	Thought well of by my teachers

Interpretation. If most of your child's self-evaluations lie in the upper half of the rating scale (3 to 5), he is very likely a person who has positive feelings about himself. He has a positive self-concept.

ABOUT ME (PART TWO). List five words or phrases that best describe you. You may choose items from the list above or think of other words that better describe you.

1. _____
2. _____
3. _____
4. _____
5. _____

ABOUT ME (PART THREE). Select five characteristics from the list of twenty-three about which you would like to feel better. Why do you think these characteristics are important?

1. _____
2. _____
3. _____
4. _____
5. _____

ABOUT ME (PART FOUR). Rate yourself on a scale of 1 to 10 on the three items listed below:

I am a competent person.

| 1 | 2 | 3 | 4 | 5 | 6 | 7 | 8 | 9 | 10 |

I am a worthwhile person.

| 1 | 2 | 3 | 4 | 5 | 6 | 7 | 8 | 9 | 10 |

I am a likable person.

| 1 | 2 | 3 | 4 | 5 | 6 | 7 | 8 | 9 | 10 |

Many experts have identified self-concept as the single most significant key to a person's behavior. Most children are found somewhere between the two extremes of positive and negative self-concept. The way a child feels about herself changes slightly from day to day. Larger changes in a child's self-concept, both positive and negative, occur over longer periods of time.

Children who feel good about themselves have a solid base on which positive learning experiences can be built. They are secure, self-confident, and happy and expect good things to happen to them. The most effective way to help your child deal with the issues related to *loss* is to help her maintain a good self-concept or improve a poor one. In fact, all of the issues discussed in this book—loss, disappointment, fear, transition, and inappropriate behavior—can be addressed by the development of a positive self-concept. (See chapter 3 for specific strategies for developing a positive self-concept.)

Going to Bed

Once little boys go to bed they must stay there. I don't know how many times I've told that to Josh. Is he deaf? Every twenty minutes he is back in the living room, trying to charm someone into that extra story or drink of apple juice.

Mealtimes and bedtimes are often the most stressful times of day for young parents. Both involve transition; bedtime involves separation. Spock (1988) believes all children are born lawyers. Particularly for the young child, who is often the first to go to bed, the goal becomes winning the privilege to stay with the rest of the family, if there is any remote possibility of doing so.

Why would the child want to stay up? The first reason is the child may not be tired. This is a very real consideration that parents often ignore (see also chapter 3). The parental position presented is that it doesn't matter if the child is not tired. He still must go to sleep. This view is similar to forcing children to eat when they are not hungry. I am not advocating keeping children awake until they drop from exhaustion. What I am advocating is understanding that the need for sleep is biological. No one can stay awake indefinitely.

If your child cannot fall asleep, your first question should be, "Why isn't Bryan tired?" not "Why isn't Bryan asleep?"

Obviously, a multitude of factors can keep even a tired child wide awake. We can all remember evenings when we, overwhelmed by work or personal endeavors, cannot fall asleep easily either. If wakefuless is occasional, true, it may be disconcerting, particularly if the parents are exhausted, but it is very normal. Everyone has difficulty falling asleep from time to time. The child may have watched a particularly exciting television program right before bedtime. She may be anticipating Steven's birthday tomorrow. Uncle Mike may be in the living room, and David hasn't seen his favorite uncle for two months. If the child is overstimulated or feels he is going to miss out on something by going to bed, then his natural instinct is to fight to stay awake.

If wakefulness is chronic, ambivalence is often the root. Children as young as three learn very quickly that parents can be worn down, particularly late at night when they are also tired. The endless requests for cookies and drinks often have the desired effect, and Rachel gets to stay up with the big people. Children do not mind repeating their requests if they know that eventually they will get what they want. They are much more persistent than we are. Children want to be with their parents. Children naturally have a strong dependence on their principle caregivers. If Mom and Dad have been at work all day, or the child has been at school, it is natural for both parents and child to have missed one another. When the child resists going to bed, she may be indicating her need to be with you. You have been separated all day. Bedtime is further separation and therefore is not welcomed.

Sleeping with Parents

Perhaps no cultural taboo is so consistently broken as the one that refuses the child's entrance into the parents' bed. Again, children want to be with their parents. Learning to sleep in one's own bed is a learned skill that parents must help their child acquire.

If the child is truly frightened, anxious, or sick, there is really nothing wrong with the child's sharing the parents' bed. Some experts may be against this practice. Others advocate children's being permitted access whenever they want it. I am not one for absolutism. Communication with children is not an all-or-nothing endeavor. More important than the act of sharing the parents' bed is the reason the child wants to be there and the reason the parents allow it.

Often, the continued crawling of a child into her parents' bed is precipitated by a traumatic event such as a nightmare, the move to a new home, or the prolonged absence of a parent. Sleeping next to parents makes the child feel safe. Children are most likely to want to sleep in their parents' bed when they are afraid or have had major changes in their lives.

The trouble arises when children want to stay with the parents long after the initial problem is gone. The most common reason parents allow young children into their beds as a matter of course is that it is convenient. It is often much easier to bring the child into one's bed than it is to help the child sleep by himself. Tired parents don't have the energy in the middle of the night to constantly bring the protesting child back to his room. A crying child annoys the parents' sleep. The parents' goal becomes their staying in bed, the absence of crying, and their getting some sleep. These goals may not include helping the child stay in her own bed. Helping a child achieve this goal requires time and energy that parents may not feel they have. The more the child sleeps in her parents' bed, the more she will want to sleep there. Any habit is very difficult to break once it has been established.

I could not do justice to this section without discussing the even more heated controversy regarding human sexuality. Humans are sexual beings from the minute they are born. Can young children be sexually aroused by sleeping with their parents? Yes, they can. The next question is "Is this wrong?" No, it's not. Children will be sexually aroused by their parents and other family members whether or not they sleep with them. Any normal human being can be aroused by a wide variety of stimuli. The natural development of sexuality depends on children's having sexual feelings, and knowing they can express them:

Sean (*squeezing his penis*): Look, look, I have a vagina.

Mom: Well, it certainly looks as if you do. You are probably thinking about what that must feel like—having a vagina.

Sean: You have a vagina.

Mom: Yes, I do. You have a penis. I don't know what it's like to have a penis. Daddy does. Each one of us is different and each one is good.

My point is that the fear of sexual arousal should not be the reason you refuse your child entrance to your bed. Sexual arousal cannot be prevented. Sexuality is a perfectly normal part of human development.

Why is it good for the child to sleep by himself? In many cultures, children sleep with their parents until they are eight years old. These are generally cultures in which autonomy is not primary in the culture's development. The reason children should learn to sleep by themselves is that the practice aids in the development of independent, self-directed behavior. Cultures that value independence also tend to value persons' learning to sleep by themselves.

You will also need to examine other reasons you allow your child to sleep with you. Does the child provide you comfort? Have you and your spouse just had a fight? Do you feel guilty leaving her all day with the baby-sitter? You may not want your child to be all that independent. The bottom line is that children sleep in their parents' beds because the parents allow it, or need it.

Starting School

I had to go to work. I felt terrible standing there, Valerie clinging to my leg. She seemed so happy before. Two of her friends were in Toby's class, and Toby was a great teacher! There were several kids sitting in a circle playing with Legos. Why wouldn't Valerie join them?

We often think that the child who does not seem to mind when we leave him that first important day of school is the one who has coped and managed the situation well. Yet separation from parents or caregivers often makes children unhappy. It is perfectly normal for children to miss their parents, to be confused, uncertain, even angry or upset, and to feel this loss acutely.

Even though many children have had baby-sitters and have been away from their parents for varying periods of time, school is different. For many children, starting school is a major loss experience that means separation from the parent and the home. Children can perceive this as abandonment: being left alone for a long period of time in a strange place with equally strange people and brand-new expectations.

Children may respond to the strangers and newness of any situation in a variety of different ways. Starting school represents stress for the child, and she is bound to exhibit some negative, or at least unexpected, behavior. Parents may announce, "She never acted this way before." The child is physically at school but emotionally wanting home. This kind of psychological fragmenting can cause a great deal of imbalance for the child. For young children, this emotional imbalance is manifested very concretely. Some children scream, tantrum, and cry. Some throw things or try to hit other children. Others appear withdrawn, suppressing angry, upset feelings. Some become agitated, running around the classroom, quickly handling and discarding objects without exploring them.

Then there is the child who walks in that first day, a sweeping smile on her face, a warm greeting for the teacher and children. A week goes by, then two weeks. Finally, in the middle of snack one day, she collapses, weeping inconsolably. This is a surprise. "Now what has happened to her?" you ask. She's been holding on as best as she can. She can't hold on anymore.

Not every child reacts negatively to starting school. Some, perhaps because of an older sibling or a fundamental enjoyment of novelty, relish this experience. The point is composure should be appreciated when it exists; it should not be expected. Almost all children react definitely to starting school. It is a milestone, a passage, a ritual of a kind.

Even though most of our schooling is eclipsed by other experiences when we reach adulthood, almost all adults have memories of those first moments of school. It is truly our first encounter with society, with society's rules.

This experience can be exciting. But underneath the excitement are some very basic concerns. Why is Daddy leaving me here? Who are these people? What should I do? No one knows my name. What if I have to go to the bathroom? Do I have to eat this snack? What if I don't listen to that big person over there? Am I allowed to touch those toys?

It is natural for people to feel comfortable with those who know them and less comfortable with those who don't. Children do not fit neatly and naturally into this placed called school. They will have to earn their place through actions. Although it is impossible for them to realize this consciously, perhaps they sense it intuitively. There is no way to foresee all the possible reactions a child may have. The ability to tolerate the stress of school separation and the ability to adjust to strange and new situations vary greatly from child to child.

Here, at school entry, lies the opportunity for great parental involvement. Positive self-concepts arise from separations that are well achieved. Children who are supported by their parents have their road paved to future success in learning.

Parents may well be upset, too:

I remember standing there being so afraid to ask Mrs. Lawrence if I could go to the bathroom. I wet myself. I was so humiliated, Mrs. Lawrence called me "a baby." I don't want Richie ever to know anyone like Mrs. Lawrence.

How the parents feel about leaving their child at school also influences how the child will react. Sometimes the child adapts very nicely. The parents do not. You cannot possibly understand your child's feelings about school until you understand your own.

The major source of worry for most parents is ambivalence. You want your child to experience the company of others. You want to pursue your own interests. You need to work to survive economically. On the other hand, you don't like leaving your child with strangers. You want to supervise her experiences and make sure they are absolutely the best. You can't do that if you leave. These feelings are particularly strong for parents who have not left their children before.

Many parents make connections with their own early school experiences. Long-buried feelings of loss, fear, anxiety, and discomfort emerge as they take their own children to school. Others initially feel good about "getting rid of the kid" and then feel bad because they feel this way. Clearly, starting school arouses a great wealth of feelings in parents as well as in children.

Because parents are the mediators for their children's earliest experiences, they must help their children understand the meaning of school and the relationships they will have with their teacher and other children. This will not happen overnight. It takes time for both children and adults to build trust. You can help your child have confidence that he is a person who can cope with uncomfortable feelings, and that he will receive help from you. With your help, your child will be well on his way to functioning without you in another safe, nurturing environment. It is your support that offers him the possibility of emotional growth and future successes with other experiences of loving and losing.

Losing Things

Objects, in and of themselves, have no real meaning. It is only when humans endow them with meaning that they take on significance. Children learn early to give objects human characteristics, and then to use these objects to comfort themselves when the loved person is not available. The ragged teddy bear and the torn and tattered blanket are stereotypical childhood attachments. The word *attachment* is important here. Children form an identity with or a love for things in a way similar to the manner in which they form relationships with people.

Not all objects are candidates for attachment, nor should they be. I suppose we can all think of the endless line of lost items that span our lives—umbrellas, scarves, sunglasses—but these are not attachment items. We may miss them, but for the most part, they can be replaced. The new pair of sunglasses is as good as the lost pair. On the other hand, the attachment item is not easily replaced. Although this item may be expensive, it is not the expense alone that causes concern when it is gone. It is the emotional connections surrounding the object that makes its absence unbearable. True, you may lose your wallet and feel extremely vulnerable. Lost money and credit cards, in particular, can cause great financial distress. But what if you had a photograph of your grandmother in the wallet, one that could never be replaced. That loss would be felt differently and sometimes more acutely than the financial one. How often have you heard something like the following?

Yes, there were money and credit cards in the bag. But that's not what mattered. I had things in that bag I can never replace. They don't mean anything to anyone but me, and now I don't have them.

The old love letters, the wedding album, the blue ribbon, the pile of greeting cards and newspaper clippings—we mark the passage of time with objects. We grow close to them. Always, these objects remind us of people or experiences we love. Children have the same kinds of attachment to objects.

The Transitional Object

The so-called security blanket is perhaps the best example of a transitional object. As children struggle to achieve separation, whatever the circumstance, they often use objects in order to shoulder the blow. The security blanket as used by Linus, the beloved Charles Schulz cartoon character, is theoretically helping him achieve separation successfully.

The degree of attachment and the kind of transitional object vary greatly from child to child. Some children become so dependent on the object that they are desperate when it is lost; others have no such object. Some children have one preferred object; others shift periodically among several. Although soft stuffed toys and blankets are the most common transitional objects, keys and small change purses are also popular. One four-year-old child, Alex, wore a plastic sword to nursery school each day. He never played with it in the classroom but never allowed anyone to touch it either. He kept it carefully strapped around his right shoulder, so that the sword swung from his left hip.

Most children relinquish their transitional object(s) somewhere between ages three and five. Some keep one handy for those times when they are particularly frustrated.

As I have reiterated staunchly, there is nothing wrong with this particular behavior. It is perfectly normal within its developmental framework. Parents should not secretly hide the object or throw it away. When the time is right, most children relinquish the object themselves, with little coaxing. Normally, the five- or six-year-old relinquishes the object and replaces it with equally prized objects such as collections of insects, model dinosaurs, or stickers that they can part with and return to. Problems arise only when the child is quite unable to live without the object, even though developmentally it may be time.

Keeping Things

Quite at the other end of the continuum is the child who loses everything. He leaves his lunch on the bus, his homework at home, his sweater in the gym. This behavior tends to be exhibited later than the security behaviors, which are exhibited almost from infancy. Although careless behavior has a variety of explanations, when a child of six or seven repeatedly loses things, he may be telling you of his fear of becoming attached to anything. Remember that when you are attached to something, you always risk losing it. That loss is painful. One way of coping with that fear is choosing not to be attached to anything. This fear of forming strong attachments to anything seems to generalize, so that even objects not normally candidates for such attachment, such as lunch, are lost with regularity.

Well, don't all kids lose things? Yes, they do. And there is nothing earth-shattering about an occasional loss. But if your child is losing things daily, although such losses are not pathological you may need to disregard the expense and inconvenience of these losses and focus on what your child may be feeling.

Losing Friends

Kevin stood on the corner a long time. The moving truck had left twenty-five minutes earlier. He crossed his legs and sat down on the grass. He didn't cry. He didn't talk. He wouldn't smile for a long time.

There are many ways to lose a friend. Lost friendships often involve disloyalty or growing apart emotionally (see also chapters 4 and 5). This section involves a very specific kind of loss, the kind that is not voluntary or mutually agreed upon. When families move, children lose friends they don't want to lose, and there is nothing they can do about it. Although moving itself involves many emotional transitions (see also chapters 8 and 9), we will look here specifically at the friend who moves away because this circumstance relates directly to the issues of loving and losing that we are discussing in this chapter.

Initially, the young child attaches to her parents, her brothers and sisters, and familiar objects. Particularly when children begin school, their social attachments widen. They become close to peers and often prefer a "best friend" to being with parents or siblings. It is a natural developmental sequence for children to become more and more peer-oriented and less family-oriented as they mature. Depending on who the peers are and how they support the child, this friend orientation influences the child positively or negatively.

During the later stage of early childhood, there is obvious movement in children's interpersonal knowledge from an understanding of the material basis for contact to an understanding of the psychological basis. Friendship for three- to five-year-olds is clearly associated with playing and sharing toys. When playing is initiated, liking and friendship, in their most fundamental form, follow almost automatically. Beginning in kindergarten, children also start to help each other when they sense another can use help.

By the time the child enters first grade, two new levels of interpersonal skills have emerged:

1. The concept that friendship exists as the reciprocal interest of two parties, and that each party must respond to the other's needs or desires.
2. The concept that friends are people who understand one another and share their inner thoughts, feelings, and secrets with one another. Friends are in a special position to help each other with special or difficult feelings.

My point here is that the three- or four-year-old is not truly capable of experiencing friendship of the kind I am about to discuss. This does not mean that the three- or four-year-old does not respond well or meaningfully to peers. There has been much research of late reinforcing the idea that even infants may relate to each other. What very young children do not do with peers is form attachments with them parallel to the ones they have formed with their families:

When Lydia was three, her close friend Ellen was moving back to England. Ellen's mom threw a big party in her apartment. At the end of the evening, I stood in the doorway weeping for the lost friendship between Lydia and Ellen. There was not a tear between them. For several weeks following, I kept asking Lydia about Ellen. She never brought her up. Finally, when a postcard arrived from overseas, Lydia looked at it and said, "Ellen's gone." Now Lydia doesn't even remember her.

Parents of young children are often more upset about the departing child than the so-called friends are. For young children, one child is as good as the next. It is very typical for Jodie to have a "best friend" without even knowing the child's name. If play is enjoyable, a friendship between Anna and Peter is fused, at least for the next hour or two.

By the time the child has reached six or seven, he has arrived at a new social plateau. Now we can talk about real friendships, those in which true attachments are forged. Children spend a great deal of time with their friends beginning at this age, after school, on weekends. By age nine or ten, children prefer the company of a close friend to that of almost anyone else. Peers help children see the world from a new perspective. Discovering that people can have different points of view is a very important social milestone for children.

We can all remember that one special person with whom we could share any thought or feeling. This person contributed to the formation of our identity. She picked up where our parents left off in setting the stage for loving relationships with spouses and with our own children. She taught us charity, compassion, loyalty, discretion, trust, dependability, and good humor.

At this age, when a friend moves away the child feels this separation deeply. This separation may be as traumatizing as those first few days of school—and is often even more traumatizing. Children rely on their friends to console them when they are upset, to make them feel good about themselves, to encourage them, to call them up on the telephone and chitchat. A good friend is the child's connection to the outside world, a world not as accepting as her family. Without these threads to the world, it is a very scary, sad, lonesome place. When a friend is not there, there is a big emotional hole to fill. New friends are not made quickly. This hole may be there a long time.

Sibling Rivalry

Glorianna: Mom, Cindy's looking at me. She's always looking at me! Stop it you little creep! You jerk!

Cindy: Leave me alone. I wasn't looking at you! Ugly pig!

Glorianna: Mom, Cindy called me a pig! Mom. Tell her to quit it!

Mom: Glorianna, leave your sister alone. Go upstairs and finish your homework.

Glorianna: Yeah, yeah. Take her side. Cindy, the little baby. I always have to get it!

We can't help laughing at the humor in this situation. Yet repeated occasions of squabbling are not at all humorous, for either parents or children. It is possible that sibling rivalry exists in all families, but its frequency, intensity, and duration varies greatly. Some children experience only surface spats that fizzle out just as quickly as they begin. Others harbor ongoing, deep-seated hostility that can fester well into adulthood.

Sibling rivalry is a struggle that exists between children because of each one's desire for parental attention and love. When a child does not perceive that she is receiving an equal amount of her parents' affections, jealousy develops, and hostility, either overt or hidden, is directed toward other siblings. Jealousy and fear of the loss of parental love are the major causes of sibling rivalry. A child secure in her parents' love exhibits a smaller degree of quarrelsome behavior toward her siblings than a child who does not perceive this love.

The key word here is *perceive.* As always, we must take the child's point of view. *Telling* your children you love each of them equally is not going to suffice if they don't feel this to be true. When Mom told Glorianna to go upstairs and do her homework, she implied that Cindy was better and more valued by Mom than Glorianna was.

A certain amount of sibling rivalry is to be expected and must be handled. What needs to be determined is when rivalry becomes unhealthy and destructive.

Birth Order

Every position in the family has advantages and disadvantages. Your impression as a parent will differ depending on which of your children you speak with. At some point, each child will feel that she is losing out.

Oldest: I do all the chores. I clean up the mess. I have to answer the phone and take messages. When Joey and Lisa do something stupid, it's cute. When I do something stupid, it's irresponsible. I hate that word *responsible!*

These reactions from an eleven-year-old are not unfounded. Research confirms that parents have higher expectations of the oldest child. They exert more pressure on her to achieve; and she usually does. Studies in the professions and big business continue to show that firstborn children are society's highest achievers. Now this achieving may be OK as long as the oldest feels nurtured as well as challenged by her parents. If the oldest continually feels short-changed in attention—that younger siblings are getting *her* attention—then she is likely to resent and antagonize younger brothers and sisters every chance she gets.

Middle: Being in the middle is lousy. Jenny gets to do all the things I want to because she is the oldest, and Matthew is the baby. Everyone loves babies.

If the oldest typically feels pressure from parents, the middle child typically feels neglect. Studies also support this impression. In general, parents don't give as much attention to the middle child as they do to the oldest and the youngest. No malevolence is intended on the part of the parents, but they do tend to spend less time with the middle child.

The middle child's typical reaction to this perceived neglect is to provoke negative attention by destroying prized possessions, doing poorly in school, or using profanity. The rationale is that any attention from parents is better than none at all.

Youngest: My sister bosses me around and teases me. I never get to play with any of her things. When her friends come over, they go into her room and lock the door. Mom never does anything. She says to leave them alone.

The youngest generally feels he loses out because everyone in the family is bigger and perhaps better than he is. Older siblings have more privileges than he does because parents give them more. Big brothers and sisters stay up later, go out with friends, and have bigger allowances than he does.

If the youngest perceives he is not getting the prized attention that older siblings are, he is likely to stage events to cast his older brothers and sisters in a bad light. If big brother is singing in the shower, little brother is likely to complain, "Make him stop, Daddy. He's giving me a headache."

Gender and spacing also affect the number of sibling quarrels a family has. Same-sex siblings quarrel a great deal more than siblings of the opposite sex. Same-sex siblings simply find themselves in a greater number of competitive situations, where there are definite winners and losers, than opposite-sex siblings. For the same reason, children close in age quarrel more than generously spaced siblings. Closely spaced siblings have more common battlegrounds. On the upside, same-sex closely spaced siblings are more likely to develop an emotional closeness later in life as the common battlegrounds emerge as common interests.

So, are you doomed to years of conflict and petty squabbles if you have two boys ages six and seven? It is important to remember that the points discussed do not *cause* sibling rivalry. Instead, they focus on the factors most likely to cause problems. Parents can do a great deal to diminish sibling rivalry by learning to eliminate potentially competitive experiences between children, and by listening carefully to their feelings.

When Conflicts Become Harmful

There is no way to eliminate quarreling completely. Your children don't like it when you and your spouse quarrel, and you don't like it when they quarrel, but the fact remains that most people who love one another quarrel. A certain amount of tension between siblings is actually healthy in helping them establish their individual uniqueness and role in the family. What parents need to determine is when this quarreling is no longer constructive. Most quarreling falls into the *nuisance* category:

Tyler: I'm watching TV. Stop tapping your foot.

Leila: I'm not bothering you. I'm just tapping.

Tyler: OK. I'm turning the volume up.

Leila: It's loud. You're hurting my ears! You big snothead!

Tyler: OK. OK. Just quit the foot.

Even noisy quarrels do not necessarily amount to destructiveness. Nuisance quarrels may be annoying, but they are not harmful. This type of petty quarreling is usually triggered by hunger, boredom, or fatigue. The hour before dinner, that long ride to Aunt Mary's, Christmas shopping—these are perfect settings for mindless squabbling. The cause of the quarrel revolves around some temporary irritability followed by equally mindless bickering and needling. The negative energy is usually vented, and there is no long-term damage.

The second type of quarrel—the debate—should actually be *encouraged:*

Linda: Those cartoons are ridiculous.

Terry: I like them.

Linda: Don't you know that if those things really happened to people, they'd be dead!

Terry: They're funny. I like them. They're funny.

Linda: You might think they're funny. But they are actually pretty sad. There are other things to watch, you know.

Terry: I don't care. I am going to watch them anyway.

Linda: All right. It's *your* brain!

You might think that Linda has a hidden agenda. She is looking to change the channel and is using manipulation to her own end. However, the message she is imparting to cartoon-crazed Terry is valid. Cartoons may not be the best things to watch. Some of them are violent. It certainly will take more debates of this sort to persuade Terry to try alternatives. But if Terry is never cautioned to think differently, he may never do so on his own. The debate involves practice in verbal communication and sharing of ideas. Initially, it may involve some bantering and manipulation. Optimally, it will involve a willingness to listen to different points of view and to form new opinions. This is *constructive argument,* the healthy desire to use one's knowledge to exchange information on a topic of interest. This kind of debate between children is never to be discouraged, but facilitated.

It is the last type of quarrel, the destructive quarrel, that needs adult intervention:

Chris: You little creep! You keep away from my friends! You're no good at sports and no one wants you! You come near me and I'll punch your lights outs.

Mark: Liar! Liar! Big shot! Everything's got to be your way. You

lost last weekend. Every team you've ever been on loses. Loser!
Loser! Liar! Liar!
(*Fistfighting ensues, along with crying, shouting, and name
calling.*)

The cause of the destructive quarrel is feelings of inadequacy and
low self-esteem. The focus degrades personal character and may
end in long-term emotional damage to the children.

Helping children lessen the amount and intensity of quarreling
involves understanding why children quarrel. Underlying problems
support the quarrel; the quarrel itself is only a symptom. When
parents simply demand that quarreling stop, the underlying cause
stays alive and will continue to fuel future quarrels.

Children's quarrels can actively provide parents with insight into
how children see the world. If we listen empathically, we may learn
that our children need attention, are feeling pressure, need closer
friendships, or are insecure. This is all useful information when we
want to help our children with everyday problems.

A Special Concern: The New Baby

There is nothing more exciting or traumatizing in family life than
the arrival of a new baby. What is often underscored is the fact that
roles in the family do shift either when new family member arrives
or when an older one leaves.

For children, the arrival of a new sibling can be difficult. Young
children are ambivalent about siblings because deep down they do
have affection or, at least, curiosity about this intruder. On the
other hand, this new person certainly does take up a lot of Mommy's and Daddy's precious time. The way older children adjust to
a new arrival depends a great deal on how parents respond both to
new baby and to the older child's sometimes fragile feelings.

Age

Research has confirmed that children between the ages of eighteen
months and three years have a much more difficult time adapting
to a new sibling than either older children or infants. The concept
of sharing is not fully developed at ages eighteen months to three

years. As a result, most younger children will do everything to keep from giving away pieces of their parents' attention.

In general, children over the age of five have it easier. They have had more time to develop independence through school and personal friendships. They are more willing to share their parents with another because their attention is drawn elsewhere. Traditionally, infants or young toddlers also adapt easily for exactly the opposite reason. They haven't had the turf long enough. The new sibling is just another person, not necessarily a threat.

Again, just because you have a three-year-old and are awaiting that precious bundle, you are not doomed. In some cases, even a teenager will adapt poorly to a new sibling. This is not a hard science. We only know what is likely to happen, not what will. Parents must be sensitive, understanding, and accepting of the child's feelings about the new baby. They can help their child sort out her confused feelings and realize she is still special and very much loved by her parents.

OK, you say, what can I do realistically? My child has to go to sleep, to school. He will lose things and friends—and kids fight. Read chapter 3.

3

Loving and Losing
Strategies and Solutions

Solving problems effectively can be difficult. Rarely does one quick, easy answer suffice. From the discussions in chapter 2, you can see that the issues related to loving and losing are complex, the causes sometimes completely unknown. The problems are not what they appear to be on the surface. Even so, if you have spent time understanding your child's behavior, you are ready to implement some specific strategies. Remember, in some cases, you may have to use several approaches, to be persistent, and to be very patient.

Bedtime

In chapter 2, we established that sleep is a biological process. Children sleep if they are tired. If they are not tired or are anxious or excited, sleep does not come naturally. We also saw that sleeping alone in a bed at a prescribed time is a learned behavior. The child must be given the opportunity to comfort herself, to become quiet, and to fall asleep. Some children are quite good at comforting themselves, climbing into their beds and using blankets, toys, and even their own lullabies to croon themselves to sleep. If children are not falling asleep well or easily, it is rarely their fault. True, some children may use bedtime as a battleground: "I won't go to sleep." But many simply don't have the skills to put themselves to sleep. When children lack skills, parents must teach.

The key "sleep" word with three- to five-year-olds is *ritual*. Preschool children need to know what to expect at bedtime each and every night. The hour before bedtime should be spent in a calming activity. If the child is expected to retire at 8:30 P.M., he should *not* be watching a stimulating television program at 8:15 P.M. Unless he is totally exhausted, he is not going to be easily coaxed into bed after the program is finished. When he is wound up, he needs time to wind down.

The evening ritual may be set by parents and child together. Jimmie takes a bath, complete with toy dinosaurs and "color foam." Dad and Jimmie sing endless strings of "Row, Row, Row Your Boat," as it echoes on the bathroom walls. Baths are generally quieting, comforting experiences. After the bath, Jimmie dresses for bed—pajamas, football jersey, ancient Beach Boys T-shirt—and climbs into the sack. Dad is there to read a good two, sometime three, stories. The *bedtime* and bedtime ritual should be the *same* each night. Surely, there will be variations, but the goal itself should remain the same.

OK, great, you say. We've taken the bath, sung, put on our football jersey, climbed into bed, and read two stories. At 8:45 P.M. Richie is in the livingroom asking for orange juice. At 9:00 P.M. Richie is back for more juice. This time he takes his juice and sits down on the couch. Richie does not want to go back to bed.

The point I've made earlier remains. Parents must help children learn responsible habits. If Richie stays up, it is because you haven't helped him to go back to bed. Each time Richie gets up, you must take his hand and walk him firmly but gently back to this bed. You will need to stay in his room until he settles down. You may have to do this ten or twelve times, but you must be consistent. The point is not to create a power struggle between yourself and your child: if Brendan stays in bed *you* win; if he stays on the couch, *he* wins. Setting sleeping schedules is not to be treated as an authoritarian practice. The attitude is not "I, the parent, set the schedule that must be obeyed." It is "I am your parent, and I am going to help you find ways to fall asleep so that you can comfort yourself eventually." The goal is independence and self-direction, not arbitrary compliance.

Children form habits from the responses we give to them. If we permit the child to stay in the living room, the message is very clear. It is OK to be in the living room, to get up several times and go back to bed several times. Finally, I end up in the living room with Mommy and Daddy. That's the way it works.

If Joel does not stay in bed easily even after you've set the ritual very carefully, you may need to rehearse this schedule with him. Remember that children are concrete reasoners. They need words and actions to be clearly defined. Early in the afternoon or on the weekend, you may need to sit down with Joel, crayons and paper in hand, and go over the entire bedtime procedure, step by step:

1. First, Joel is going to take a bath with some of his favorite toys. What toys are you going to take? Why don't we draw some pictures of what you want to take into the tub?

2. Let's pretend that Joel is out of the tub. What towel does he have? The green one? He's drying himself with the green towel. Daddy is helping. Let's draw another picture of Joel and the big towel.

3. Now Joel is going to get into his bedtime T-shirt. The one Grandma bought, or another one? We have two pictures now. Let us make picture number three with Joel and his bedtime T-shirt.

4. It's time to get into bed. What books are we going to take? Let's draw a picture of that, too.

5. Joel is so tired. Let's draw a picture of you with your eyes closed. You have had such a long day.

Once all of the pictures are complete, review each with Joel and transcribe what he says onto each picture. For example, if Joel says, "I want to read *Frances* and *Goodnight Moon*," then that's what the picture says.

When you are finished reviewing the schedule, take all the pictures and post them in sequential order in a conspicuous place. At least once a day in advance of bedtime, review the pictures in Joel's own words. Have him tell you his own bedtime story, over and over again.

More pictures may be drawn, posted, and reviewed for particular circumstances:

1. After Joel has gone to bed, he comes into the living room and asks for some juice. Let's draw a picture of you asking for your juice.

2. Mommie brings Joel his juice and walks him back to his room. Mommie fixes the special yellow timer. When it

rings, she will go. That's picture number two. Let's draw a picture of you, the juice, and the timer.

3. Joel comes back into the living room. He asks for more juice. Joel gets juice the first time he asks, *not* the second. This time Mommie takes Joel back to his room right away. She sets the yellow timer. When it rings, she will go. Let's draw this picture, too.

4. If Joel comes into the living room the second time, he does *not* get a drink. He is taken back to bed.

Again, this second set of pictures should be posted and reviewed frequently. Remember that all habits are difficult to break, good ones as well as bad ones. Most children will respond very nicely to reviewing their prescribed rituals and will be content knowing the expected outcome. Children find tremendous comfort in the familiar.

In the Middle of the Night

Some children fall asleep quite readily but are unable to remain asleep. Children are biologically able to sleep through the night before they are a year old. Again, if they cannot comfort themselves sufficiently to fall back to sleep on their own, it is generally because they don't know how. I have known parents to complain that seven-year-olds are waking them several times during the night without falling back to sleep. Certainly, children have nightmares. I discuss this phenomenon in chapters 6 and 7. But many don't. They are awake because the alternative has not been learned adequately.

When your child awakens in the middle of the night and is not having a nightmare, the procedure is similar to the ones practiced at bedtime's initiation, with one additional complication. You will be even more exhausted and, as a result, more susceptible to your child's protests. You must interpret these protests as a plea for help. As much difficulty as your child has falling asleep she may have falling back to sleep. Taking her into bed with you or getting up and switching on "David Letterman" for the two of you to view is not help. It is avoiding a difficult learning experience. Everytime the child gets up, he must be lovingly but firmly taken back to his own bed, a drink of water the first time, and the timer.

Humans are extremely resilient, resourceful creatures. Left alone, Joanne will find ways to comfort herself and put herself back to sleep. Current research has alerted us to the fact that most of us do awaken several times during any given night. This alert state is very brief, followed just as quickly by sleep. This is a learned response pattern. If it is not learned, we stay awake and look for others to "put us to sleep."

Again, when several sleepless nights have been the result of bringing Cary back to his own bed, parents may begin the rehearsal process described earlier. Learning requires the absorption of ideas. Conscious rehearsal of what happens when Renata wakes up in the middle of the night will help her to know what to expect.

Older Children

Six- to eight-year-olds need consistent bedtimes as well, mutually arrived at but consistent. A nice practice is to have children sit in bed and read quietly for fifteen to thirty minutes. This is a blissful habit, one as strong and as lasting as television, and one that children revisit the rest of their lives.

After nine years, parents should not expect a specific bedtime. Lights are doused somewhere between nine and ten. The hour before should be fairly quiet, spent by the child in her own room, listening to cassettes, reading until sleepy.

A nine-year-old may have difficulty with this independence at first, staying awake until the last possible moment and oversleeping in the morning. If this happens, bring the hour forward by thirty minutes "until you need a little less sleep." If bedtime doesn't become an issue now, neither will curfews later.

By making his nightly retirement gradual, you not only help your child monitor his body, but you allow him to wind down at his own pace, and to adjust to his home schedule and the one at school. Even a night owl can learn to regulate his body clock with proper gentle intervention.

In Bed in the Morning

One nice development of late, perhaps in reaction to this overload of advice on bedtime, is the idea that it is good for children to join their parents in bed *in the morning,* particularly on Saturdays and Sundays. Even Spock (1988) promoted this practice.

It seems that our Puritan-based American culture is and has been too hung up about sex, particularly with regard to affection between males. The proverbial pendulum has swung, as it often does, in another direction. Families need to get together—physically—and express affection. The family bed in the morning seems to have struck that delicate balance. For those parents who wish to institute this practice, I suggest it as something to offer children without having to have them spend the entire night with you. In this way, independence and physical connectedness are both nurtured equally.

Starting School

Parents can set the tone for how their children will feel about those first few days of school. By respecting a child's individual concerns and responding adequately to them, parents can prevent unnecessary anxiety, while addressing concerns that continue to exist. The following strategies are appropriate for children three, four, and five years old. Younger children require a separate set of strategies. As this book is aimed at three- to twelve-year-olds, strategies for younger children are *not* included here.

Prevention

Select your child care program carefully. Make certain it is one that respects the networking of parents, children, and teachers. Adequate preparation for school is the key to comfort and predictability. Every effort should be made for parents and children to have teacher and classroom contact before that exciting, yet tension-provoking, first day. Many schools, both public and private, give tours to prospective parents. If the school does not invite parental observation, it is clear that it is not supportive of parental intervention. Your first impressions as a parent touring the school can be quite revealing:

> At 8:35 A.M. all those little bottoms were planted in a row on the cold floor outside the classroom. Every few seconds the

teacher would steal a glance from a crack behind the closed door. She didn't want to spend one minute more with those children than she absolutely had to. A few blocks away, another kindergarten teacher had a door wide open. Parents, entire families, were in the classroom. The teacher was very involved, but he had a yellow chart next to the door that announced, "Sometimes I'm busy. If I am, leave me a note. I always want to speak with you."

There is no way parents can know what their child is doing every minute of the day—that is unrealistic and unfair to demand of any teacher. Yet good early childhood teachers know how to avail parents of necessary and meaningful communication no matter how busy they are. The behavior of individual teachers often indicates the overall school policy on parental involvement. Some schools have a very strict closed-door policy. Parents drop their children off at the classroom and retrieve them at the end of the day. That is all the involvement parents are expected or allowed to have. Parents in these environments are rarely allowed into the classroom except at the appointed times during the year. In some cases, parents may not even be allowed in the building. Other schools realize that, although opening doors to parents requires intensive planning and a sensitivity that not all administrators, teachers, and parents can develop easily, the potential benefits are worth the initial time and effort. Teachers and parents can learn from each other and support children's integration into the world of school.

This section deals exclusively with school *separation* and cannot provide all the criteria for school *selection*. (For more information, see the appendix and reference sections.)

Once you've made some preliminary decisions, check on each school's separation policy before registration. A sensible, yet sensitive school policy reflects the following.

School Policy

All new families are invited to visit the classroom before the beginning of the school year. Sometimes families visit as a class or in small groups or pairs. During this time, children are invited to explore the room while parents sit and talk with the teacher. The purpose of this visit is simply to familiarize the family with some of the classroom routines. Teachers may talk to parents about what a typical day is like and show each child where her cubby is. Parents may be given questionnaires at this time to be reviewed then or to be returned at a later date (see the sample questionnaire below). A good practice is for the child to bring a recent photograph of herself or her family. During the visit, the teacher will encourage each child to tape the photo inside her cubby. Sometimes, teachers have visiting children draw their own pictures, one to take home and one for their cubby. In this way, children are given an immediate sense of ownership in this place called school. When they arrive on that big first day, a place is waiting for them.

Some settings encourage brief (no more than thirty-minute) home visits by the teacher. These visits should not be mandatory but are often helpful in establishing that vital bridge between home and school.

New Children

For the first two days of school, all parents of new children attend. Special preparations are made so that the parents can be seated in one section of the room while the children participate in the scheduled activities. Parents and children leave at lunchtime. For the next two days, the parents are on the premises, but in a separate room. Again, all leave midday. The last day is set up so that parents advise their children that they are leaving but that they will return for them after work. The children begin their normal schedule after this first week of transition. Children admitted to the program in midyear follow this same transition format.

Transition Difficulties

Children who experience difficulties after this initial period are placed on an extended transition schedule. The transition process is individualized according to the needs of the family.

Parental Questionnaire

This questionnaire has been designed to help teachers know more about the children who will be entering their classroom for the first time. It may alert the teacher to reactions that your child may have when you leave him at school. Its purpose is to sensitize teachers and parents to the meaning of the school entry and separation process. It is based, in part, on the Parental Anxiety Rating Scale reported in the work of Doris et. al. (1971).

1. How old was your child when you first left him or her with a sitter or someone other than you?
   How did she or he react at that time?
   How does she or he react now?
   Have there been any changes in the people who take care of him or her?
   If yes, how does she or he react to those changes?
   How do you feel when you leave him or her with another person for care?
2. Does your child have a favorite blanket or toy to which she or he is attached?
   Under what circumstances does she or he use it?
3. How does your child react to people she or he does not know, either in or outside your home?
4. How does your child behave when she or he is asked to mix with a new group, such as at a birthday party?
5. Has your child ever stayed overnight at the home of a friend or relative?
   If yes, describe his or her reactions to the experience.
6. Have either or both parents been away overnight or for a period of time?
   If yes, how old was the child at the time?
   How did she or he react to this separation?
   Who cared for him or her at that time?
7. Has your child ever been hospitalized?
   If yes, at what age?
   For what reason?
   For what length of time?
   Were parents allowed to stay with the child?
   Describe the circumstances, including his or her reactions to this hospitalization.
   How did she or he behave when she or he came home?
8. Was either parent ever hospitalized?

For what length of time?

What was the child told?

Was she or he permitted to visit?

What were his or her reactions?

9. Has there been a death of anyone close to your family, or of a pet?

   If yes, what was the child's relationship to that person?

   What was he or she told?

   What were his or her reactions to the death?

10. If you and your spouse have separated or divorced, what is the living arrangement for your child?

    What has been his or her reaction to this situation?

    In what way do you think it will affect his or her entry into school and his or her separation from you?

11. Have you moved during the child's lifetime?

    If yes, how many times?

    How old was he or she?

    How did she or he react to the move?

12. What does your child do when she or he is angry?

    Afraid?

    Sad?

    Happy?

13. What makes your child fearful?

14. How does your child recover from emotional stress?

15. How do you think your child will react to beginning school?

    How do you think he or she will react when you leave him or her in school without you?

16. What else would you like us to know about your child that would help us in planning for his or her most comfortable entry into school and the most comfortable separation for both of you?

Existing Problems

School policy alone is no guarantee that children will adjust to separation readily and easily. Even if your child completes the initial transition process, there will be times when it is difficult for her to allow you to leave.

Sneaking Out

One may be tempted when a child seems absorbed in an engaging activity to avoid the ramifications of saying good-bye. Parents and teachers often feel it is easier to avoid a problem than to face it.

As always, we must take the child's point of view. Surely, it may be more comfortable for parents to tiptoe out. Children view the experience differently. Suppose you were in a doctor's office and were told you needed to receive an injection. You know this won't be pleasant. You brace yourself. You may choose to look the other way, but you have been made aware of the inevitability of the injection.

What if the doctor chose not to tell you about the injection. When you weren't looking, she simply came over to you and *wham!* Chances are you would not trust this physician. Chances are you would never see this physician again. There is no doubt that the injection is needed. The fault is with the approach.

The same holds true when you are leaving a child at school or, for that matter, anywhere. Parents and children both need the opportunity to say good-bye to one another. Each will struggle to resolve their feelings. Yet the child who struggles to overcome his discomfort and adjusts to school with the help of a supportive teacher has achieved self-esteem. In essence, he can say, "This was tough but I did it." When a parent sneaks out, the child never has this important opportunity.

So far, we have focused exclusively on leaving your child at school. However, we cannot neglect what happens at the end of the day:

> *Jeremy left easily enough in the morning, looking for the Lego house he had begun the day before, but when I came to pick him up, he didn't even look at me. He sat on the floor, refusing to put his puzzle away, saying he didn't want to go home, didn't want his coat or dinner.*

Refusing to go home and giving parents a hard time are behaviors that state, "OK, you left me. Now it's my turn to give you a dose of what you gave me this morning." All of this is perfectly normal. Remember that all day the child may have very sad, angry feelings. Each day she copes, the better she becomes at coping:

- When your child is anxious after your having said good-bye, simply state, "Now it's time for you to go to school and for me to go to work. You will see me again after outdoor play, when I come to pick you up." Encourage the teacher to come over to the two of you. A sharp teacher will already be with you, reiterating what you have just said. As she directs the child to the day's activity, bid adieu, leave quickly and smoothly.

- Arrive about ten minutes early for both dropping off and picking up your child. Often teachers will use this time to speak briefly with the parents, and to greet or say good-bye to the children. Avoid rushing in or out or lingering too long. Both can add to the anxiety of separation.

- Security objects from home, such as small toys, stuffed animals or blankets, or special "Mom and Daddy things" like old house keys or memo pads, help children form that important bridge from home to school. The teacher should not expect these items to be shared. These belong to the individual child. They are a symbol of home and family.

- Encourage your child to make things at school to bring home. This school-to-home activity provides the final scaffolding between school-and-home and home-and-school. Make certain that school-made items are posted prominently at home and at your workplace. Displaying your child's work not only boosts his self-esteem but lets him know that schoolwork is "special."

- Write a note or draw a picture and place it in your child's lunchbox. The teacher can read this note to your child at snack or lunchtime. If you've made a picture, your child can post it in his cubby. Your note need not say more than "Have a nice day" or "Daddy misses you." The child will feel that you have not completely deserted him, and that he has had contact with you during the day.

- Whenever you can, have your child visit your workplace. This is important. Your child needs to know where you go every day. Children are very concrete reasoners. No matter how you explain where you go and what you do, an explanation is no substitute for actually seeing and experiencing your workplace firsthand. Your child should see his drawings and photographs in your office. As he takes parts of you to school, you take parts of him to work.

When the Child Is Really and Truly Not Ready

Sometimes, the child does not seem ready to begin. In some cases, a particular school may not be meeting the child's needs. If this is the case, a change in setting may be in order. In others, the schedule may be too overwhelming. If the child is attending four days a week, maybe three days would be more reasonable in this situation.

In a few cases, for any number of reasons, children may simply not be ready for school at all. They don't seem interested in classroom materials or enter easily into classroom activities. They seem upset by the very thought of going to school. If changing the setting or modifying the schedule does not make a reasonable difference in her response, then you may have to listen to your child. She is telling you, "I'm not ready."

The realization that you child is not ready for a regular nursery-school program can be very painful. You want to avail your child of every opportunity. What is most essential is not to feel defeated or rejected. In fact, your attempts to orchestrate alternatives for your child's socialization are more likely to produce success than pressing her into a situation that, for her, is not developmentally correct.

If a nursery program permits, have her introduced on a very minimal schedule one morning or afternoon a week. Begin some recreational programs, such as forty-five-minute gymnastic, dance, or music classes. Arrange play dates in your home first, then in others' homes. For most children who experience this level of difficulty with separation, it is not the separation experience alone that is troubling. It is the amount of time away from the parent and the number of children with whom the child is expected to interact that accelerate the stress and make school intolerable. If your child is introduced to more manageable separation experiences, the larger ones will be more manageable as well.

When My Child Will Be Ready

Certain developmental abilities are cited as necessary for a child to be able to cope with a traditional nursery-school experience. Anna

Freud (1966) believed a child should be able to feed herself and have both bowel and bladder control. Some schools assist in this toileting process and may not require complete bowel and bladder control as a prerequisite to entry.

The ability to relate to other children, to use play materials in a directed manner, to wait turns, to tolerate frustration, and to express negative feelings are also cited by other researchers and child psychologists as indications that young children are ready for school. We all know children who fit these guidelines and other who don't. Unfortunately, no one really knows who's ready and who's not until after the first few weeks of school. The reality is that many children are ready and, with the appropriate support from parents and teachers, will embrace learning now and for a lifetime. School separation is an adventure and a challenge. The ability to separate provides your child with the foundation to develop as an autonomous, self-reliant, whole person.

Losing Things

Children between the ages of three and five are bound to lose things they love. Their reaction is particularly distressing if the lost object is one to which they have become extremely attached. As I stated earlier, some children may find it unbearable to live without the beloved object even for a short time.

This section does not address the loss of *nonattachment items,* such as puzzle pieces or small manipulatives. All children are expected to lose such items. These losses are not related to the issue of loving and losing and therefore are not discussed here.

The best cure for loss is prevention. Even young children can begin to learn the virtues of responsibility, especially if they've been the victims of several prolonged searches for coveted items. Children learn to care first for the items to which they are attached. Helping the child establish cubbies or special places for special things is one of the first steps in helping them toward responsible behavior. A good activity is to have Kathi construct and decorate her own special place for Lou-Lou, the dinosaur doll. When Kathi is not playing with Lou-Lou, this is where Lou-Lou is going to live—in the special house Kathi has made for her. This special Lou-Lou house is always next to Kathi's bed. Special places may be inside closets, under beds, on shelves, or wherever the child selects. When Craig knows Monk the monkey will always be safe and sound in his special place, Craig is very likely to place Monk there for safe keeping, rather than risk losing him by leaving him somewhere else.

Broken Toys

My former opinion on this subject was simply not to buy toys easily broken. Experience has taught me that this practice is not easily applied. Attachment objects are handled often. They are thrown, jumped on, hugged, soaked in water, painted, and fed assorted breakfast cereals. Most young children don't care what these special objects look like. In fact, many children prefer the worn look.

If, however, an arm or an ear is torn from Bo-Bo the clown and Beverly is upset, her parents should take her seriously. Remember the last time your car wasn't running properly. You weren't too happy either. Do not offer to buy a new doll immediately. Beverly has specific feelings for Bo-Bo that cannot be transferred willingly or easily to a new toy.

If at all possible, try to fix the broken toy right away. Tell Jason exactly what you are going to do to the toy and have him help you. This fixing is actually the most fundamental form of problem solving, teaching the young child very concretely that solutions do exist. If you cannot fix the toy immediately, help your child lay the toy in its special place until you can fix it.

Allow the child to ask for the toy to be fixed. Or ask if there is anything you can do to help. Remember, the child may not be upset by the lost buttons at all. You are there to respond to the child's feelings, not your own.

If the toy cannot be fixed effectively by you and your child continues to be concerned, there are several things you can do. You can take the toy to someone who can fix it. Your child may not be willing to do this, particularly if the toy must be left. Or you can offer to purchase a new toy with the stipulation that the old one will not be discarded until the child is ready. (The practice of keeping the old toy even though a duplicate has been purchased is specifically for attachment objects. To implement this procedure for *all* childrens' toys is not reasonable or practical.) Dealing with the broken attachment object in this manner allows the young child to see that

- Things that are hurt can be fixed.
- Important things that are hurt or broken are not simply cast aside.

Here the child's attachment objects are addressed as items of value, because they are valued by the child. In turn, the child sees himself as valued and respected.

Separation

There does come a time when the child's need for an attachment object is no longer developmentally appropriate. Most children relinquish this object themselves somewhere between three and four years old. Up to this time, parents and teachers should be patient and accommodating. The more patient and accommodating parents and teachers are, the more easily is the object relinquished. If children feel that their object is in any way resented or threatened, they will be concerned when it is not with them. This anxiety can prolong the attachment to the object.

Some children can be weaned away from the object in much the same way they made the transition to school, a little at a time. The most creative practice I ever heard of is the mom who, together with her son, cut his adored blanket into numerous pocket-sized pieces. In this way, the child always had a small piece with him, until finally he didn't even need that. The basic idea is to slowly wean the child from the object by having him keep smaller pieces of it, just as the parent spends a shorter and shorter amount of time at school as the child makes the transition.

This practice helps the child come to understand that he can survive without the object. He gains confidence as he is able to exist with smaller and smaller fragments of the beloved toy. This does not mean that you take Bo-Bo the clown and tear him up. Most objects do have something that can be removed and placed in a pocket or purse. If not, with your child, you can design something pocket-sized from the toy. All of these actions tell your child that you respect his feelings for the things he loves. The self-esteem he gains from your respect will aid in his growth toward autonomy and in the eventual relinquishing of the attachment object.

Lost Friendship

> *Gregory was the largest boy in our fourth-grade class. He wasn't fat, just bigger, taller, and wider than everyone else. He was good-natured, athletic, not the big-bully type, so almost everyone liked him. One day Gregory came to school very, very quiet. While we were writing in our notebooks, Gregory lumbered to the front of the room and lurched over to the teacher's desk. Within seconds, he was weeping, controlled but weeping. "Jeff, Jeff's gone," he whimpered. He fell into the teacher's lap. She contained his large body as best she could. Jeff was Gregory's best friend. He had moved to Michigan.*

Of the many experiences I had in grade school, I remember this one in detail. The sight of poor Gregory taking over Sister Marietta's chair is something at which my fourth-grade class could have smirked, or at least giggled. But we didn't. Maybe we were just plain shocked. Or maybe we identified with Gregory. The mobility of people in this country is vast. It is very probable that a child will lose at least one good friend during the middle-school years.

For all the middle-school set may try to act like adults, they still identify most with their friends, wearing the same kind of jeans and sneakers, having the same haircuts, the same video games as the other children in their class and neighborhood. If friends are not physically together, they visit together on the telephone. Friendships begin to be built on verbal exchanges as well as common interests and activities.

Children this age constantly think in terms of others. A picnic is fun only if Lisa can invite a guest, or better still if she can go picnicking with her friends' families. This need to be with friends is part of the familiar compulsion to conform, to organize, to be in a group. That is why school, the anxiety zone of the three-year-old, becomes the comfort zone of the nine-year-old. Nothing else in the middle-schooler's life is so socially organized.

Clubs emerge, and girls especially can literally block the sidewalk as they walk arm in arm, a veritable parade of friendship. Although many children have a circle of friends, within it there is inevitably one or two "bests." The alliances that form during this time may last for many years. Middle-school children choose friends with great care and give these friends complete loyalty. They throw themselves into relationships. Friends seldom leave their thoughts. Girls, whose friendships at this time take on a greater intensity than boys' (some experts state not only at this time but during a lifetime), spend hours selecting just the right card, the right present for that very special friend. At this age, children ask their friends for advice, as well as asking their parents or older siblings.

My point here is that the middle-school child is extremely reliant on her friends, almost as much as she is on family. The loss of a friend is not a trivial, easily resolved dilemma. Parents who console the child with "You'll find new friends" aren't accepting reality. Yes, the child may find new friends. That is not the issue. A person with a freshly broken leg does not respond well to "You'll feel better soon." First, you must deal with the pain.

Children are often aware early of the potential move. This period before the move is spent in close contact with the friend. Parents can prepare the child for separation by either taking photographs and videos of the friends together or having the friends themselves take them, and by making certain each friend exchanges items that are to become the special attachment objects of late childhood.

Friendship albums or a friendship collage can be made from the collected photos. My daughter has such a collage framed on her desk, one in which she has photos of all her friends who have moved away. When parents help their child prepare in this way, they are telling her, "Your feelings are important to us."

No matter how integrated the preparation is for the move, the day the friend leaves will always be a difficult one. Feelings are strongest now—anger, despair, fear of loneliness. Right now your child is not sure she can deal with the separation. Her emotions are a potent mixture of sadness and fear. It is important not to counter these fresh feelings of vulnerability, but to accept them:

Eileen (crying): I am going to miss Meghan so much.
Mom: You spent so much time with Meghan. She was just like one of the family. This is very hard, isn't it?
Eileen (crying): Yeah!

Mom: Nothing I could say would make you feel better. I wish it could. When a good friend moves, it's rough!

One of the mistakes parents make is thinking that there *is* a right thing to say. Say this magical thing, and Donna will perk up and forget about Sandy. It's very difficult for parents to deal with their child's unhappiness. Children's emotions rekindle feelings of our own loneliness and vulnerability:

Eileen: What am I going to do?

Mom: You are going to be very upset for a while. I don't know how long. You are going to miss Meghan and wish she were here. You will write to her and call her on the phone, but it's not going to be the same as having her two blocks away. You will make new friends, but it's not going to be as soon as you'd like.

Here Mom is giving Eileen a very realistic picture of what is in store for her. She is comforting but honest. When parents give children a candy-coated picture of a dilemma, they teach children to expect something quite different from what is likely to happen. If Eileen is promised brand-new friends to replace Meghan and then doesn't get them, two things are likely to occur. First, Eileen will begin to think something is wrong with her. After all, she is supposed to have these wonderful new friends and she doesn't have them. She must be doing something terribly wrong. Second, she won't trust you with her feelings the next time. You don't seem to have the right crystal ball in front of you. Maybe you know what could happen to others, but you don't know anything about her.

Sometimes parents are overly zealous in their quest for an optimistic outlook. Chad is invited to phone Jerry each and every night. Every weekend Dad has a houseful of new friends over for ball games and video parties. These tactics can confuse the child. After all, he's lost someone important. Why the camouflage?

When you tell your child that she is going to be upset and she is, true, the feelings themselves are very uncomfortable, but at least Stacey knows that these are the right feelings. She's on the right track!

If I could give only one piece of advice to parents, it would be this: *There is no way to keep your child from being hurt.* Your child has feelings, some of them very painful. You may not want to march right up to Max and state, "You are going to be miserable, Max, miserable, understand!" But telling your child what feelings to have and what ones not to does not build trust or certainty about life's events.

Once your child has passed through the initial feelings of fear and sadness, he will be willing to explore options. Now is the time to suggest visits from potential friends and going to the movies or the mall. Your child now has the confidence that he can come through a difficult time. Using this new emotional strength, he can now take the risk of building a new friendship.

The child's final coping stage consists of evaluating the experience and coming to terms with it. Tiffany has moved away. Carolyn can write to her often and call her occasionally. She may see Tiffany once a year. Then again, she may never see her. Their relationship will change because of the distance between them. There is nothing Carolyn can do about this. Carolyn will remember and cherish Tiffany's friendship, but she also knows that she has the ability to go out and make new friends. This will take time and patience, but good friendships like the one she had with Tiffany are worth the effort.

How to Keep the Kids from Quarreling

As was indicated in chapter 2, no household is truly quarrel-free. Siblings are natural targets for conflict, as children quite naturally feel that they compete with their siblings for their parents' love and attention. When children are frustrated, for whatever reason, it is easy to vent this frustration on a sibling. Whether the child is jealous, angry, tired, or hungry, the sibling is a convenient target. However, many conflicts can be eliminated, and others vastly diminished, if parents take the time to review when, where, and how most sibling quarrels emerge.

Fatigue

Evan: How much longer is it?
Dad: You just asked three minutes ago.

Evan: How much longer? Andrea keeps rocking back and forth. It's so annoying. I can't stand it. Why did we have to go to Grandma's? Why couldn't she come to our house? Sitting back here for two hours with Andrea would make anyone sick.

Andrea: I am not rocking. I am not. You smell bad, Evan. You stink!

Dad: OK, I've had it. I'm trying to drive, or can't you see that? Andrea sit still and Evan just be quiet! Next time we are leaving Grandma's right after dinner.

Studies on the relationship between lack of sleep, exhaustion, and irritability unquestionably support the idea that children quarrel more when they are tired. It is not that, when he is tired, Jonathan automatically sees how much more attention you pay to Connie, his younger sister. It is simply that when Jonathan is tired, he is more sensitive to these issues. When Connie is tired, she will be sensitive to these issues, too.

Fortunately, there is a simple, if not easily applied, cure for quarrels caused by fatigue. Quite obviously the tired child must get more rest.

What is enough sleep for a child? That depends on the age of the child and her own personal metabolism. The following chart indicates the average amount of sleep per day for children of different ages:

3–4 years	12 hours
5–7 years	11 hours
8–10 years	10 hours
11 and above	8 hours

This chart indicates whether a child is departing drastically from the average amount of sleep required for children her age. However, it cannot account for individual differences and specific circumstances. For example, a child who engages in a great amount of physical activity needs much more sleep than the one who engages in an ordinary amount. When Bobbie comes home from lacrosse practice, he is going to be more irritable the moment he walks through the door than he will be a few hours later. If his sister Tina is anxious to jump on Bobbie the minute she sees him, Tina is in for a big disappointment!

In addition, as children reach early adolescence, new hormonal activity can cause fatigue and thus a greater need for sleep. Any parent who has attempted to get an eleven- or twelve-year-old up on a Saturday morning can attest to this.

Parents get into the most trouble when they try to establish sleeping schedules for individual children regardless of what their child's behavior may be telling them. If your child does not fall asleep within fifteen minutes of his bedtime, there is something wrong with the bedtime, not with the child. Younger children rely on their parents (See "Going to Bed" in chapters 2 and "Bedtime" in this chapter) to help them regulate their sleep cycles. Older children can be prepared to set their own bedtimes as long as they accept the responsibility of getting to school and other activities alert and on time. If they do not meet their responsibilities adequately, you will orchestrate their schedule until they can demonstrate these time management activities.

A *few* guidelines:

- Help children establish a *consistent* bedtime *with* you. Children should know that *they* have contributed to the decision for *their* bedtime. Modifications may be made in special circumstances.
- When children tell you they are tired, let them sleep. Homework may be a priority; however, some children require a brief nap when they come home from school. To deprive them of it and insist on the immediate completion of homework is not feasible. If the child is using the nap to avoid doing homework, that is a separate issue. You can easily determine whether your child truly needs a nap by seeing if and how the homework is completed. If the homework is completed carefully and with interest, you know the nap has been useful.
- Long trips are often necessary. However, in order to avoid that all-too-common "nasty fight in the back seat," leave early; bring blankets, pillows, and bedtime stores; and when planning vacations, make a major consideration the time traveling *to and from*. A miserable, tension-ridden ride can cancel the joy of an entire excursion.

Hunger

The time is 5:45 P.M.:

Marie: Mommy, Joey took my blue sippie straw. I wanted the blue one, the blue one . . . now!

Mommie: Marie, what's wrong with the red sippie straw? You like red. Red is your favorite color.

Marie: No, no. Joey. Joey. That's mine. I had it first.

Joey: I always have the blue one. Daddy bought them—he gave it to me. I don't want the red one. (*Steps on the blue "sippie straw" and breaks it. He heads for the refrigerator and takes a package of cookies off the lower shelf.*)

Mommie: Joey, put those Oreos away. I'm making noodles. You are going to spoil your dinner. (*Marie is screaming now and also grabbing cookies.*) Marie, Marie! (*Mommie grabs the cookies. Everyone is crying and/or screaming now.*) Give me those straws. No one gets cookies or straws until after dinner! Now go inside and watch TV.

If this scenario does not sound all-too-familiar to you, I would be suspicious of your claim to be a parent. Western culture has always been preoccupied with the *what, where,* and *when* of mealtimes. The problem with the previous scenario is that everyone involved is hungry and irritable. No one is listening to anyone; no one cares to listen.

The evening dinner hour has a mythology that seldom bears fruit in the real world. In theory, the family comes together at the evening meal to share the pieces of wisdom gathered during the day. Food is shared as ideas are, freely and calmly. Now, there are occasions when this does occur. But typically, hungry older children race through the meal to watch a favorite television program or finish homework. Younger children fall asleep, fuss with their food, or cry to leave the tedium of the table. The myth is shattered, and many parents are left wondering where they went awry.

The average working family may not eat dinner until seven or eight at night. You may want the family to be together at dinner, but asking children to wait that long to eat is not reasonable. Most children need something nutritious the minute they come home from school. As children need sleep when they are tired, they need food when they are hungry. There are many nutritious foods that need little or no preparation: cheese, fruit, peanut butter. High-sugar, high-fat snacks should be kept to a minimum. Whether or not a child is hungry at dinner should not be the issue; whether or not a child is nourished should be. If children are hungry when they come home from school and eat well then, there is no need to be concerned about what they eat or don't eat at the scheduled mealtime. Forcing children to abstain from eating when they are hungry, and forcing them to eat when they are not, does not teach children to regulate their eating habits appropriately.

I am not advocating the elimination of traditional mealtimes. What I do advocate is modification of the typical mealtime focus. Attention should be on people, not food and its consumption. Younger children, in particular, do not need or appreciate gourmet preparations. The family should come together at a certain hour for conversation. A light meal may be served. Those who are hungry will eat; those who are not are welcome to come and chat. Nutritious snacks should be available beforehand so that no one has to come to the table ravenous. Older children are, in fact, capable of determining when they are hungry and can, with moderate direction from adults, make appropriate food selections. Obviously, younger children need more adult intervention; however, even three- or four-year-olds left to their own devices will not starve, given the availability of nutritious food.

The purpose of this book is not to provide meal plans or guidance on child nutrition; it is to help parents create an environment in which sibling quarrels are addressed wisely and with sensitivity. As was suggested in chapter 2, many sibling quarrels are of the nuisance variety, caused by hunger and fatigue. If you notice heightened squabbling around dinnertime, you might consider the following:

- If possible, have the whole family eat early and have a light snack available later.
- If family members are working or going to school late, make sure younger family members are given their meal earlier and are not made to wait until the entire family is available.

- Make meals simple. Spend time with the family, not cooking elaborate feasts.
- Make sure there is a wide variety of nutritious snacks available. Limit sugar and caffeine, which cause irritability.
- Have family members participate in meal planning and preparation. Ten-year-olds are perfectly capable of preparing simple meals both for themselves and for younger siblings. A six- or seven-year-old can help slicing peppers for a salad or making a yogurt dip for celery stalks. Three- and four-year-olds can set the table with durable serving ware.
- To reiterate, mealtime ought to be person-focused, not food-focused. As long as the food is nutritious and good-tasting, energy should be expended elsewhere.

Once the tension that revolves around food and its presentation is lifted, families do find they are able to listen more to each other, and mealtimes are more enjoyable for both children and parents.

Fatigue and human quarrels, though annoying, are not rooted in deep, underlying emotional difficulties and do not result in serious, long-term damage to children. Diminishing such quarrels between siblings is *relatively* simple: Remove the physical cause, and the quarrels lessen.

Unfortunately, there are quarrels between siblings that do have long-range effects and need careful intervention by parents.

Anger

Judy comes home from school in a hurry. She is anxious to get on her bike and ride over to Marilyn's house to begin their project for the science fair. When she goes into the garage, she discovers her bike is gone. Tommy, next door, lets Judy know that Pam, Judy's sister, took the bike a half hour ago. Judy is furious. This is the second time Pam has taken her bike without permission. Now Judy has to walk to Marilyn's and she is already late.

Anger is a very primitive, yet highly necessary emotion. Its presence has ensured the preservation of the human race since ancient times. There is nothing wrong with anger. Most of us can understand why Judy would be angry in this circumstance. But the issue is not whether Judy is angry but how she chooses to express this powerful emotion.

Children express their anger in many different ways, some constructive, some not. Some children attempt to hide their anger, but it surfaces in other forms: extreme competitiveness, compulsive eating, ulcers, headaches, or extreme shyness. Others are physical in their expression, slamming doors, throwing toys, punching, or verbally degrading their siblings' personal character, calling them stupid, ugly, an idiot, or moron or using profanity.

Fewer are specific and direct regarding their anger:

Judy: I am very angry, Pam. This is the second time you've taken my bike without asking me first.

Pam: But you weren't home.

Judy: If I'm not home, you cannot take my bike because you don't know if I will need it.

Pam: What if it's an emergency?

Judy: Pam, get air in your own bicycle tires and you won't have to worry about an emergency.

Just as we learn almost everything else, we *learn* to express anger. Research supports the view that families pass down patterns of expressing conflict. Children are fabulous imitators. It is frightening to think that our children are watching us and copying our personal behavior. No matter how we shout, "Do what I say, not what I do," children inevitably do the opposite.

When you walk into your son's room and holler, "How can you be such a slob?" you are giving him a message loud and clear: When you are angry at someone, tear him apart verbally. Don't be surprised if your children argue using similar tactics.

Parental anger can be expressed in constructive ways that do not hurt children. Civilized expressions of anger become desirable models for children to copy. When children see their parents express anger constructively, they are more likely to express their own anger in this way.

Constructive Anger

Dad comes home from work. The kitchen is a mess. The television is blasting. Ted and Randy are sitting in the den. Popcorn, chips, and soda are everywhere. Dad is very upset. He told the boys this morning he wanted the kitchen clean and food kept either out of the den or on the coffee table, and off the floor.

Dad expresses his anger constructively:

Dad (*shuts off TV*): OK. I am very tired and very angry. I told the two of you this morning that I wanted the kitchen clean when I came home. You have completely ignored this.

Randy: We will clean it later. We will, Dad.

Dad: That is not what I asked. I asked that the kitchen be clean when I came home. I am home and it's not clean. I also asked that you either not bring food into the den or keep it on the coffee table.

Ted: But we were hungry, Dad.

Dad: I understand that you were hungry. I am not questioning your eating. I am questioning the way you are eating. Now I have to waste time cleaning up when I could be taking a shower and getting ready to make dinner. The TV does not go back on until you help me clean this place to my satisfaction. Your dinner will be late. Next time, I want the kitchen clean the minute I come home.

Dad was angry because his specific requests had been ignored. He expressed his anger openly but constructively:

1. He told the boys *why* he was angry: "You have completely ignored this" (cleaning the kitchen and keeping the den tidy).
2. He told the boys exactly what was wrong with their behavior: "I asked that the kitchen be clean when I came home. I am home and it's not clean."
3. He gave the boys specific information regarding the desired behavior: "Next time, I want the kitchen clean the minute I come home."
4. He gave the boys concrete information regarding the consequences of their behavior: "The TV does not go back on until you help me clean this place to my satisfaction. Your dinner will be late."

Children do imitate their parents' methods of dealing with anger. Children who use antisocial aggression and assaultive behavior tend to come from families where there are parents who act as aggressive models. All parents get angry at their children. It is not harmful for your children to know that you are angry and that your anger has to do with their behavior. It is harmful for children when parents express their anger through abusive physical or verbal attacks.

Notice that Dad in the previous scenario did not disapprove of Ted or Randy themselves, calling them "lazy, irresponsible, good-for-nothings." He disapproved of their behavior in this one instance. Both boys can continue their day knowing they have made a mistake, but their-self concepts are not diminished.

Constructive expressions of anger focus on the behavior rather than the worth of the person. Enraged expressions of anger toward the child himself distracts the child's attention away from *what* is being said to *how* it is being said. The child is so concerned about whether he will be struck or destroyed verbally that he no longer has the energy to think about *what* he has done.

If children observe their parents expressing anger in nonconstructive ways, they often imitate such behavior and have loud, enraged conflicts with their brothers and sisters. They spend so much time yelling and hitting each other that they cannot focus on the real problem. If you yourself cannot express your anger constructively, there is no way you can expect this from your children. Next time you are *yelling* upstairs for the children "to stop screaming," pause. Think about what you are really doing.

Television Violence

The average American child will watch fifteen thousand hours of television before she or he completes high school. During these hours, children are given countless examples of violence: beatings, stabbings, gunfire, often graphic displays of human cruelty. Here they learn the various models of how adults handle their anger.

Research findings confirm that children do imitate what they see on television, good and bad. Children sample the behavior they see demonstrated. If they are comfortable with the behavior, they keep it. If they do not feel comfortable with it, they discard it. This does not mean that a child witnessing a murder on television is doomed to perform this horrendous act at some point in the future. It does mean that children need careful adult supervision when watching television.

If a child's parents are strong models of behavior that is different from what he sees on television and violent programming is kept to a minimum, it is rare that a child will choose to exhibit violence. However, if the television is the strongest model of adult behavior the child has, and he witnesses an excess of violent programming, chances are that this child will choose aggressive behavior.

Peers

Even if parents handle their anger appropriately, as children approach the middle-school years they become increasingly shaped by the behavior of their peers. It becomes very important for children to dress, talk, and act like other children. Children of this age in particular feel at least some pressure to conform to the peer group's expectations. For some children, this pressure is accentuated by the fact that they do not have the skills that allow them to conform to peer group expectation (see also "Losing Friends," chapter 2; "Lost Friendship," in this chapter; and chapters 4 and 5, "Feeling Left Out").

Children may choose to hide their anger from their peers, recognizing that its display will cause further isolation from the desired peer group. Children trapped socially in this way often use siblings as targets, goading and teasing them, as others do them at school. As strategies related to peer group pressure are addressed at length in chapters 4 and 5, they will not be discussed here. Even so, it is important for parents to recognize that peer group difficulties can result in accelerated quarrels between siblings.

Sampling Behaviors

Even parents' providing healthy models of dealing with anger is no guarantee that children will imitate this appropriate behavior. If children have sampled aggressive behaviors and discovered they work, they will be repeated:

Ian: I don't want to share my cookies. I don't wanna.

Mom: Ian, there are only two cookies. Give one to your sister. (*Ian takes cookies and smashes them on the table.*)

Next time, for fear of provoking another outburst, Mom does not ask Ian to share. Because this physical display worked for Ian in this instance, he is likely to use the same behavior in the future when he is angry.

When children are allowed to use physical or verbal aggression in their conflicts, they learn that it's OK to harm another person physically; it's OK to hurt another person's feelings; it's OK to do anything you want to the person who has made you angry.

Nothing of positive value is learned from hostile battles between siblings. The vicious fight does nothing more than give children a practice ground for destructive anger. Children should be encouraged to settle their own problems, but only if those children possess the skills to do so constructively. Although the most powerful deterrent to aggressive behavior between siblings is appropriate parental modeling, no matter how constructive your own channeling of anger may be, you must be prepared to *teach* as well as model this behavior when necessary.

How Can Parents Help

Mom hears Alice and Claire screaming in their bedroom. They are calling each other names and hurling toys at one another.

Mom can

1. Let them fight it out on their own. Someone will eventually get hurt, and the children won't be so quick to fight next time.
2. March in and announce, "OK, you have three minutes to resolve this. If I hear anymore screaming, you are both grounded for the weekend."
3. Take sides without any acknowledgment of what has taken place: "Claire, you are always picking on your sister. Now stop it."
4. Intercede. Tell the girls that they seem angry about

something. You'd like to help. Have each girl state her
side calmly, no name calling, no screaming. Each girl
should also state *how* she feels. Ask each girl what the
other sister could do to make her feel better. Together
work on the problem until you find a satisfactory
resolution. If you can't solve the problem then and there,
make a time to meet again.

At this point, it must be obvious that techniques 1, 2, and 3 are
all blatantly inappropriate. Yet these parental strategies are often
used as means of settling conflicts. Technique 1 actually encourages
aggressive behavior. The girls are "being told" to continue the fight
because their mother, in essence, has condoned fighting by turning
her back on it. Strategy 2 will no doubt terminate the screaming, at
least for the moment. Yet the problem the girls are having remains
unaddressed. They will continue to release their anger on each
other in future bitter quarrels. The same is true of strategy 3. No-
where are anyone's feelings being addressed. In this case, Claire
feels even more animosity toward her sister than she did at the beginning of the quarrel. Chances are that the quarreling will continue.

Only the final solution helps children deal with their anger and
solve problems constructively. Here the children are taught to express their feelings without causing damage to anyone. They are
taught that they have a right to angry feelings. Everyone gets angry.
What they do not have a right to do is to inflict their anger on
anyone else.

Such efforts are extremely time-consuming. As was stated earlier,
most things of value are. Human emotions are not responsive to a
"quick fix." If parents take the time early to help their children deal
appropriately with angry feelings, there will be fewer hostile quarrels in the future. Using the constructive model they have seen their
parents apply, children will be better able to settle conflicts on their
own.

We spend hours teaching children to tie their shoes or wash their
hands, recognizing full well that such time invested now produces
a lifetime of self-sufficiency. Teaching children to resolve the sibling
conflicts produced by anger gives them even more important lifelong tools: compassion and justice. They are well worth the time.

Jealousy

Anger and jealousy often go hand in hand. One of the most common expressions of jealousy between siblings is quarreling. This is easy to understand. The child who feels he must struggle for his "fair share" of parental love will undoubtedly have hostile feelings toward his siblings, with whom he must compete. Often, he will tease and antagonize the sibling and degrade her personal character. Unconsciously, the jealous child chooses ways to behave that will attract his parents' attention, and fighting among brothers and sisters usually does attract attention.

Some parents believe it reflects badly on them when their children show signs of sibling rivalry, so they try to root out all signs of rivalry among their children. Children in such families try to hide their jealousy of a sibling because they know their parents do not approve of such feelings. Although it is possible for parents to get rid of most open signs of sibling rivalry, the jealous feelings remain. Eventually, these feelings appear in behavior that is more destructive than simple, open expressions of rivalry. For example, the child may express jealousy by becoming overly "good." She kisses and hugs her younger sibling and runs to answer his every whimper. Or she rushes to comply with all her older sibling's demands. Parents may interpret this overly good behavior as an abundance of sibling love, when in fact the child acts this way in order to win parental approval. She is desperately seeking love and approval and believes that her parents like children who are good. The child works hard to look good in her parents' eyes. Other subtle expressions of jealousy include nightmares, excessive competitiveness, extreme shyness, or excessive generosity.

These subtle expressions of jealousy are less obvious and may appear to be less troublesome than the overt confrontation. However, they are evidence that the child may be feeling less loved by her parents. It is important for the parents to notice these less conspicuous signs of jealousy and to help the child deal with these jealous feelings.

Helping Children Deal with Jealousy

Encourage children to express their feelings about their siblings. The first step that one can take in helping children deal with feeling jealous is to admit that such feelings probably do exist, to some degree. Next, children must be encouraged to express their feelings openly, being assured that these feelings will not be judged or criticized. Parents need, as always, to listen with an *empathic* ear and to try to understand why children feel the way they do.

By encouraging children to express their feelings about their siblings, parents learn how children may have acquired jealous feelings. Parents may discover that some of their children's jealousy has developed because the children have misinterpreted certain words or actions to mean that other siblings are loved more than they are. For example:

> Dad comes home from Danny's trumpet concert, praising and carrying on about Danny's performance. Emily has never been gifted in music. She interprets Dad's enthusiasm as a sign that what Danny does is more important to Dad than what she does.

Does this mean parents must never express joy over one child's particular gift? Should we compliment each of our children in secret for fear their siblings may know of our positive feelings and feel belittled? Of course not. Expressing positive feelings toward children helps them to feel loved.

What parents must remember, however, is that when they give positive messages to one child, they are simultaneously giving messages to the other. Parents must be sensitive to what those messages may say to the observing child. If, for example, Melissa always receives hand-me-downs from Corey, her older sister, Melissa is not going to see the sense of this practice. What she is more likely to see is that Corey always get new clothes, and that she gets Corey's old things. If using hand-me-downs is a feasible practice, and it is, then Melissa should be as involved in the clothing purchase as Corey is. If Melissa is involved, she is less likely to view the clothing as Corey's belongings. After all, Mom purchased the clothes for both Corey *and* Melissa.

Children are less likely to misinterpret positive messages given to their siblings if they themselves feel secure in their parents' love. Children whose need for parental love is being fulfilled develop a minimum of jealousy toward their siblings and experience much less sibling rivalry.

The New Arrival

The beginning of intense sibling rivalry can often be traced back to the first few weeks and months after the birth of a new sibling. The child who feels insecure about his parents' love has a difficult time accepting and loving a new sibling. When the child sees his parents loving the new baby, he becomes even more insecure about his parents' love. The insecure child finds it difficult to share parental love because he feels there was already not enough to go around.

If instead the child receives as much love as he needs and desires before the baby arrives, the child is less concerned about the new sibling's also receiving love from his parents. He feels secure that there is enough parental love for both of them.

The child is less confused over the birth of a new brother or sister if the parents take time to prepare her for this experience. One way to introduce children to what babies are like is to show them their own baby books. Even older children enjoy looking at their baby books as you tell them what they were like as babies. Children of all ages like to hear how much they were loved as babies, how cute they were and are, and how much you enjoy and love them, whatever age they are.

Look at this baby boy. What a smart face you had. And what a smart face you have right now.

Children should be told ahead of time that they will have a new baby brother or sister, so that they can take part in the family preparation. Children feel included in this special event when they select clothing or contribute some of their own belongings, like a stuffed animal or a blanket.

For the young child, Mommy's sudden disappearance to the hospital can be frightening. Even if the child is allowed to visit Mommy and the new baby, leaving Mommy at the hospital and going home is very confusing. If there have not been adequate explanations, the child may believe that the hospital is where Mommy will live. It is best to tell children exactly what will happen beforehand so they can plan mentally. Some hospitals permit a family tour so that siblings have a picture of where Mommy will be. The child should know who will be taking care of him while the parents are at the hospital. Children should be able to contribute to this decision. If the child is permitted to observe his sibling's birth, as some hospitals encourage, he should be presented with adequate information regarding the birthing process. It is important to recognize that, although a certain hospital or physician may encourage a family birthing, compliance here is an individual matter. Many children may not be ready to accept this experience. This is perfectly all right. Many adults have difficulty observing a loved one in great discomfort, so it is perfectly natural for children to be concerned.

When the child visits Mom and baby at the hospital, he should understand that there will be a time when he and the rest of the family must leave. Mommy and the baby will rest for a few days, but soon the whole family will be back together again. The child may, in fact, protest leaving, but he should not be denied knowing the inevitable. Children cannot learn to trust unless they are given the truth.

The first few days with the new baby at home are often the most important in helping the young child to accept her new sibling and to feel secure that she is loved by her parents. Parents should never assume, "Of course, we still love Peggie. She knows that." Although this may be true and very clear in parents' minds, the child needs to be reassured of it. Particularly when the baby is home and time is at a premium, plans need to be made so that each parent has time for each child. Children feel loved when parents spend time with them. During that time, children need to know that they are special, that they bring joy, and that their parents care a great deal about them. (See "Making Time" and "Being Together" in chapter 1.)

The Home

Many of the reasons that children quarrel have been addressed:

1. They are tired or hungry.
2. They are unable to express their anger constructively.
3. They are jealous of their siblings.

Yet the emotional tone found in a household also strongly affects the quality of sibling relationships. In families where the general home atmosphere is positive, warm, and supportive, there will be less conflict between siblings. In contrast, a negative, critical, hostile atmosphere will foster heightened levels of sibling conflict.

Every member of the family contributes to some extent to the overall quality of the home. Yet parents often have the greatest influence as they set the stage for initiating and encouraging either positive or negative behavior.

Behaving in positive ways is not easy. It is especially difficult when parents are faced with the difficulties of family life: financial worries, career concerns, and juggling schedules. When consumed in this way, parents cannot bolster the energy or focus to work on creating a positive home atmosphere.

However, most parents can improve the quality of the home atmosphere. It does require getting to know each family member well and spending time communicating with each other. It is worth remembering that it takes as much time for families to grow together as it does for them to grow apart.

Two major competitors for family time are extracurricular activities and television. Special interests are wonderful for the development of self-concept, but an overabundance of these produces family members that simply pass one another while going in and out, never sharing experiences, and eventually never really caring about each other.

Television also competes for family time. It is not enough for families all to watch the same program together, although even this is a rarity nowadays. Parents and children must talk to each another, about what they do, what they think, and what they feel.

It is true. Family atmosphere does change, sometimes daily. Even so, parents must plan regular family times, maybe not once a week but once a month perhaps. The family time doesn't need to be a full day, perhaps part of one. Older children may be resentful of such plans, particularly if they feel the family outing is cutting into their free time with friends. Yet if all family members contribute to the planning, it can certainly be less tension-provoking. It may mean that parents may have to alter their expectations regarding the nature and content of the traditional family outing. The old cabin and the fishing trip may no longer pass muster. Parents need to listen to what their children may want.

Each day, each parent must spend some time with each and every child—talking, reading, playing cards, something. If parents do not do this, they have no way of even guessing what is going on in their child's life. Children should know that this time is sharing time— for feelings and ideas.

Self-Concept

Notice that the many causes of difficulty with loving and losing involve one common element: *how children feel about themselves.* When children feed bad about themselves, they often become frustrated and angry when presented with the stressful circumstances involving loss.

There are a number of ways parents can help their children develop self-concepts that are more positive. Children with improved self-concepts have fewer, less intense conflicts regarding loving and losing and are in a better position to develop constructive approaches to problem solving.

THE FIVE SELF-STRENGTHENERS

1. *Allow your children to help you.* Don't give them trivial tasks. Give them something meaningful to do for you that is within their developmental framework. Young children are generally very pleased to be included in adult activity. Older children are often stereotyped as notorious work shirkers, but this doesn't have to be. Generally, if children know they are truly needed, they will give time to a task.

2. *Help children feel good about their bodies.* Self-concept begins with the most concrete manifestation of the self: the human body. Remind young children of how steadily they are growing and how much more they can do now than they ever could before. Compliment older children on their appearance, clothing selection, or physical abilities.

3. *Allow children to make their own choices.* Allowing children to make decisions tells them that you have confidence in them. Even children as young as three or four can be given alternatives from which to select. For example, there are several pairs of pants on the chair. Which would you like to wear?

4. *Tell your child you love her and show her often.* People do not

magically know that you love them. They need verbal and physical expressions.

5. *Listen to children and acknowledge their feelings.* I don't think I can ever say this enough, so here it is once again.

Disappointment

"I Expected Something Different. Why Didn't I Get It?"

Anan sat at his desk and scribbled in the margins. The other children set quickly to the task at hand, reading and answering the required questions. After about ten minutes, Anan stood up and brought his paper to the front of the room. "You didn't answer the questions, Anan. You didn't even try," said his teacher. "Trying hurts," said Anan and walked back to his desk.

In the previous chapters, we have examined the issues related to loving and losing. We learned that to feel loss, one must first feel attachment, connectedness to a person or a thing. Without attachment, there is *no* love, or loss. Disappointment is different. Disappointment involves wanting something—often something we have never had—and not getting it. As loving and losing are linked to our experiences with attachment, disappointment is tied to our experiences with success and failure. As always, the child's ability to grapple with this lifelong problem involves her development of self-concept.

Whatever the child desires in life is a result of her own self-evaluation. For the most part, the child's ability to evaluate herself does not develop until external reinforcement is in place. The child's desire to attain something, whether it be an A in science, a swimming trophy, or a special friend, is planted every time a parent communicates something positive to her. The smile of elation when you tape the "pony" drawing to the refrigerator urges Allen "to make an even better pony" next time. That slap on the back when you finish your morning run with Irene allows her to run further and longer tomorrow. If anything that parents do is magic, *encouragement is.*

All humans love praise. We may think compliments have their hidden agenda, but inwardly we hunger for others to look at us and tell us how wonderful we are. It's the reason Bobbie gives in and dons the new shirt and tie, the reason Patti slides into her new outfit with little coaxing. Children want adults to tell them that they look "good," that they think "good," that they are "good." A desire for learning and achievement needs continual bolstering in the early years in order to be sustained later in life. Young children need approval from significant others to define for them exactly how competently they are performing. Remember, children want to be like the adults they love. They won't know if they are doing well unless someone "knowing" tells them they are.

This is not to say that external reinforcement is the goal. It's not. When Mom alerts Bonnie to the many good things she does each day, Mom is inadvertently telling Bonnie exactly what competency is. The next time Bonnie does a good thing, she may be able to measure her own performance. If Bonnie likes what she has done, she can *give herself* a compliment. If she doesn't, she can give herself support and encouragement to continue. This is what self-reinforcement is all about, being able to tell yourself, "You're doing a great job. Keep going," or "OK, this is not what I want. Let's do it again."

Young children do not have the capacity to reinforce themselves in the ways that adults and older children do. Until they develop this ability, they need consciously directed reinforcement and praise from adults. If children receive this kind of support early, they won't require an inordinate amount of it later on.

We all know perfectly wonderful, capable people in our lives who are never happy with how they look, what they think, or what they do. Before they choose the suit to wear to the dinner, take on that special project, or leave for that well-deserved vacation, they need a dozen opinions and confirmations regarding their decision. The message these people may have received in childhood was "You're not capable. You do not do good things." This essential lesson of competency has never been learned by these people because it has never been taught.

Constant reassurance is needed by people like this because they really don't know what it looks like or feels like to do well. What they do know, and know very well, is failure. As with loving and losing, children cope each and every day with success and failure. Very early in development, the child understands whether he is an "almost always doer" or a "not" or "seldom doer." Results don't occur merely from telling children they are worthy but from the establishment of an atmosphere that fosters security, acceptance, independence, and responsibility and where warmth, praise, and appropriate limits are ever-present. A parent doesn't need to criticize a child verbally for the child to get the message loud and clear: "You are not going to make it."

> *I remember standing next to my father's desk, holding my history test. It was an 88, the best mark I had got that term. He never got off the phone, not ever. The people at the other end of the phone were so much better than I was. Dad couldn't be bothered with my measly 88.*

Again, there are many success and failure issues that could be discussed here. Those selected most reflect the concerns likely to have the most enduring impact upon lifelong development: school performance, competing, disloyal friends, feeling left out, and feeling humiliated.

Before we examine each of these circumstances individually, let's take a longer look at the central issue: success and failure.

Praise and Criticism

There is an expression: "Nothing succeeds like success." The reverse is also true: "Nothing fails like failure." Current research points to the realization that negative adult reactions regarding achievement produce a significant decrease in children's expectations of success. In other words, if a child is continually criticized, she will learn not to anticipate achievement. This perception initiates a vicious circle of failure.

For example, suppose René learns that she does not express herself well in front of people. René sees that other people are confused when she speaks to them. She learns not to expect adequate communication with others. She begins to keep quiet and avoids circumstances where she might have to interact. The prophecy is fulfilled. People speak of René as "unfriendly, withdrawn, shy." René does not communicate well with others.

But what if René learns something else? Suppose she learns that she has a nice, quiet way about her. People like that. Good listeners are hard to find. So René begins to listen very attentively when people speak to her. And guess what? René becomes a very good listener. She has many friends who speak of her as "sensitive, warm, and intuitive." Here the prophecy is also fulfilled. René does have "a nice quiet way about her." People like that.

These two stories of René illustrate the fact that success and failure are seldom related to actual ability, as is common held. René is René. She is either supported for who she is or condemned for it. Criticism does not, as some parents think, help children change their behavior. In fact, chronic criticism may accelerate the very behavior that is disturbing to parents.

The second part of this predicament of failure is even more upsetting than the first. The most current studies reveal that once a child has, in essence, learned to fail, he can no longer respond to praise in the same way as the child who has learned to succeed. Everyone loves a winner. The winners know this and continue to win and to gain confidence in themselves.

"I look great, don't I?" chirped Natalie, as she fixed her ribbon. Natalie always looked great, and she always knew she did.

Conversely, children who learn to fail also learn not to accept the praise they so desperately need. As ironic as it may sound, the children who hunger for praise the most continue to starve; the banquet of reinforcement is before them, and they cannot nourish themselves. In contrast, confident children accept and revel in the praise they don't really need.

Failure is not the result of the absence of praise. Once children learn to fail they do so in spite of the fact that reinforcement exists.

Learning Success

Marisol sat on the floor pulling at the knot in her lacing toy. She looked at the knot from every possible angle, tugging at one end and then the other. After about fifteen minutes, she placed the toy on the chair in her bedroom and walked away.

About an hour later, she came back and began the process again. This time she managed to loosen the knot and untie it. Marisol smiled excitedly, sat down, and tied the toy up all over again.

There is the continuing controversy regarding the development of human personality. What role does genetics play in its evolvement, and what role does experience play? The present controversy stems from an old one, dating back to John Locke in the 19th Century: Are our personalities fixed at birth, or do we enter this world an "empty slate" to be drawn upon? No one truly knows the answers to these questions, and my speculation is that speculating about the hows and whys of human personality will continue for another few centuries.

What we do know and have known for some time is that each and every human being is unique. This uniqueness is observable at birth. No two babies are *exactly* alike in each and every way, even identical twins who come from the same fertilized egg.

Yet, even with this great diversity of human characteristics, there are some features of humanness that apply to almost everyone, like the need to be attached, to protect oneself from harm, and to live in the proximity of other humans. It is these common features that unite us as a species and these unique ones that define us as individuals that constitute the domain of human personality.

Which aspects of personality are available at birth and which are products of experience are still unclear. What is clear is that many of these personality traits appear strikingly early in development and tend to resist change. The child who readily and assertively engages adults at age two is the adult who readily and assertively engages colleagues at forty-two.

Any group of children—or adults, for that matter—is composed of a wide variety of personality types. Some are flamboyant and excitable; others are quieter and intuitive. This is not to say that children do not have many sides to their individual personalities. They do. The most gentle of children has a tough, swaggering side; the most assertive, a warm, endearing one. Yet most of us can characterize ourselves as displaying certain personality features more than others.

The problem is not the existence of so many different, sometimes contrasting, personalities, but society's consistent rewarding of certain personality types and rare rewarding of others—particularly in childhood. Fun-loving, outgoing types get lots of attention, and the more sensitive types slip through the cracks.

Parents' contact with a child in his earliest years will help him determine his self-worth before he has other meaningful ties, so parents are the primary mediators of their child's experiences with success and failure. Because our culture has been so overt in its adoration of the jovial, life-of-the party, big-leader type, parents are often concerned when their child doesn't exhibit these features.

Jerome Kagan (1986), the noted psychologist from Harvard University, has spent almost a decade researching the idea that shyness in children may have an innate component, not determined by experience. Psychologists, including Kagan, have yet to agree on a definition of shyness. What they do know are its symptoms. People who say they are shy find social contact uncomfortable—they may blush, their hearts race, their palms sweat, and so on. They feel awkward and continually monitor the "impression I'm making." Shy people are not necessarily introverted. True introverts don't like people as a rule and prefer solitude. Shy people often wish they were different, that they could be more outgoing. Kagan also supports the notion that this early shyness need not be a scar for life. Parents can help children become socially competent by nurturing self-esteem and a sense of belonging. Many people described as shy in early childhood grow up to surpass early expectations and to form wonderfully secure relationships during late childhood and for a lifetime.

First and foremost, the shy child is extremely private. She doesn't open herself up to other people easily. And although this private nature lends itself to many desirable characteristics, such as concentration and introspection, it has also helped to create a misunderstanding regarding the nature and motive of shy children.

In my own research, I found an extremely biased—though, I must admit, an extremely traditional—evaluation of one quiet young man. Evan, a charming, blue-eyed, black-haired, three-and-a-half-year-old had participated, with his parents' consent, in a research project conducted at his university-based preschool. This project was designed to measure levels of social ability in preschool children. I interviewed Evan's parents shortly after the project's conclusion. Here are their own words:

Mom: Evan is such a happy child, he really is. He's just quiet. Oh, he has friends. But he's more of a follower, you know.

Dad: We're just a little concerned. We have the results of that study, the one they did with Evan's class. He did really poorly on the social responsiveness scale. I've seen him in class, and he does wander around an awful lot.

Mom: He plays by himself.

Dad: Yeah, he does, but the other kids like him well enough. I just don't understand. What does this mean for Evan?

My curiosity, of course, got the better of me, and I got hold of that test. I was distressed, but not particularly surprised, by what I uncovered. Children's social abilities were rated on the following six-point scale, which was designed to measure young children's degree of "socialness." A child received one point for ignoring other children when they tried to engage her, two points for "just watching," three for being disruptive, four for what was described as a "minimal" response, and five for an "active" response. Now, you don't have to be a rocket scientist to figure out that the quiet, observant child, who gets only two points for watching, is at a great disadvantage. Sweet little Evan would have been a good deal better off if he had kicked another child. Remember, on this test a child got three points for being disruptive.

About a week after my interview with Evan's parents, I went to see him in his preschool class. He was, as the test indicated, generally on the outskirts of activity, quietly playing by himself. But did that make him socially incompetent? I remembered the proclamation on the glossy cover of the social responsiveness scale: "Social interactions are intended to elicit *active* rather than minimal responses. Social competence is indicated by the degree to which the child is able to elicit *active* responses."

As always, the popular child with many friends gets the prize. I decided to stay and watch Evan for a while. He smiled often and made eye contact with many children. And more often than not, his smiles and glances were returned. And although he didn't speak much or "act silly" to draw attention to himself, as other children did, he seemed to like the closeness of others. Several children approached Evan during my visit, and twice he accepted their invitations. When one girl pinched her finger between two Lego pieces, Evan was the first at her side, gently consoling and reassuring her. I spoke to Evan's teacher about him, and about the research project:

Teacher: Unfortunately, Evan is the kind of child who can get lost. Most of the time, I don't even know he's here. Kids like Evan deserve more attention—certainly not because they exert a weightier influence on the group than others, but simply because they're so often ignored. Obviously, the kids who are more traditionally social did better on this test. But I've been teaching for almost fifteen years, and I've seen kids like Evan before. They're very perceptive. You know what he said to me the other day? I had picked out a book to read to the children, and he came over to me. "Don't read that," he said. "Tobie and Alysse don't like that story. It makes them very sad." And you know, he was right.

I suspect that many parents, including myself, have held the rather naive view that human social development is a kind of popularity contest. Social ability is measured by counting how many friends you have or how many party invitations you receive. And surely both popular and unpopular children exist, but most children would be better off described in terms of the type of social person they are and the kinds of social relationships they are likely to have. Each child has a unique constellation of social abilities that, if supported appropriately by his parents, can provide him with the tools to form satisfying relationships. Not everyone can be the Big Leader or the Social Butterfly, nor should everyone be encouraged to be.

No matter what kind of personality your child has, the only way she will learn success is if you value that personality and do not attempt to change it. Please note that I am not referring to specific personality disorders, which may indeed warrant intervention. This book deals exclusively with behavior on the continuum of normal development and cannot address this issue (please see the appendix and reference sections for more specific information regarding personality, and see also chapters 10 and 11 on inappropriate behavior).

When you ask your child to change himself—which *is* what you are doing when you request that he alter his natural inclination—you are telling him that he is not a success as a person, but a failure:

When Cerita takes Janie's plastic spoon away from her and begins to play with it in the sandbox nearby, Janie doesn't move a muscle. She sits, as she always does, quietly watching, waiting and planning. Cerita soon tires of the spoon and walks away from the sandbox. Now Janie makes her move. Catlike, she tiptoes to the sandbox when no one is watching and retrieves her coveted spoon.

Janie coped with this situation by avoiding confrontation altogether. She waited until no one was looking, and then she took her spoon back. Janie is three years old. You could say some very good things about the way she handled herself. You could say how maturely Janie behaved. After all, she was patient, reserved, and calm. She didn't hit Cerita or try to wrench the spoon away, nor did she throw herself into a tantrum on the floor, as perhaps another child would. And she didn't bury her face in her hands, without a spoon, as a less confident child would. Janie very carefully planned her strategy and took care of herself. You could also applaud Janie's keen assessment of a common social predicament. Janie knew that it was only a matter of time before Cerita left her spoon in the sandbox.

This avoidance strategy works well for many quiet children, like Janie, but if used too often, it can present difficulties. How could you allow Janie to know that she is a success as a quiet person while still helping her become aware of options?

Let's look at the spoon situation with a slightly different backdrop. For example, suppose you know that Cerita, our "spoon taker," often takes things from Janie. And even though Janie appears calm, she never really confronts the situation. Cerita continually takes Janie's things without asking, and this must make Janie very uncomfortable. After all, when someone takes something away from you and doesn't even ask your permission, it's natural to get upset. The quiet child's indirect style, which often works to the child's advantage, can also backfire. A parent's instinct with Janie is to try to teach her "to stand up for herself": "If she takes your spoon, you take it back." And although direct confrontation may work for more assertive children, it rarely has the same effect for children like Janie. Remember, the quiet child is an extremely private one; she is uncomfortable with the attention that confrontation will draw.

Another way that parents traditionally try to deal with this kind of situation is to encourage Janie to hash it out with Cerita: "Find out why she took your spoon. Make her answer you. Tell her how awful it made you feel." And again, although this kind of intensive therapeutic approach may work for some, quiet children are not talkers. Both of these fairly traditional and well-intentioned approaches will not teach Janie either to value her own personal style or to be more direct when confronted by another child.

So what can you do? Janie can confront the problem, but the confrontation has to be brief and subtle—just like Janie herself. You can tell Janie, "The next time Cerita takes your spoon, just ask, Cerita, why do you want my spoon?" If Cerita doesn't answer or shouts at you, say, "I don't like that, Cerita" and walk away from her. The issue here is no longer the spoon but Janie's being able to express her feelings. Quiet children tend to be gunny-sackers, storing up old angers—never really saying what's on their minds. And this behavior can be observed in children as young as Janie. It is by recognizing both the pros and the cons of being quiet that you can be your child's greatest advocate. This is true no matter what kind of personality your child has.

All children have the ability to form meaningful social relationships, no matter what their stylistic differences. That is why it is so important for parents and teachers to be able to sense each child's individual social preferences and to establish strategies to help children use their particular style to their own advantage. One of the most important jobs we have as parents is helping our children discover who they are and how to like themselves. Through much labor and much love, I came up with a simple tool to help parents see their children from a stylistic point of view. *Please* note that the following very brief descriptions do not discuss a style as inherently good or bad; each has specific strengths and weaknesses, which I indicate:

1. *Style A: The social leader.* The leaders, as their name implies, want to lead. They are good at establishing rules and getting others

to cooperate. They are meticulous planners and extremely well organized. But they can also be autocratic, never allowing collaboration on ideas and feeling threatened by contributions of others. Their need to control can translate into aggressive activity.

2. *Style B: The social linker.* The linkers' function is affiliation. They are good at making and maintaining social ties. In fact, they often create social ties simply because they enjoy making them so much! However, they may often get so wrapped up in the social flurry that they lose their ability to be reflective, empathic, or insightful. They may then be perceived as superficial, as not really caring.

3. *Style C: The social observer* (quiet child). Social observers, again as the name implies, are onlookers. Unlike the linkers, they are extremely reflective and empathic toward others. They may have difficulty initiating contacts but may have enough socially appealing behaviors to attract others. Their problem is that they may become so socially independent that they become isolated.

You may recognize your child already—and then again, you may find she has components of two or all three of these styles. In order to illustrate these social profiles, I have purposely made this identification process a great deal simpler than it really is. Children are not adults. They have not formalized their ways of relating socially. They are still—and will be for a long time to come—social learners. Yet, even at this early stage, children show distinct preferences and patterns in social activity.

The first step in this assessment process may seem almost too rudimentary: Just sit back and think about your child. Now try to think how your child reacts in these everyday social situations:

- Does he make friends easily?
- Is he comfortable with large groups of children?
- When other children approach him, does he readily accept their invitation?
- Does he share his toys readily, or does he need coaxing?

How he copes with the resolution of these fundamental social experiences is the key to his stylistic preference.

The next step is to observe your child during play periods in which she is free to make her own selection of playmates and activities. Try to vary these observation periods, so that you are not watching your child in the same situation all the time.

During these observations answer these questions:

1. How often does she approach the other children to play?
   _____ more than 50% of the time   (linker)
   _____ 25%–50% of the time   (leader)
   _____ less than 25% of the time   (observer)
2. How often do other children approach her to play?
   _____ more than 50% of the time   (linker)
   _____ 25%–50% of the time   (leader)
   _____ less than 25% of the time   (observer)
3. How often is she engaged in solitary play?
   _____ more than 50% of the time   (observer)
   _____ 25%–50% of the time   (leader)
   _____ less than 25% of the time   (linker)
4. How often does she observe the play of the other children?
   _____ more than 50% of the time   (observer)
   _____ 25%–50% of the time   (leader)
   _____ less than 25% of the time   (linker)
5. How often does she initiate new activities with another child?
   _____ more than 50% of the time   (leader)
   _____ 25%–50% of the time   (linker)
   _____ less than 25% of the time   (observer)
6. Children interact with my child by:
   _____ eagerly following and accepting her ideas   (leader)
   _____ laughing and joking, generally fooling around with her   (linker)
   _____ approaching her to seek her opinion or for comfort   (observer)
7. The overall nature or content of my child's conversation with other children is:
   _____ mature, intellectual—talks mostly about ideas   (observer)
   _____ chatty, people-oriented—focused on the hows and whys of other children   (linker)
   _____ strategic, activity-oriented—focused on what to do and how to get it done   (leader)

8. When my child is anxious or threatened—for example, has a toy taken away from her by another child or is hit by another child—she is likely to:

_____ withdraw completely, refusing comfort   (observer)

_____ cry and seek comfort   (linker)

_____ lash out or tantrum   (leader)

Now tally your findings. Your child should fall more strongly into one of the three styles indicated. If your child scored the same in each category, simply reobserve her. Almost all children will demonstrate an inclination for one style over the others. Remember that the term *average child* is merely a tool to make statisticians happy. There really is *no* totally average person.

Remember also that these styles are not written in stone. Although in trying to understand your child's individual social preferences you learn to respect her uniqueness and focus on her particular strengths and interests, this does not mean that characteristics of other social preferences do not play a role in her social learning. They do. But while characteristics of all styles play a role in learning, knowing your child's preferred style will help you support her and instill self-esteem.

Winning

As there are some old sayings that bear fruit in the real world, there are some that truly don't. How about "It's not whether you win or lose, it's how you play the game"? Adults say this to children often, but the message children receive from society is quite different. Along the success continuum, there are only two points: *winning* and *losing*. As used here, *knowing you're a winner* and *winning* are two very different ideas. The first describes a secure sense of self; the second, an external reward. True, external rewards, particularly the praise I have indicated, are important in the development of self-esteem. However, we can become so focused on these rewards that they alone constitute our yardstick for success. *What* you do or *how* you do it don't count; it's *how much* you get. Many people in our society are willing to lead perfectly meaningless existences if they get paid well enough. This is not to say that making a good living and supporting a family are not admirable goals. They are. My point is that Americans have become overly *product-oriented* and underly *process-oriented*. We care about destinations, not journeys; landings, not steps. Yet the path one takes to reach a goal is just as important as its achievement, if not more important:

> *I remember seeing Esther Williams on a television interview. I had always loved her, loved her movies. Yet when she was asked if she had any advice for young people, she responded, "Be a champion!" At first I thought, "encouraging" but then "how unfair!"*

We *tell* our children we care about "playing the game," and then we focus our attention on getting high grades, making the team, and winning the trophies. No matter how well Tori runs, winning the race feels so much better than simply being a great runner. Don't get me wrong, there is a place for competition in everyone's life. There are also outstanding people in this world who deserve the admiration and respect of their peers. Yet Ms. Williams's advice to be a "champion," however well intentioned, isn't fair, isn't realistic for a large percentage of children. Not everyone wins awards or receives high grades, nor should everyone be expected to achieve in that particular way. The question remains how we can help *all* children *play the game* of pursuing their individual potential. The child who never becomes a concert pianist but continues to play and practice the piano is certainly as worthy of distinction in his own right as the child who wins international recognition. Our society does not give flashy immediate rewards for perseverance. If society doesn't, parents must.

Effort

Recent research has uncovered a difference between American and Japanese students that has been termed the *effort gap*. Stanford University researchers asked mothers in Japan and in the United States to explain their childrens' achievements in mathematics. The questions posed were "Why does your child do as well as he or she does?" and "Why doesn't he or she do better?" Mothers could choose from among these answers: ability, effort, luck, and schooling. The two groups of mothers responded very differently. American mothers voted overwhelmingly for ability and schooling. Japanese mothers voted for effort. Each group of children shared their mothers' views. American children felt that if you did well in math, you had natural ability; Japanese children felt the only way to achieve was to apply yourself, in other words, effort.

Certainly, there are children with God-given "gifts," so to speak. As I have indicated, the battle of "nature versus nurture" is continually fought. The issue here is not so theoretical, however. This issue involves attitude. If Jimmie believes that the only way he can achieve in life is if he is given some great gift, what could possibly give him incentive when math problems "don't come easy"? Effort. Jimmie must believe that hard work pays off. If Jimmie needs God-given gifts, what is the use?

Unfortunately, the good old-fashioned Horatio Alger story that some parents grew up with has been replaced by one in which a superhero presses a few buttons and, in seconds, becomes a millionaire, even a billionaire. Yes, there are individuals who strike it rich overnight, but most success stories begin and end with a solid day's work and solid years of work.

Research also demonstrates that telling children they are working hard, like praise, has magical results. In one study performed in a Texas elementary school, children who were told, "You've been working hard" actually did work harder. After being so encouraged, they solved 63 percent more math problems and got three times as many problems right than they had before being "aware" of this *hard work* they were doing.

Parents can literally talk their children into making a greater effort. Knowing that hard word, not luck or ability, is responsible for an outcome allows Ginnie to be in control. Natural ability and luck are not concepts children or adults feel they can influence effectively. However, if Kenny doesn't do as well as he'd like in history, he can always work harder.

It has been suggested that American children don't know what effort feels like anymore. If they did, maybe they wouldn't be so afraid of it. Effort feels good. The marathon runner, the model-ship builder, the painter, the man who spends thirty minutes organizing his bureau—all testify that taking that extra step feels absolutely wonderful and exhilarating!

Children can understand that success is not mysterious or illusive. It is almost always the result of effort.

Stress

We often think the child who has undergone the ordeal of divorce or death is scarred in some irrevocable way. Although this book is not about crises, an ordinary concern of parents is whether their child could hold up—even reach for the stars—if the worst were to happen. How can parents know if their child has the fuel to weather the storm, if and when it occurs.

Researchers have known for quite some time that there are sharp differences in the way children bear up under stress. The so-called resilient child, the one who takes almost anything in stride, has been widely investigated of late. It is believed that this child of steel may hold the answer to the seemingly opposite question of why children fail.

As there are risk factors at play in development, there are also protective factors that serve as buffers against potentially adverse conditions. Obviously, the calm, easygoing child tends to handle stress better than the nervous, overreactive one. The good news is that even the child with a high-strung temperament can acquire resilience if he has a consistent stabilizing element in his life, like an attentive, patient parent.

One of the most interesting findings of the current research is that resilient children tend to have the traditional characteristics of both sexes. They are independent, yet nurturant; persistent, yet reflective. Interesting also is the similarity of these findings to the research on creative children. The qualities necessary to be both resilient and innovative seem to involve choice. The opportunity to choose is a critical factor in ensuring success and perseverance in children.

Strengths and Weaknesses

Whem I am sad, I am so cold
my fingers hurt and I hold
my face close to my chest.
I am so little when I am sad
and cold. The front of myself is all gone
when I push my nose
to see my knee.
        —Alma, age seven

Alma is very gifted. She worked several weeks composing her poem. Alma is a child who knows what effort feels like, and she likes the result. Few of the children in Alma's class, working even a month's time, could compose the quality of poem that Alma can. Alma is uniquely gifted. Yet Alma can't do everything well. No one can.

Howard Gardner, Harvard psychologist and educator, states in his book, *Frames of Mind* (1983), that there is a body of "human intelligences, independent of one another, yet capable of being combined in a multiplicity of ways" (p. 8–9). It is Gardner's conviction that we are all gifted. We all have aptitudes in one or more intelligences. Gardner does warn in the opening of his book that the concept of "multiple intelligences" is hardly a scientific fact. It is, nonetheless, an excellent way of describing the uniqueness and diversity of human abilities evident in children..

According to Gardner's theory, Alma, our young poet, has an extraordinary degree of linguistic intelligence. This particular intelligence is one often taught in school. As each of us needs a command of language to exist in the world, children with strengths in linguistic intelligence often do well. Children with logical mathematical intelligence also do well because mathematics is a skill that our culture recognizes and tests in school. But what of children with what Gardner describes as

- *Musical intelligence,* the ability to use nonlinguistic forms to communicate. Musicians and dancers need this.
- *Spatial intelligence,* the ability to organize, navigate, and represent mental images. Artists, architects, and pilots have this.
- *Tactile-kinesthetic intelligence,* the ability to coordinate and maneuver one's body in space; fine motor coordination. Athletes, painters, and construction workers need this.
- *Interpersonal intelligence,* the ability to deal with and know people well. Salespeople, waiters, and public relations people have this.
- *Intrapersonal intelligence,* the ability to know oneself. We *all* need this.

Gardner thinks that his intelligences have a conditioning aspect. That is, children learn to be intelligent in certain areas because a culture insists on it.

For example, musical "illiteracy" is acceptable in our culture. Yet the Anong of Nigeria insist on musicianship. Anthropologists have never reported a nonmusical member of this tribe.

As with personality types, certain intelligences are rewarded in our society. Others are not. The outgoing child with a flair for language or sports will get more positive reinforcement than the quiet child who likes to sit and draw.

Certainly, parents cannot change society's perceptions overnight, but they can learn to focus on their child's special gifts, whether or not these gifts are tested in school or evidenced on a football field.

School Performance

> The institution is psychopathic, it has no conscience. It rings a bell and a young man in the middle of writing a poem must close his notebook and move to a different cell where he must memorize that man and monkey derive from a common ancestor. (Gatto, 1990)

On accepting the 1990 New York City Teacher of the Year Award, John Taylor Gatto made a number of thoughtful, yet distressing, statements regarding the nature of American education. It is not earth-shattering to hear that the American school is society's new scapegoat. We've all heard it before. Yet Gatto's reflections cannot be ignored. He believes that, with the obvious exception of some truly marvelous teachers—which there are now and always have been—schools do not educate, do not teach children to think. Instead, they teach children to obey orders.

I think of one of my graduate students' standing in front of her peers and telling them and me that her greatest regret in schooling was that she never learned to make her own decisions. All through school, she was told what to do and she did it. It is expected that that's what good students do: exactly what they are told to do.

Pablo Casals, Isadora Duncan, Thomas Edison, Pablo Picasso, Albert Einstein, F. Scott Fitzgerald, Sir Isaac Newton—recognize any of these individuals? They were all bad students. They either flunked out or did extremely poorly in school. It is difficult to find females for this list of bad students. Generally, females, like my graduate student, are more compliant than males. Even though (with the exception of Isadora Duncan) there is an absence of gifted females here, for perhaps some obvious reasons, the litany of talented individuals who can't make it in school is frightening. The problem that Gatto identified is a very old one. What exactly are we teaching our children in school, and *why*?

Good or bad, children feel a great deal of pressure from parents and teachers to do well in school, "to get good marks." The grades a child received are a very potent part of her self-concept. Good grades make Erica feel good.

Now, I may sound as if I am contradicting myself with all my previous talk about effort, but *all* children can't always receive A's. And even if they could, what would the A mean? To me, an A means a truly outstanding performance by a student. And outstanding does not imply merely spitting back the same information the teacher first spit at you. *Outstanding* implies thinking, problem solving, and applying ideas. Again, our product-oriented society has made the process of learning secondary to the product of grades. I often think, "What if there were no grades? Would children still want to work? Would parents still encourage them?"

Do I sound cranky? I am. School performance is yet another area where only certain types succeed. Compliant, well-organized children who spit back the right answers make it. Spontaneous, questioning types are often silenced. Children's self-concepts cannot be nurtured in environments that clearly select one group over another. Although parents cannot overthrow the educational system (Mr. Gatto states, "I don't think we'll get rid of schools anytime soon"), we do need to understand the meaning of marks and their impact on and often injustice to children.

Suppose tomorrow morning you come to work and your boss tells you you must do ten pages of math problems within a given time limit, make no mistakes, or lose your job. If you could decide how many of these problems you wanted to do or felt comfortable doing, and when, you might be OK. But under the stated conditions, all that is created is anxiety, less sharpness of attention, and fear of making mistakes.

The reality of grades, testing, and school performance is rather stark. Tests and the resulting grades generally measure how quickly children can solve relatively unimportant problems, making as few errors as possible, rather than measuring how people grapple with relatively important problems, making as many productive errors as necessary, with no time factor—which is what we do in real life.

Grades can get children into the "right" schools, which may or may not be important to future employers. Yet research has shown time and again that grades have little predictive value in determining how people will succeed in everyday life. In fact, the average college grade for persons currently listed in *Who's Who in America* is a very ordinary C. Surprised?

Now, I am not diminishing the value of high grades or the joy that children feel when they achieve them. What concerns me is that parents often focus more on marks than they do on whether Joey knows or is learning anything. Grades may indicate a child's ability in a very specific area of human development. They do not indicate a child's intelligence or a child's ability to succeed in life.

Even more damaging than the previously discussed "product-before-process" approach is the perception of the *child as grade*. What do I mean? Well, at the beginning of every school year, teachers receive their classroom lists with each child's grades from the previous year:

Banks, Keri	A
Connelly, Brian	C
Davido, Lisa	B
Hseih, Li-Li	A
Jimenez, Julio	A
Parker, Matthew	D
Romeo, Frank	C
Sharp, Scott	D
Wilburn, Judy	A

Do you know which children you are going to have trouble with? Teachers do. Certainly not with sweet little Keri Banks. The child is her grade. Without even meeting Keri, her teacher makes a judgment regarding her.

This example is just another illustration of the big bad self-fulfilling prophecy. In one famous study, teachers were not given grades. They were simply told their class was gifted. And you know something? By the end of the year, they were!

Unfortunately, the only reason grades are so important is that people think so much of them. As parents, we need to strike a delicate balance between society's excessive and often inappropriate valuing of school performance and the very real issue of learning for learning's sake. Children need to know

1. They are not their grades.
2. Grades do not indicate intelligence.
3. High grades are *very* important for *very specific things,* like getting into good colleges.
4. High grades are not the only thing necessary for success in life.

If your child is learning and working hard, you know he has the right grades. Rewards should not be reserved for "all A's and B's." They should be given as deserved.

Competing

I loved baseball more than anything, playing down at the dead-end late on summer nights with all the guys. But, God, did I hate Little League. Crazy, hah? All those adults yelling and screaming, "Hit the ball, hit it." I mean, whose game was it?

It is quite fitting that my discussion of school performance leads naturally into a discussion of competition. There is the inevitable academic competition previously discussed. Then there is the gamut of so-called extracurricular activities or avocations. There are also hobbies, like stamp or coin collecting. All of these may have competitive aspects to them.

As I stated earlier, there is nothing inherently wrong in competition—or high marks, for that matter. It is the manner in which we engage these life events that either sweetens them or turns them sour.

The act of parents' helping their children understand their strengths enables children to feel good about themselves and strong enough to compete. Competition is part of life, whether we like it or not.

Parents also need to understand that competing in the classroom is not the same as competing on the tennis court. Children learn very early, particularly in athletics, that the results are what is important, who wins and who loses. But what if you don't win, never win? Do you still compete?

All children must be able to compete in life. The act of competing is what is crucial, not the act of winning. Life does not have one finish line. It has many. Every day people win and people lose. You don't have to be a mathematical genius to figure out that the more you play, and continue to play, the more chances you have to win eventually. Stop playing and you forfeit your chances.

To compete, children must be able to lose. Children must be willing to fail without feeling like failures. We cannot promise our children that they will never fail. We can teach them how to fall and how to get up.

Disloyal Friends

Nicole stood in the shopping mall. What she witnessed was upsetting but not particularly surprising. There was Rebecca with that new girl, Holly. All the whispering and snickering was true. Rebecca had a new best friend.

Friendship is extremely important to middle-school children. As discussed in chapters 2 and 3, friends create an identity for children this age. Without her friends, Nicole feels lost and often worthless. Yet the experience of friends' moving away, as discussed earlier, is quite different from the experience of a friend's moving away psychologically.

Separation breeds loss, regardless of context. Loss due to disloyalty breeds disappointment and failure. If Nicole is not invited to spend time with Rebecca and Holly, the message is clear. Nicole is unwanted. She has failed as a friend.

When children's friends reject them, a number of internal conflicts emerge. Often children blame themselves:

- What did I do wrong?
- What's wrong with me?
- Why is this new person better than I am?

This kind of torment is extremely painful for the child who almost always believes the worst. Nicole may sit for days attempting to calculate just when things went wrong. Was it when she didn't return Rebecca's gray sweater or couldn't go with her on that picnic?

It is not unusual for relationships to fizzle with little or no explanation. One weekend, Nicole and Rebecca are dressing up in each other's outfits; the next, Nicole can't even get Rebecca on the phone.

Children and many adults are afraid of their feelings. Very few people have a strong desire to hurt another. What exactly can you say to this old friend who's been so good to you? "Listen, I'm much more interested in this new person. I find her more exciting than I do you right now. Give me a little time. I'll tire of her, and then I'll come back to you"? It's much simpler to say nothing at all, and to act surprised, angry, or hurt when confronted.

As with every other problem we've discussed so far, don't tell your child that everything will be OK. No one feels OK when he has been rejected by a friend. Feeling bad in this particular situation is a "very OK feeling." Bad is what you are supposed to feel.

Feeling Left Out

Jordan had tried to be nice to Danny. He lent him his science homework. He campaigned for him for student council. He always said hello to him. Jordan liked Danny. He really did. But when it came time for the party after the big game, Jordan wasn't invited, again. Alex told Jordan to forget it. Danny was never going to invite Jordan anywhere, no matter what he did.

The social observer I described earlier in this chapter is clearly different from Jordan. Normally, quiet children either haven't acquired the social skills necessary to interact effectively or aren't interested in the same levels of interaction that their peers are. Jordan does have social skills and does want to interact. His invitations are not being reciprocated. If this problem were a simple one, there wouldn't be the cascade of books available on this subject with titles like *How to Be Popular* and *How to Win Friends and Influence People*.

Another important, yet painful, lesson children need to learn is that no matter how honest and genuine we may be in our efforts to make certain friendships, we are not always or automatically victorious. Not everyone will want our friendship. This is not an easy reality to swallow. It would be wonderful if every wanted friend spontaneously clung to us devotedly. But that's not how it happens. Children need to know that rejection is as much a part of life as acceptance. Rejection is something we all feel miserable about. It is not something to be ashamed of. If your child knows you understand her feelings, she won't have to pretend that she doesn't care about this friend. She does. And her acknowledgment of these caring feelings will help her initiate other friendships, if one doesn't work out. Again, we can't promise our children all the friends they want. The only thing we can do is encourage them when attempts at specific friendships are thwarted, and simultaneously to teach them to nurture the friends they already have.

Children also need to examine their motives for wanting friendships. Particularly in middle school, with its urgency for peer group acceptance, children may begin to seek friends for ulterior motives. The "in-crowd" can be very seductive; it's priced high emotionally but is perceived as "well worth it." Is your child strong enough interpersonally to bear the extraordinary social demands of this group while still retaining his individuality? Some children can, and some may be crushed.

Feeling Humiliated

Kevin hated the schoolyard. Every afternoon the kids chose sides for softball. The captains selected their teammates one by excruciating one. How easy it was for the ones picked early! How difficult for the ones picked last! The worst part for Kevin was never the game itself, but this lineup. Yet he was used to it by now. As the line dwindled and the cheers changed to sneers, Kevin stood. The message was clear. No one wanted him. He was no good. But he had either to withstand the pain or forfeit the privilege of play. Kevin wanted to play with those kids badly, but he was always happiest on rainy days.

We all know Kevin. Some of us may have been Kevin at one time. We can hear our own parents and ourselves echoing, "Children can be so cruel." Why is it that humans need to knock someone else down to feel better about themselves? Why do we continually carry this tape measure in our back pockets, contrasting all ability against our own, making certain to exalt those like us and trample on those who are different? Is it human nature? Is it tribal instinct? We have all heard stories of the primitive tribes that leave their weak and wounded on the mountainside to perish. Yet there are also tribes that take the most handicapped among them and give them a special place in their society. Which kind of culture do we wish to have? How would we like our own children to be treated? How would we like them to treat each other?

The child who becomes a scapegoat tends to develop a low self-concept as a result. He may be more persuadable and conforming than the child with high self-esteem. Some experts believe that this compliance may be a defensive behavior aimed at pleasing everyone. When children lack personal adequacy, they have a strong need for approval. Or he may decide he's had enough abuse and begin to lash out at his peers, which doesn't endear him to them either.

In contrast, the child who feels good about himself tends to be adjusted socially and to be more accepted by his peers. This social acceptance improves his self-concept. We see another vicious circle developing. As the child succeeds with his peers, he feels better about himself and continues interacting with them. The child who is worried about failing because of past experiences of fear feels like a failure, so she either doesn't get involved in a group, or interacts with them in an inappropriate or hostile way. The more of a social failure she perceives herself to be, the more inadequate she feels, and the less she gets involved in a meaningful way.

If this tale does not sound promising, it is not meant to. The child who is continually picked on by his peers is going to have a tough time and needs a most encouraging, sensitive parent. The first thing parents must understand and accept is that the child who becomes a scapegoat is different in some way from her peers. This difference may be physical; she may be very small or poorly coordinated. The difference may be academic; she may be having an absolutely horrific time in math class. It may be social; she may be gifted and simply not share the interests of her peers. Or she may be quiet and not know exactly *how* to be friendly. Whatever the problem is, telling your child she is just like everyone else when it is very clear to her that she is not is not going to be helpful at all. When a child is different, she knows it. Equally unproductive is attempting to make this different child the same. Placing Joey in the soccer league when he is absolutely atrocious at soccer is only going to provide another area in which Joey can be hurt and humiliated. This is not to say that Joey will never be available to play soccer. With the proper intervention from loving adults, Joey may be able to play soccer—

and like it. Placing Joey on the soccer field is not the first step to take when, clearly, this is the one place Joey feels most miserable. If you have just cut your finger, you apply some medication and wrap it in a bandage. You don't rub salt into it.

All children, especially those who are not ordinarily given positive messages by their peers, need to find their special niche, so to speak. Cliché as it might sound, everyone is good at something. A child needs to find consolation in a particular endeavor. Her strength in this activity may bolster her when support from peers is not available:

I remember Diana. She decided to dance a whole section of the "Nutcracker Suite" right in front of the class. This is not something the sixth-grade boys were too thrilled with—to say the least! They laughed and barked. After she finished, Diana went to the girl's room to change. I ran in after her, expecting to find her in a puddle of tears. I should have known better. "Oh, come on, Mrs. Paley," she said. "Those guys are a bunch of dorks. In a few years they are going to be chasing after me so fast their ankles will be swollen." What a smart cookie!

Helping our children to be winners, without insisting that they win all the time, is not easy. Often, parents try to live vicariously through their children, hoping Craig and Lucy will do all the things Mom and Dad wished they had accomplished. This is a heavy burden for children to carry.

Yet there are ways to help children to come to terms with their grades, their performance, their friends, and their social lives. Remember, children will have to cope with *not winning* more times in life than with *winning*. The coping begins and ends with feeling good:

> My mother loves me.
> I feel good.
> I feel good because she loves me.
> I am good because I feel good
> I feel good because I am good
> My mother loves me because I am good.
> My mother does not love me.
> I feel bad.
> I feel bad because she does not love me

I am bad because I feel bad
I feel bad because I am bad
I am bad because she does not love me
She does not love me because I am bad.
—(Laing, 1972, p. 9)

5

Disappointment

Strategies and Solutions

There is no way we can teach our children to win all the time. Likewise, sheltering them from life's ordinary disappointments is not realistic either. What parents can do is teach children the act of competing. The act of competing is what is crucial in life, not the act of winning. There are many more opportunities for children to compete than there are for them to win. As long as Danielle competes, she succeeds. As long as she succeeds, she wins.

School Performance

Ten forty, ten more minutes in math class. They were the longest minutes on earth. It was as if you had to switch your life off for forty-five minutes. Those who could bear the boredom must have been the ones who did the best.

Remember the story of the tortoise and the hare—the hare with his bravado, falling asleep in the middle of the race, while the ever-consistent tortoise takes over? *Motto:* "Slow but steady wins the race." In school, children must stay motivated, work against discouragement, and face competition and challenge squarely. School is our children's first testing ground for meeting the demands of society. True, some "fail" in school and do famously in life, as evidenced by the unsuspected overachievers discussed in chapter 4. Other children receive incredibly wonderful instruction from incredibly wonderful teachers.

But what if you are just like most of us are, perfectly wonderful ordinary parents, with perfectly wonderful ordinary children, who go to perfectly wonderful ordinary schools, with perfectly wonderful ordinary teachers? How are you going to make sure Robert is getting the most out of school? Ask him, "How was school?" Does he respond, "OK," "good," "boring"? Does Robert like school, look forward to it? Is this what you want? When things don't go perfectly well at school, should parents turn around and blame the teachers, the system? Educational reform, even when it is as much wanted by parents and teachers as it is today, is an incredibly long, and often unsatisfying, process. Experts say school change can take as much as thirty years. Can Robert wait that long? The educational reform that cannot start at your school tomorrow can start at your house tonight.

School reform at home involves the following:

1. *Teaching* schoolwork without *using* schoolwork. Parents must use activities at home that don't directly mimic what children have already done at school. Parents need to help their children learn in ways other than nagging: "Did you do your homework?" "Did you study for your history test?"

2. *Teaching in parts.* Whatever you want your child to learn, break the activity down into small, manageable pieces. In this way, success is achieved earlier, faster. Voilà, Elizabeth is motivated sooner!

3. *Easy to do.* Parents can teach and children can learn without worry or hassle. Activities like kneading bread dough, painting wooden clothes pins, and the like are for martyrs, not parents. Whatever you do, it should be able to be accomplished alongside ordinary household routines, using whatever you have at home.

Attitude

Wadyaget? *That's what I remember. After every test, everyone out in the hallway comparing,* Wadyaget?

Good, bad, or indifferent, perception is everything. All of us, no matter how secure we are, use each other as mirrors from time to time. Parents and children have been using grades as mirrors of self-worth in the classroom for a very long time. When grades go up, Nina is pretty. When they go down, Nina is ugly. No mention is given to the very real possibility that the 97 Nina received was good luck, a fluke of the multiple-choice gamble, while the 80 she received was the result of many evenings of study and problem solving. The important thing is grades. Although no one can completely eliminate the power of grades as mirrors of the self in society, they do not warrant this power at home. The questions for parents should be: "Is my child working hard?" and "Is my child learning?" Not "How pretty are her grades?"

Draw an Ugly Picture

Drawing an ugly picture is an activity I do with very young children and graduate students alike. I hand out paper and crayons or markers with one simple direction: "Draw an ugly picture." In the years since I have introduced this activity, I have never had anyone resist.

This activity can also be done at home. Once your family has drawn their "ugly" pictures, post them together somewhere for everyone to take a look at. What you will discover is that family members don't ordinarily find each other's pictures "ugly." Dad sees Janie's picture as "creative." Marc finds Mom's picture "colorful." When we see ourselves using another's eyes, we often find our own mirrors very cloudy.

When Peggie is not receiving the grades either she or you have expected, you both must shift your focus from the product of grades to the process of learning. It is only when Peggie hasn't worked to capacity or hasn't truly learned anything that you can say her performance is ugly. Otherwise, her C can be just as glorious as any A.

As there are many excellent books on school performance, it is not my purpose here to discuss this topic thoroughly. What I will do is address the four areas where I believe parents can have the greatest influence: autonomy, effort, perseverance, and reading and writing.

Autonomy

I couldn't help it. It was a pop quiz.
She never told us about this project.
All four teachers gave us homework. I couldn't finish it all.

Does this list go on? You bet it does. It is very easy to fix blame upon others. Some of us become masters at it. The phenomenon of blame functions on two principles: (1) we can be responsible only for ourselves, and (2) we cannot control the behavior of other people very well or very long.

Blame is sensible. If we can control only ourselves and we don't want to do that, we can blame someone else. That way, when we don't want to do something, we are not obliged to. That's someone else's business. Imagine, next time your ten-year-old marches into the living room and says, "I couldn't help it. It was a pop quiz." You say, "What an outrage! I hope you went right to the front of the room and handed that test right back to her!"

Of course, Terry will think you've gone right off the deep end. But your point is made. The teacher did not do anything wrong. Neither did Terry. What Terry did was make an excuse rather than take responsibility. One can never be autonomous until one takes responsibility.

Next time, instead of saying, "I couldn't help it. It was a pop quiz," Terry says, "This is the mark I can get when I don't really know the material being covered in class." No one can control when teachers choose to give pop quizzes or whether they choose to give them at all. The only thing that can be controlled is knowledge of the material being covered. If your child knows his material, pop quiz or no pop quiz, he knows it anywhere, not only at test-taking time.

Children become responsible for their actions through an accumulation of experiences. Autonomy is self-reliance, knowing that you are your own instrument of change. The following few activities may not seem school-related. They're not, but the practice received in self-reliance is carried over into schoolwork.

CHOOSING YOUR CLOTHES. Although middle-school children have ordinarily overcome this hurdle, most small children need practice in choosing what to wear each day. Early in the clothes selection process, parents can lay out several clothing alternatives: "OK, Joannie, I've laid out three outfits. You pick one." This practice is helpful in preventing the choice of a cotton playsuit in mid-January. Later on, Tommie can lay out selected outfits in advance. A word of caution: Interfere as little as possible! Remember, we're focusing on the process of selecting one's clothing for oneself, not on whether Andrea's tights match her fluffy hair ribbon.

THE SCHOOL–HOME BOX. Children are notorious for coming into the house and tossing school items everywhere. In the morning, things mysteriously disappear. The solution? Make a school–home box.

The school–home box is generally cardboard, large enough to hold school supplies and unsoiled, undrenched outer clothing. Johnnie decorates this box with pictures, and his name in bold letters. The home–school box is located right outside Johnnie's bedroom door (or in any equally convenient place).

When Johnnie comes home, the box is the first stop for school items. It is the last stop on the way out the door in the morning. Finished homework and supplies needed for school are put in the box at night, ready for the next day.

No one is too old for a box. Each parent can make a work–home box. I have one for my glasses and keys. You can't imagine how much time and temperament this box has saved me over the years.

Each box also serves another important family function. The boxes in my house have become message centers. I drop a note in my son's box. He drops a note in mine. Notes don't even need to contain information. The best notes are the love variety: "You're terrific! Love, Mom" or "Mom, you're a perfect 10!"

THE WAKE-UP GAME. At times, we must be responsible not only for ourselves but for other people as well. A good activity for children seven and older is the wake-up game. One child is given the alarm clock, taught how to set it, and given the responsibility of waking everyone else up. Talk to your child beforehand. Tell her how important her role is: "What would happen if you didn't wake Mommy and Daddy up?"

It is smart to have a backup system the first several times you try this game, particularly if you have an important appointment. Most children find this game incredibly satisfying. Its message is simple yet extraordinarily profound: "You have an important job. Everyone in the family really needs you."

I WILL. "I will" statements are designed to reinforce the positive aspect of self-correction. How often are children taught what not to do rather than what to do? "Don't run in the hall" rather than "Walk in the hall" or "Don't be late" rather than "Be on time." Both adults and children can learn to use the positive "I will" when correcting as opposed to the negative, "Don't" and "I won't."

Over my fifteen years in teaching this seemingly simple concept, I have discovered that it is difficult, not only for children but also for parents. Changing the negative pattern of "I won't" to a positive "I will" takes a conscious act of will. When Christopher says, "I won't do it anymore," guide the awareness of his choice by asking, "What will you do?" Usually he'll repeat, "I won't ever, ever do it again." Again say, "If you aren't going to do it, what will you do?" Continue asking in such a way as to evoke an "I will" statement, such as, "I will listen," "I will read," or "I will wait for my turn."

This is a simple activity, but not easy. It involves a focused act of will, and there will be resistance in both children and adults. Our language is so full of shoulds, oughts, and nots. I hear myself saying, "*Should* is a word we shouldn't have." Internally I interrupt myself, rephrase, and say, "It would be better to have something else." "I will" statements give power, freedom, and open-endedness and evoke creativity. The following activity offers an opportunity to use the will as an act of concentration. It develops self-awareness and self-discipline and has the potential of enhancing self-esteem. It involves planning. Plans and goals give a much needed lift to life, and children with many plans tend to be zestful and purposeful.

The object is for your child to write a simple goal on a piece of paper. The goal may involve any subject the child chooses: academic, friends, home. Often children write goals that can have very little follow-through. For example, Doreen wrote the goal "To be nice." True, we all want to be nice, nicest even. But what does nice mean? How do you be nice? How do you know when you've been nice?

Obviously, we all have very different impressions of what nice might be. For Doreen, being nice meant saying hello to Lauren, the new girl in her class, each day. Doreen did do this. And because saying hello each day was a much more measurable goal than "being nice," Doreen was much more satisfied. She saw the results of her labor.

The point of these suggested activities is not to directly teach your children to lay out their clothes, to make school–home boxes, to wake the family up, to say "I will," or to write goals for themselves. It is to teach them to follow through, to take responsibility for themselves and others, to use positive language, and to choose specific, achievable goals. These process-oriented activities build a strong sense of autonomy in children. When Adrian learns to rely on himself, he takes power and joy from his own learning.

Effort

I know this is going to sound silly. But when I'm feeling really confused, I take all my clothing out of my bureau and fold it neatly in piles. I feel so much better afterward. I don't know why.

There is something powerful about a job well done, a job begun, finished, and perfectly executed. Twelve-year-old Marcie knows this. That's why she feels so good about organizing her bureau.

We recognize and applaud effort when we see it, for example, the waitress who takes the time to give us exactly what we want; the salesperson who spends that extra minute fluffing and arranging the bow on our package; or the student who goes that extra mile on a project and hands in something truly superlative. *And* we recognize when we don't see effort, for example, the toys that have been flung carelessly into the cupboard when a more orderly cleanup has been requested; the cashier who is consistently abrupt and rude; and the students whose homework is so sloppy that it cannot be read.

My hunch is that the "effort appliers" here have discovered that a good job is magical and has its own rewards. On the other hand, the "effort avoiders" just don't know how good it feels to do "good." These people avoid work because they have learned that work feels bad.

Some interesting research has revealed that people who enjoy their work work often, and steadily. People who like to work also like to play. Their outside interests are as rich and fulfilling as their work. People who have the least time do the most.

The researchers had expected people to have specific work and hobby interests and to devote themselves accordingly, for example, that people who liked to garden would spend a lot of time gardening, and that people who liked to go to concerts would spend a lot of time doing that. In fact, the people who gardened often also went to a great many concerts, and vice versa. People who didn't do much of anything, except perhaps watch television, just didn't do anything no matter how much time they had. The researchers compared their findings to a Newtonian principle: "A body in motion stays in motion." The more one does, the more one can do. The less one does, the less one can do.

For children to find the joy in work, they must have good work-loving models. They need to see parents who find the "doing" exhilarating.

THE LITTLE THINGS. It is important to celebrate our raise, our promotion, the big deal we closed. But these great big things don't happen every day. Effort in day-to-day life is composed of little things: the cranky customer who gave you a smile, the copy machine you fixed, that third mile you ran even when you were absolutely exhausted, and the great memo you wrote.

Don't be stingy on letting Becky in on the little goings-on at work and home that illustrate effort and the sense of satisfaction that comes with it. Not all daily problems can be solved quickly or easily. Let Tony know your frustrations, too. Perhaps your car didn't get fixed properly, you were stood up at an appointment, or you had to stand in an extremely long line at the supermarket.

Talk about your own problems with your children. Ask them for suggestions. What would they do if their secretary was late all the time? If their boss gave them unrealistic deadlines? Love of work is lurking in every problem that is managed and eventually solved.

Ask your children about their day. Urge them to discuss their little successes. Remember that Judy can't win a game or ace an exam every day. But she can always be a winner by talking to a new person at lunch, answering a question in class, or helping Marc find his history book.

Effort is that extraspecial mile. It is not looking for the easy way out.

HOMEWORK. Homework is one area where parents can have a great effect on school performance. Parents can't do a lot about what goes on in the classroom, but homework is parent territory.

I am not advocating that parents do their children's homework, although some parents do. Doing your children's homework for them does not teach them to apply effort. It teaches them to avoid it.

Again, recent research can shed light on the question of homework. Many parents feel that their child is getting too much. I, personally, have never heard a parent complain that their child has too little.

The remarkable school performance of recently arrived Asian

students who came to this country with little or no command of English has prompted some heated discussion. A Stanford University study of San Francisco high-school students found that Asian-Americans consistently received better grades than other students, regardless of their parents' level of education or income. In reality, the more English spoken in the home, the less well the students did. There was no fancy methodology applied or special materials purchased in the Asian homes. The Asian parents were simply able to make their children work longer, period.

I may sound as if I am contradicting myself with all my discussion of the "child as grade." What difference would it make to me if these Asian students did receive better grades? What could these grades mean? Well, if high grades were the only outcome of this study, perhaps I wouldn't be so intrigued.

The Stanford study measured the hours high-schoolers spent on homework. The differences were startling. Asian-American males spent almost twelve hours a week on homework, American white males spent eight, and American black males spent a little over six. For females, it was found that Asian-Americans spent over twelve hours a week on homework; white Americans, eight hours; and American blacks, over nine hours.

There are continuing discussions about whether Asians have higher IQs than Americans. These arguments are bound to accelerate with each new study. However, whatever we will discover regarding the innate capacity of certain cultural groups, this information will never help us enable students to apply effort. We can't change children's IQs (or at least, experts don't perceive we can at the moment). What the Stanford study can help parents understand is that achievement is directly related to the amount of time children spend doing something. The more time children spend on schoolwork, the more of a chance they will have to learn the material.

Another study unearthed an even more revealing finding about homework. A University of Michigan study investigated elementary-school students in the United States, Taiwan, and Japan. American children scored the lowest of the three groups in math. The American first-graders spent about fourteen minutes a night on homework. They hated it. The Japanese children spent thirty-seven minutes; the Taiwanese, seventy-seven. They loved homework. Asian children go to school 240 days annually. American children go 180 days. Asian parents believe effort makes a difference. They let their children know this.

I do believe the Horatio Alger story is still alive for many of us. In order to keep it alive, we must stop looking for shortcuts. There is no substitute for hard work and for the time that work takes. Maybe a lot of stress is caused by our thinking—our children's thinking—that there are shortcuts for everything. Everything should take a little time and be easy to do. If something seems hard and long, well, we just haven't discovered the shortcut. Yet the reality is, as it has always been, that little comes easily or quickly.

A recent article about the success of the Japanese in wooing business in China, despite the long-standing animosity between the two countries, points out the fact that the Japanese count on persistence and patience to win the day. They just plain outwork everyone else. They have a long-term perspective, and they're consistent. They work long hours. They live in accommodations Americans would not accept. Where American executives might quit, Japanese executives endure.

I am not making a case for Japanese upbringing or schooling. There are also many studies indicating that Asians as a group may suffer emotionally from too much work and too little play. Yet Asian parents do appear to be able to teach their children the value of endurance. That is one thing we Americans tend not to teach. We need to teach our children endurance and effort. Homework gives practice in both. Children need to know that homework is serious business. It is not something to be slid through so that they can get to the "really important stuff," like softball and television. There should be a set amount of time for homework each day. An hour and a half to two hours is effective for ten- to twelve-year-olds; forty-five minutes to an hour for seven- to nine-year-olds; and thirty minutes for first-graders. School-related work is done each day at that time, whether or not homework is assigned, and whether or not the assigned work is finished before the assigned time ends. If there is no official work, children should read, draw, write a story, or engage in some other active yet reflective activity.

Talk with your children about their assignments as well as their self-initiated work. Did they find their assignment difficult? Easy? Would they like to know more about this topic? Do they enjoy the book they are reading? Why? Why not?

A LEARNING PLACE. Every child needs her or his own place to do homework. Walk through your home with your child. Find that special pace, that special study corner. It need not be big, but it needs to be personal, a desk blotter, a plant, a sticker book, your child's own artwork. A child needs to take ownership of her learning space. When she does, she psychologically takes ownership of her learning.

Your entire home is a learning place. There should be books and magazines everywhere. Although this material need not be all new, stock should be replenished regularly. Just as there should be fresh food in your house, there should be fresh reading material. Let your children see you reading, and talk to them about what you've read.

You want your children to be writing often as well. Keep blank notebooks, lined yellow pads, and pencils in a number of places around the house. Encourage your children to write down their spontaneous thoughts, to keep an idea book. Have them keep pads next to their beds for those brilliant middle-of-the-night thoughts.

Use bulletin boards to display compositions and artwork, or better yet, hang an indoor clothesline! Children love to post their work here! Frame some of your children's artwork and compositions, and display them in prominent areas.

The job you have as parents is to let your home convey the message that this is a place where people learn.

Perseverance

The clay on the science project looked OK in the beginning. But when it hardened, it cracked and fell off. Melissa was upset. She carefully removed the brittle clay and threw it into the garbage. She looked at her model of the human eye for about twenty minutes and began to make a list. After she finished, she went to her mom, who said, "You know, there are alternatives to the clay. This whole project is a kind of experiment— finding out what works best!"

There will always be others who are more talented than we are, who are better looking, who have more education. Yet even with this edge, they still need perseverance in order to accomplish and to create.

Effort and perseverance are very similar. Effort involves *applica-*

tion and *hard work.* Perseverance involves *time, stick-to-itiveness,* and another all important *p* word: *patience.* It often seems that certain people experience overnight success. But when the whole story is revealed, these people will admit that it took a long time and a great deal of practice to achieve that so-called overnight success.

Helping your children persevere is a challenge today. Everything happens so quickly and is expected to. We fly across the country in several hours, across the world in half a day. We pick up the telephone and speak to someone in New Zealand immediately. We have express mail, overnight service, fax machines. The Jell-O that used to take hours to thicken now takes minutes. I have actually come to a point in my life where I can't imagine a kitchen without a microwave.

I am genuinely fond of these modern conveniences. I like the shuttle service to Washington, D.C.; my word processor; my calculator; and the instant money machine at the bank. These devices help me to do my work and to organize my life better. Instead of spending my lunch hour at the bank, I can actually eat lunch.

But even with all of these time-saving wonders, my own experience has shown me that some goals take much longer to accomplish, and that to achieve these goals we have to keep working at them. I'm not sure whether our children have as many patience-building experiences as they need to help them prepare for the long-range goals that life has in store for them.

What is particularly worrisome to me is that we seem to accept that our children have short attention spans. Certainly, there is a grain of truth in this statement. Children under the age of seven have not developed a concept of time parallel to the adult's concept. Even so, television, even educational television, has depressed children's attention spans further. No television segment or commercial is to be longer than a certain number of minutes or seconds. Instead, we should emphasize building our children's level and length of attention and their ability to concentrate over a period of time.

There are activities that, by their very nature, teach perseverance and patience. These activities cannot be completed in a rush because they demand detail and the passage of time.

PUTTING IN ORDER. Some of the hardest jobs, the ones that never seem to get done, the ones we avoid doing for as long as possible, involve putting many little things in order.

Do you have several cardboard cartons with miscellaneous photos and scrapbook items stored in them? Take your children to the local variety store and purchase several inexpensive but sturdy photo albums. Sewn composition books are also good.

On a large tabletop, distribute the photos and scrapbook items so they can be talked about individually. Figure out a way to organize the material. Most of the time, chronological order is easiest, merging *all* material, starting with the earliest and moving forward. However, each family member can also make her own photo scrapbook, organized in her own unique way.

Attach the photos and other paraphernalia to the album pages, along with captions. Young children can dictate their captions. Not only does it take a great deal of time to do this activity, but the activity itself illustrates the passages of time.

GARDENING. Young children enjoy watching seeds sprout. This activity allows children to comprehend the passage of time and to receive an intrinsic reward simultaneously.

You need two or three packets of seeds, small pots or milk cartons cut down, a ruler, and, depending on the season, a sunny windowsill or an outdoor garden.

Empty your seeds on a table, and have each child fill each pot with about two inches of soil. Together, read the directions on the seed packet. Plant a few seeds in each pot. Place the pots on a sunny window sill. Talk about what you have to do to make sure the seeds will grow.

Water the seeds according to the directions. Then, day by day, watch for the seeds to begin to sprout. Seeds grow slowly. Depending on the variety, it will take about ten days to see the sprouts.

Plants have a way of saying, "We love you and we care." Encourage your children to share their plants with friends, neighbors, and relatives.

INCOMPLETE. Some may think it's easier to do an incomplete job than a complete one. I'm not so sure. I see students who have to think of all kinds of excuses for why their work is late. Just think of the effort exerted in coming up with excuses. I wonder if they wouldn't find it faster simply to complete a job.

I am not convinced that we always must finish what we start, but we must learn to finish many things. A lot depends on the individual situation. As an adult, if I am not enjoying a book I am reading for pleasure, I may stop reading it. But as a student, I know I have to complete all assigned readings. As an employee, I must complete all tasks assigned to me.

Every family needs to decide on its own options: what must be completed, what is discretionary. But there need to be some tasks that children know they must complete. For example, if Jake has begged for tennis lessons and you sign him up, he should not be able to quit after his first lesson. Just as you can't expect penicillin to work after the first dose, children need to understand that they need to give things a chance to work.

Rome was not built in a day, but as an avid TV watcher you may believe it was built in an hour, or in a miniseries at most. Perhaps more than any other generation, our children need to learn that things don't happen all at once, and many not very quickly. Practice may not *make* perfect, but it makes, it builds, it creates, it accomplishes, it completes. And in doing that, it makes us feel good about the job and about ourselves.

Reading and Writing

I don't think I need to begin yet another treatise on how miserable our children's reading and writing skills are at present. According to the latest studies close to one third of them have trouble deciphering the directions on a can of soup. This situation is dismal.

Yet, outside of those children who are truly learning-disabled or economically and hence socially disadvantaged, I am not convinced that American children are so much *illiterate* and *aliterate*. Many children can read and write. They simply choose not to:

> *Once, on a white Caribbean beach, I met a charming ten-year-old named Carla. Every morning Carla would come down to the sand and sit for at least an hour reading. I watched her glide through three good-sized novels in the span of a week. I asked Carla, "Why do you like reading so much?" "Oh," she replied, "isn't it the most interesting thing to do?"*

Sadly, I can't say Carla was American. She wasn't. Perhaps in Europe, children aren't quite as overwhelmed with the wealth of media as they are in this country. European children may still perceive reading to be interesting.

American children are used to *being* entertained, not necessarily entertaining themselves. This being the case, perhaps parents need to make reading more entertaining. Reading aloud to children is a form of entertainment. The highly acclaimed national best-seller *The Read-Aloud Handbook* (1979), by Jim Trelease, attests to this fact.

Children of all ages need to hear the written word spoken aloud, sometimes without pictures, sometimes with. One night I took *The Adventures of Huckleberry Finn* down from the shelf, sat my two children down on the living-room floor, and began to read. I broke into a southern drawl as best I could. They were mesmerized. Huckleberry Finn is great literature, replete with social conflicts: slavery, child abuse, alcoholism, charlatanism. My performance was an enactment of the eleven o'clock news that was written more than one hundred years ago. My eleven-year-old stole the book and escaped to bed with it. This was one of the best things I had ever done for her. My six-year-old was used to having stories read aloud to him. Everyone reads stories to young children. Parents often forget that older children enjoy and benefit from the oral tradition, and that younger children can listen to stories that don't have pictures.

Together, my children and I have listened to many great novels, from *Anne of Green Gables* to *Captains Courageous* to *The Hobbit*.

Every night I read aloud to my children for at least thirty minutes. This does require some effort. One must learn to read with expression, using various voices and facial cues along with appropriate gestures. The stories I read during this time have no pictures, so the children learn to focus on the words. If my daughter likes, she may read aloud also. Later on in the evening, closer to bedtime, I read a picture book to my son. Pictures often tell a different story from words, particularly for small children. He often reads another picture book to me, and my daughter reads one to both of us. When I tell this to parents, the response is "You do this every night?" Just about. It is interesting that parents don't find watching television every night quite as time-consuming. And children and families invest a great deal more time in television than they do in reading.

Writing is also a skill on the decline in this country. Just as I think children know how to read, I think there are many children who know how to write. They just don't write. Writing is extremely important because, good or bad, it is the primary way we indicate knowledge in this society. Oral exams are rare. Written exams and essays are standard.

Long ago, or perhaps not so long ago, people wrote letters to friends and family. The advent of the telephone has all but eliminated this practice. How often do we write a friendly letter? In my house, we write notes and messages to each other all the time. My son will leave me an index card right by the bathroom mirror: "Have a great day, Mom!" For whatever reason, written messages have more intimacy than the spoken ones. Writing a note is an intimate act. Humans recognize and respect that the written word is an expression of themselves.

Along with story reading goes story writing. Young children love to illustrate and write their own stories. A pencil and spiral notebook or a few looseleaf pages stapled together are all the tools necessary for a great home-grown, home-written story. Writing is also a great television link. If you watched a program on dolphins, for example, why not write a story about them?

Older children, particularly girls, like to keep diaries that can be locked. Of course, you, the parent, may never see this writing, and it is not your prerogative to investigate this material. Your goal is to see your children electing to put their thoughts on paper, whatever the form.

One terrific activity for the entire family is the following. Distribute paper and crayons or markers to everyone. The assignment is: If you were to write your autobiography and there could be only three illustrations, what would they be? Children, young and old, can engage in this activity. Adults may be a little uncomfortable with the drawing part, but this early distress is easily overcome. After the illustrations are finished, everyone holds up his drawings and is asked to talk about them. This is a very enlightening activity. You often discover the moments in life that are truly important to your family. You may be surprised!

After all have discussed their drawings, everyone has to write a story about one of her illustrations. Younger children can dictate their stories to older children or parents. The stories need not be finished in a single sitting. They may be worked on for days, or even weeks. When you give writing this very personal autobiographical slant, you teach children and adults to become emotionally invested in their writing. Some children take their writing very seriously and bind their finished products with elaborately decorated covers. Once they do, the reading–writing cycle begins anew. You now have original child-written material to read aloud. If you receive enough bound materials, you can start your own family library.

If we want our children to feel successful in school, we have to impart to them the basic success tools for this arena: self reliance, hard work, and patience. Your children will need these very same skills to succeed on all fronts in all areas.

Competition

When Laurie came off the field, the tears were streaming down her face. "I missed it! I missed it! How could I have missed it!" I wrapped my arms around her. She was shaking. Tara was there, blue ribbon in hand. I could see she wanted to talk to Laurie. She froze. She must have known there was nothing she could say.

Although you can fail a quiz quietly, there is something uniquely humiliating about a performance of some kind. Who knows? Laurie may have worked harder than Tara. It is a possibility.

Didn't Laurie deserve to win then? It all seems so unfair.

Yet competition of any kind yields the same fundamental question: "Do we play merely to win?" *or* "Do we play to play?" The winning of an award can certainly lend itself to a child's development of self-esteem. As I have said so many times before, *children are concrete reasoners*. The trophy, the medal, the certificate, the applause offer special tangible reinforcement to the child that verbal praise often can't match.

Adults are the child's models for behavior. Parents often create "such a big deal" with regard to awards, is it any wonder that our children follow suit? When was the last time there was a pep rally in preparation for a history exam, a cheer-leading squad assembled to pay tribute to saving enough money to buy Mom that extraspecial birthday present, or shiny silver trophies handed out for being kind to the little boy next door. All of the aforementioned experiences are just as important as the track meet or the ball game, yet because there is no concrete recognition for these other accomplishments, children don't view them with the same intensity as they do performances or sports.

Forgive me if I sound like a broken record, but again the attitude toward competition is largely an issue of process versus product. Certainly, you can't do much to avert society's need to exalt the "quarterback." To paraphrase Gatto (1990), "I don't think we'll get rid of football anytime soon." The only thing families do have control over is what happens in their own homes. Sometimes we may feel powerless there as well.

If at all possible, try to help your children begin to measure their own performance *day to day*. Help them compete with themselves rather than with others. Remember, there is absolutely no way we can guarantee our children success in the performance area if success is measured only by one standard, that is, the *first* to cross the finish line.

Ask process-oriented questions: "Was your run any different today, honey?" "How did it feel different?" "How do you think you could change your routine? I really liked your arm movements in the second section." and "Do you think you're working better with Larry? How does it feel?"—*rather than* "Are you ready for that big game on Sunday? Gonna beat the crap out of those losers, huh?" "Maybe you should take lessons from Tim Cameron. He's been working with Karen. Her backhand has got much better than yours," or "You really need new sneakers. You'll never win with those old things."

Allow your child to enjoy the whole process of learning, experiencing the adrenalin and the excitement of athletics rather than a stark vision of winning or losing. It's hard to be happy for the so-called winners, when you are standing on the sidelines watching them receive ribbons and adoration. Yet the finish lines in life are not so narrow. There is much more room to succeed, without feeling pressure to win medals. When you teach your child to appreciate her own performance, you teach her to appreciate herself and to overcome obstacles even when there is no applause.

Disloyalty

Michael sat in his room. He was sure if he sat long enough Richie would call. Richie and he had fought often enough before. Richie always apologized, or Michael apologized. But this time Richie told all the guys, "Mike is stupid. He doesn't belong with us." This was three days ago, and no Richie since. Michael was very angry at Richie, but he missed him very much.

There is nothing more guilt-provoking to a parent than a sulking child. Unhappy children are very difficult to have around. One of the reasons we like to have children laughing and playing is that their pleasure gives us reason to take joy in living. An unhappy child draws so many unhappy images for us. We know all too well what the child is going through. Remember those painful evenings waiting by the phone that was never to ring? We don't want that unhappiness rekindled for our own children. No one does.

When we lose someone close to us because that person has indicated she doesn't really care about us anymore, there is virtually no way we can escape feeling like a failure—at least temporarily. This is an important concept for parents to embrace. Feeling bad is what is supposed to happen here. If your child doesn't give any indication of feeling bad, *then* you should be concerned.

Sulking is good. Surprised? Sometimes I think more harm is done by trying to keep children from sulking than by just leaving them alone. Most parents are afraid of sulking. What are they afraid of? The sulking child may become depressed or morbid. Maybe. But I really don't believe it's that that parents fear the most. I believe that most parents feel that a child—or any person, for that matter—shouldn't feel bad about anything. Mental health is perceived as feeling good no matter what happens. Nothing could be further from the truth, which is why our culture has traditionally had such problems addressing the very bad feelings associated with death and illness. There is a fear that bad feelings will hurt us.

Bad feelings do hurt, but they don't necessarily have to hurt us. As we must allow our children to feel loss, we must allow them to feel failure, to feel disappointed. When Lindy goes to her room, shuts the door, and indicates she doesn't want any dinner, the worst thing to do is stand outside her door bellowing, "What do your mean your don't want any dinner! You have to have dinner!" Good health and nutrition aside, Lindy doesn't need dinner. She does need to be alone to sort out her feelings. The best you can do is say, "Listen, if you need anything, honey, just let me know. If you want to talk to someone, I'm here. If you don't want anything and don't want to talk to anybody, that's also fine."

Another technique parents often execute at this time is what I will call the *party tactic:* Let's get all dressed up and go out!

June had just told me she didn't want to be my best friend anymore. I remember my mother literally dressing me and making me go to this party. I was miserable. I sat at a table eating M & M's. I ate so many and was so upset to begin with that I went into the bathroom and threw up.

When parents overreact to bad feelings, they inadvertently tell their children that these feelings are to be feared and avoided. Yet children need to experience these feelings to know they have the ability to cope with them.

There is no perfect amount of time to give your child to be alone and sad. Some children are finished after a day or two. Others need several weeks. During this sulking time, it is important for your child to know that you support him. If he doesn't want to eat, which is a symptom, bring a snack tray up. Maybe Carl doesn't want to sit down with the whole family yet but wants to speak with one person quietly. You can offer to take him out somewhere or join him in his room. Sometimes, it won't be you he wants to speak with. It may be a sibling. Give them a place and some quiet time together.

Often a child will want to speak with another friend. If she wants to make a phone call, give her some privacy. Try to remember the last time you felt rejection. Most of us need space, respect, and someone to talk to. These are exactly the things your child needs. Once your child has spent some time sorting out her feelings, there are some very concrete things you can do.

The first and foremost is to *listen, listen,* and *listen* some more. As I have reiterated countless times, children do not necessarily want advice; they want and need good listeners.

The second is to be honest. Tell them that bad feelings don't go away easily. They hurt. New friends are not easy to make. Everyone is afraid of being alone. What is different about this situation, compared to the friendship dissolved or diminished because of distance, is that here we have the element of rejection, that is, failure. No matter how wonderful we are, there is no way that all the people we want to like us will like us. The fact that "not everyone likes us" is a human condition. Often, when one important person in our lives tells us he doesn't need us anymore, it feels as if *no one* likes us. Yet most caring people in the world are liked, loved even, by at least some of the people that are important to them.

Don't expect your child to perk right up after you deliver these great truths. These concepts are not the happiest ones for children to have to come to terms with. It will take some time for Suzanne to digest them, and even longer for her to act on them effectively.

If Suzanne asks you directly, "What should I do?" Your best response is "What do you think?" Sometimes, children think that parents actually know exactly how to win friends back. Children should understand that no one knows this. There is no magical formula for winning friends back.

There is one specific suggestion I do think effective. Often the friend who has initiated the "breakup" will refuse to speak to the friend who still wants the relationship. He avoids him at school and won't return phone calls. The reason for this behavior is quite obvious. It is not comfortable to stand squarely in front of someone and tell him you liked him once but you don't like him anymore. The jilted child is left hanging, never able to bring closure to the experience. However painful closure may be, it is a far more emotionally satisfying experience than the lack of it.

Tell your child you have a suggestion, and a suggestion only. It's up to her to decide what she wants to do. This is her life, not yours. Write the friend a letter. It doesn't need to be a long one. It does need to be a sincere one that deals with feelings. Boys have a great deal more difficulty with this than girls. However, if we want our young men to express themselves better than their predecessors, this is a good place to start. Boys are more comfortable with a short, straightforward note, girls may be more elaborate:

Dear Dorothy,
I'm sorry you feel the way you do. I still want to be your friend.
I think we have had many good times together. I was hoping there could be many more. I would like to see you. You said some pretty mean things to me and I was very upset. I would like to see if we could patch things up. If I don't receive a phone call from you by Wednesday, I will know you don't want to see me and don't want to patch things up.
  —Carly

In some cases, a short note like this can bridge the difficulty or actually begin to mend the friendship. It is certainly not guaranteed. Your child should understand this. However, even if the note is never answered, your child has had the opportunity to close the relationship, to get "things off her chest." Once there is closure, Carly can begin the process of going out and seeking new friends.

Feeling Left Out

Johanna had a winning part in the school play. All her class-mates had congratulated her. Her parents and teachers were all very proud of her. Yet, after the performance, kids scattered. Johanna heard a lot of kids were going over to Andrea's house. Johanna wasn't invited. She ended up at the Burger Barn with Carol and Meg, as always. No matter what she did, Johanna just never seemed to make it with the really popular kids.

There is something devastating about preadolescence. You always wonder: Just how did all of those popular kids get so popular? Were they all taller, better looking, richer, or smarter than everyone else? I don't think anyone emerges from junior high school not wanting to be popular, to travel in that inner circle. Exclusion is hurtful because it forces children to acknowledge that others may not see them the way they see themselves. This is perhaps even more painful to accept when the young person has spent a relatively long time providing himself with positive esteem-building outlets.

It is perhaps natural for humans to think the grass is greener, to feel they are missing out on something when seemingly important others don't include them. It is equally important to keep the front, to pretend that we don't care and that we are having a perfectly good time on our own. How many times did we answer the question "How was your weekend?" with "Great!" when we did nothing but watch television. How often did we feel extreme pressure to go out on Saturday night when, honestly, we might have preferred sitting at home and reading a good book. This continual exaggeration accelerates anxiety. If the other children are standing around telling your child how terrific their weekend was, she, too, will be compelled to invent an equally diverting tale, then come home to you and lament how miserable her life is.

Again, parents cannot control what other children choose to say and do. What parents can do is let their children in on one extremely powerful truth, about children and adults. The best of us are painfully self-absorbed. We actually spend very little time during the day thinking about the wants and needs of others. A large percentage of our mental energy is devoted to our own problems, our own plans. What *we* do counts very little in terms of *other* people. True, Matt may have wanted to go to that party. But why? Often it's because he thinks others will view him differently if he does:

> *No one was happier than I to be invited to Sam's party. Sam was a great basketball player, but he was nice—not stand-offish like some of the other guys. Eileen was the only other friend of mine who was invited. I felt special, real special. I thought that party would be my initiation. After that, everything would change. I would have new friends, new exciting things to do. Nothing changed. That was the greatest shock of all.*

Another intriguing finding is how few kids truly perceive themselves as part of that *in*-crowd. When interviewed, close to 70 percent of American twelve-year-olds felt they did not run with the popular crowd. How interesting that so many see themselves as being surrounded by kids perceived as so much more popular than themselves?

There is no magic way to deal with the child who feels left out. Feeling excluded occurs at many points in development. The best things to do are to

1. *Empathize.* Let your child know that almost everyone, even these envied popular souls, have this empty feeling. Life has good and bad feelings. This is one of the bad ones.
2. *Help your child shift perspective,* for example, "You know, you do have some very good friends. I know that they don't give what you think are the greatest parties. They do care an awful lot about you. If ever anything happened to you, Jeannie would be there. You can count on her."

Another, perhaps harsh, reality is that this feeling of exclusion is as much a part of being human as the feeling of inclusion. If exclusion were not so potent a feeling, maybe we wouldn't value inclusion as much as we do.

Being Humiliated

Karina had another stomachache. She had had three stomach-aches and one headache in one week. I was at my wit's end.

I'd taken her to the doctor. Nothing. Yet, every morning for the past four days, stomachaches, headaches. I finally said to her, "Karina, this is enough. You've missed so much school." She burst into tears. "Mom, please, I can't go on the school bus. I just can't." I drove her to school myself. "It's my stupid haircut, Mom. They all laughed."

There is perhaps nothing worse than being teased, feeling rejected and inadequate. No matter how strong one's self-image is, being humiliated hurts, and hurts badly. There is the child who is consistently humiliated because he is very different and the child who is occasionally humiliated, like Karina, because of some generally minor social infraction, which, to the peer group, unfortunately warrants temporary ostracism.

We will begin with the latter because it is the simpler problem. As parents, we are apt to dismiss the expectations of the peer group as ridiculous and sometimes outrageous. We may also be angry with this anonymous group as it seems to be quietly usurping a great deal of our perceived power and influence as parents. After all, parents do know more than this bunch of kids, or do we?

In order for humans to become totally integrated individuals, they must at some preadolescent time form strong bonds with those outside their family. Being with peers at this time is seen by the child as a more important experience than being with family, particularly parents. Parents begin to represent a tie to early childhood that middle-school children may eagerly wish to sever. They are not babies anymore. They want privileges that even adults don't have, but they believe that they need these in order to snap that umbilical cord.

When the children we love begin to send out "keep-away" messages, it is natural for us to feel hurt, even threatened. As a result, when Keith is humiliated by his peer group, it may be easy for us to tell him to forget about it. These kids don't know anything! See, we told you!

Yet the middle-school child needs as much support and praise from his peer group as the very young child needs from his parents. This does not mean that Billy needs to be adored by every single member of his fifth-grade class. It does mean that he has a small group of personal friends on whom he can rely. This special group of peers cannot always shoulder the blow of humiliation from others, but they do help. They pick up the responsibility from parents by allowing Billy to know that even though he may be hurt by outsiders, he is secure and loved by them.

Why do children humiliate each other? If the humiliation is an isolated incident, it may simply be for amusement; when children become bored, humiliating another is often perceived as fun. Jealousy is another reason. Because children's strivings for conforming are so strong at this time, any child asserting her individuality is seen as a threat; it is certainly OK to wear the hottest new clothes, but only as long as that is exactly what everyone else is wearing. The last reason that humiliation exists is that immature or insecure humans feel superior when they are capable of humiliating someone else. This seeming superiority is false because the one humiliated is almost always at a clear disadvantage when compared to the one doing the humiliating: younger, smaller, less socially adept, or simply isolated from his natural supporters.

A child who has been humiliated learns very quickly never to engage in the ridiculed behavior again: Wear cool clothes but not too cool; don't disagree with anyone a foot taller than you are.

Being humiliated is extremely distressing to children. Karina may wonder if this will become routine. In most cases, it doesn't. However, in order to understand the plight of the humiliated, parents must understand the psychology of the bully. No matter how loud their bravado, bullies are extremely frightened children. Their self-concepts are extremely low. One of the few ways they can feel good—feel successful—is to put someone else down. They get away with this behavior because children are gullible. They believe what they hear. The bully gets a reputation, and like all self-fulfilling prophecies, it becomes true. The bully is feared. Bullies also like to tease those too young or too small to be a potential threat. Bullies love to pick on little kids. They're the easiest targets of all.

I am not going to address physical fighting here. I address that in chapters 10 and 11 as inappropriate behavior. If your child has been physically hurt by another child, that's not only humiliation, that's assault. Assault requires specific handling. What I am discussing here is verbal humiliation, teasing, and name calling.

At the beginning of this book, I talked about my bully experience. I had my nose twisted with pliers in front of a group of peers. Amazingly, I was not physically hurt. But I was humiliated. My mother told me "to keep away from that boy." Well, from the standpoint of behavior, Mom did have the right idea. We cannot ask our children to reform bullies. When Alice has been humiliated, it is important to tell her to steer clear of this child and to stay in the company of her friends. Yet telling her to avoid this child is not enough. Alice may wonder why she has been humiliated? Why not someone else? These are natural questions that should be answered.

Alice needs to know that she has not been personally selected for this humiliation. Whoever confronted her did so randomly in the sense that *any person* could be a potential target—anyone in the wrong place at the wrong time doing the wrong thing. Has she seen this child pick on other children? Most often, she has. Ask her to describe exactly what happened to her. Most humiliations have a mob appeal. One child begins. Soon, there is a host of children laughing and pointing. Children join in the mockery because they are afraid of being targets themselves. One way to avoid being a target is to become a bully yourself.

There is a different set of variables involved when a child is routinely humiliated. Children who are routinely humiliated are often loners, different from their peers in some distinct way. They may be smarter, less coordinated, or shorter, or they may like to read and write poetry. They tend not to have well-developed social skills and, hence, few good friends.

As a result, these children need specific instruction in the development of social skills. Isolated children are a natural target for teasing. They have few supporters. Bullies are cowards. They are not going to attack a socially integrated child. It's too risky. Generally, they attack only when they know they can win. When you teach Alex appropriate social skills, you also teach him the potential of friendship. Friends are a kind of armor in the peer-oriented world. You are not asking him to completely alter his social style by helping him with these skills. He may not be a social butterfly. That's fine. Quiet people are great friends. However, these skills can help him when he does see someone that he might like to become friends with. The first two social skills described here are introducing and sending an "I'm interested" message. They are good to review for all children—and even some adults.

Introducing

No one ever knows anybody the first time they see him. Children should know (1) how to introduce themselves to someone they don't know and (2) how to introduce two people that don't know each other.

To introduce himself, the child

1. uses a pleasant face and voice
2. looks at the person
3. tells the person his name
4. asks for the person's name

To introduce two people who don't know each other, the child

1. uses a pleasant face and voice
2. looks at each person
3. tells each person the other's name

Family members can practice this activity at home with each other, taking various parts. After the children become comfortable with this routine, you might like to try some role plays:

You're walking home from school with a friend, and a younger child joins you. She doesn't know your friend.

Two kids you don't know are playing a game that you would really like to join.

You met a new kid last week. Today you see him and realize that you have forgotten his name.

You have just introduced yourself to a new kid. A friend of yours walks by. You need to introduce them to each other.

You go with your dad to visit his friends. You don't know the kids, but your dad tells you to go out and play with them.

Your dad takes you to the park but says he'd rather read his book than play. While you are playing alone, a little girl comes by and stops to watch you.

A friend invites you to a birthday party. He's the only person you know there. You'd like to meet the girl near you.

You've asked your older sister to take you to your friend's house. His mom is out in the yard and hasn't met your sister.

Families can problem-solve these role plays together and add to this list considerably. Ask your children to keep a mental log of the new people they introduce themselves to, answering such questions as: Where were you? Whom did you meet? What did you say? What did the other person say or do? They may also keep a log of the people they introduce to each other: What did you do and say? What did they do and say?

First attempts are apt to be rough around the edges. Practice does help us reach a goal. Children who are isolated are often that way because they really don't know what to do to meet new people.

Sending an "I'm Interested" Message

Another important social skill is allowing a speaker to know you are listening and paying attention to what she is saying.

Family members can also practice this activity at home, using the following role plays and adding to them:

A younger child is telling you how she hit a home run in a softball game.

A friend is helping you finish some math problems that you didn't know how to do.

A friend whom you like to play with is telling you the rules of a new game. You already know how to play this game.

Your friend is telling a ghost story that you've heard before.

Here's another terrific "I'm interested" activity.

1. Cut out some pictures from old magazines. Paste pictures of someone feeling happy, tired, sad, and calm on separate pieces of paper. (If you do not want to use magazines or newspapers, you may draw the pictures.)

2. Draw a circle around the person(s) you would like to play with. What were the reasons for your choice?

_____

_____

_____

3. Find or draw a picture of two people who look interested in each other and paste it on a sheet of paper. List two ways you can tell they are interested in each other.

   1. _____

   _____

   2. _____

   _____

The next three social skills described are important to implement when your child becomes the victim of a humiliation, no matter what the frequency: sending an ignoring message, handling name calling and teasing, and saying no to stay out of trouble.

Sending an Ignoring Message

The child who teases others often does so because of the reaction of the child who is teased. If the teased child does not react in the expected manner—crying, yelling back, and so on—often the teaser will simply quit because of lack of amusement. To send an ignoring message, the child

1. keeps a neutral face
2. looks or walks away from the person
3. says nothing
4. pretends she is not listening

Again the best way to use ignoring messages when you need them is to practice them at home with family members. Here are a few role plays to start with, along with some activities. You can add to this list:

Your teacher asks a question to which you know the answer.
    The boy behind you keeps kicking your chair.
You just got braces. You go to the store and see some kids
    from your neighborhood. They start laughing at you.
You're playing a game with a friend. Your friend loses, get
    angry, starts swearing, and calls you an idiot.

1. List three things you would do to send an ignoring message.
    1. _____
       _____
    2. _____
       _____
       _____
    3. _____
       _____

2. Give three examples of times when you would want to send an ignoring message to someone.
    1. _____
       _____

2. _____
   _____

3. _____
   _____

3. Describe a time when you sent an ignoring message:
   Whom or what were you ignoring?_____
   _____
   _____

   What did you do?_____
   _____
   _____

   What happened?_____
4. If you send an ignoring message to someone but the
   person keeps bothering you, what are three things you can
   do?
   1. _____
      _____
   2. _____
      _____
   3. _____
      _____

Handling Name Calling and Teasing

When someone teases your child, he must learn to keep calm, ignore her, and walk away if possible. He also needs to use a technique called positive self-talk, which is thinking good things about
oneself, for example, "I'm calm. I can handle this. I can ignore her."
To handle name calling and teasing, the child

1. keeps a neutral face
2. takes a deep breath to get calm
3. looks or walks away
4. uses positive self-talk.

Role plays to be practiced at home and added to include

You're playing basketball, and you miss a shot.
   One of your teammates starts yelling at you and says you're
   a lousy player.
You got a neat toy while on vacation. You take it to school to
   show your friends, but they all tease you about it.

Two kids cut school during lunch and ask you to join
    them. When you say no, they make fun of you for being
    a chicken.

You're walking down the hall at school. You pass by two kids;
    they begin laughing and making fun of your clothes.

You get a new hat and wear it out to play. Some kids yank your hat
    off, begin to toss it around, and say how silly it looks.

1. What are three things you would do if someone teased
   you or called you a name?

   1. _____
      _____

   2. _____
      _____

   3. _____
      _____

2. What if you did everything right to handle name calling
   and teasing, but the other person still called you names.
   What are two things you could do?

   1. _____
      _____

   2. _____
      _____

Saying No to Stay Out of Trouble

Sometimes just saying no to the peer group can be the cause
of humiliation. Children generally say yes when they feel that
saying no may mean big trouble but are just not comfortable refusing.

To say no to stay out of trouble, the child

1. uses a neutral face and voice
2. takes a deep breath to stay calm
3. looks at the person
4. keeps saying no
5. suggests something else to do

If suggesting something else doesn't work, the child

6. ignores the person and walks away

Try these role plays and activities:

Your friends want you to spray-paint the school. You say no, and they call you a sissy.

Some kids want you to smoke a cigarette with them. They call you a chicken when you say no.

Some kids try to get you to throw rocks at the school window. You say no, and they threaten not to be your friends anymore.

When someone asks you to do something you know is wrong, what are three things you can do?

1. _____
   _____
2. _____
   _____
3. _____
   _____

Winning and *losing, success* and *failure*—perhaps all the glories and agonies of life are contained here. Learning to shoulder failure and temper success is life's greatest secret. In helping our children in this process, we may, in fact, be helping ourselves.

6

Fear

"I Don't Know What This Is. And I Don't Want to Know."

I felt a warm slightly weighted body atop mine. It was Keri. This was the third night in a row. A fuzzy, friendly-looking enough pussy cat had scratched her over the weekend. Luckily, Keri was on an antibiotic for an ear infection. Our pediatrician said that penicillin would kill anything. The cut was deep enough. I treated it and wrapped it in a bandage for a while. Now the wound was healing nicely, exposed to the air. But inside, Keri wasn't healing as quickly as I would have liked. She was so scared. That lousy cat was crawling through her sleep every single night.

Most children have common fears, of the dark, of snakes, or of being left alone, for example. These are healthy fears that protect a child as long as they do not get in the way of her abilities to play, have friends, and be reasonably independent for her age. Fears are also healthy as long as they are connected to reality—if some possibility of danger or harm really does exist.

Fear develops because children have active imaginations. They have an increasing awareness of the many ways they can be hurt, have conflicts within themselves over being independent but still needing adult protection, and are often egocentric; that is, they see themselves at the center of the world and therefore believe that all dangers are somehow directed at them.

Some extremely bright children develop extreme fears of fairly sophisticated threats, such as pollution, nuclear holocaust, or cancer. Although these children possess an advanced intellect, they also have the emotional development of children. They understand certain concepts from a cognitive point of view, but they lack the ability to put these concepts in the appropriate perspective.

The quality and tone of children's fears many appear urgent at times. Fear may seem literally to swallow them, as it did our little cat-friend Keri. Many fears are resolved as children mature, but it is fascinating how many persist throughout childhood. Depending on how parents handle their child's fears, the child will either emerge safe and secure or continue to be troubled.

Most of us consider *fear* bad, like losing and failure, as it certainly doesn't feel good. Yet, when we pass from "what we fear" to "why we fear," we discover that fear is a practical, useful emotion. Fear serves a distinct function in the human psyche.

A young animal runs to its mother when danger threatens. Humans, young and old, also run to one another when they are afraid. Fear is a strong force for cohesion, which has also been misused— by politicians and fanatical religious leaders, among others—to induce order.

Fear has always warned humans and other animals of danger. The physiological reactions associated with fear are rapid heartbeat, loss of breath, and paralysis or muscle tension. Fear has functioned as our adaptive signal system to alert us to hazards, prompting us to fight or flee a dangerous situation. In essence, fear has helped humans survive.

Some researchers have concluded that fear is a by-product not only of our mammalian ancestry, but of maturation and learning. We do learn to be afraid of the stove, of the electrical outlet. These things do not provoke fear in and of themselves. We learn to fear them through repeated interactions with them.

Fairly typical developmental fears, such as fears of dogs, spiders, darkness, masks, or water, develop for the same reason. For young children, the world is very uncertain. They've seen water whisked away—down the drain. They wonder: Will that happen to me when I go in the swimming pool? Or if Halloween is beckoning, has my brother taken someone else's face (a mask) and put it on top of his neck? Where is his own face?

If the conflict of *loss* is *loving* and *losing* and the conflict of *disap-*

pointment is *success* and *failure,* the conflict of *fear* is *reality* and *fantasy.*

Real and Not Real

My art history teacher had a saying: "If you discover reality, call me—anywhere, any hour of the night—call me." Humor aside, his point is well taken. We tread a fine line between the real and the not real. What is reality for one person may be total fantasy for another. Yet parents must admit that there are very *real* dangers in this world, especially for children: the environment, drugs, strangers. The world is not perceived to be as safe as it was even ten years ago. We lock our doors and our cars, we buy alarms for our windows, and we take our cassette players from our dashboards when we go to the supermarket.

On the six o'clock news, Michael can see dozens of horrific experiences enacted at the touch of a button. At eight o'clock, big sister Jody watches a horror film whose graphic displays will leave nothing to his imagination. Children do not need to look far to find something to be afraid of. The world is indeed a very scary place to live.

At the same time the child is made aware of real danger, she must also know what kinds of things are pretend, what may look like things to be afraid of but aren't. Making this distinction between real and not real is not easy. Although our senses are expected to communicate to us what is real and what is not, our senses often trick us. We can misinterpret that bump in the night, the shadows on the wall. There could be a monster living in our bedroom closet. The initial anxiety provoked by these misinterpretations may prove no threat whatsoever. At the same time, a perfectly innocent-looking puppy dog might start to growl when we try to pet him. This is not what we expected either. Knowing what is real and what is not is largely the product of experience and practice. As children don't have a great deal of experience and practice in the world, they often misjudge the realness or unrealness of something.

The resolution of fear is also the product of trust. There are many things a child can never experience or practice in order to find out that these things should be feared and avoided. We cannot stick our hand into a direct flame or stay underwater for too long. We cannot drink too many bottles of window cleaner or play with rattlesnakes. A child must trust his parents enough to believe that what they say to fear should in fact be feared. Of course, there is the inevitable testing of limits during the early stages of development, of the "Let's see how hot the stove is" variety, but essentially the child does come to rely on her parents for information about the nature of fear and its major issue of conflict: *reality* versus *fantasy*.

As in the previous chapters, there are many areas that could be discussed in both this chapter and the next. Children, as a group, are afraid of many things—from flushing toilets to masks to Aunt Matilda. The issues addressed here are those that have the most influence on overall development. These issues also reflect the *process* of developing fear rather than the *product* or content of the fears. Parents can use the concepts laid out in this chapter and the activities or strategies described in the next in a multitude of circumstances, rather than using only the "spider section," for example, if they have a child who is frightened of spiders.

The topics addressed are nightmares, being alone, trying something new, and "real" fears.

Nightmares

The evening before I began this chapter, I went to sleep thinking that, whereas I'd had personal experience with many of the topics I had already addressed, I hadn't had a great deal of experience with nightmares with my own children.

Someone or something must have been listening to my thoughts. That very night, Jared, my six-year-old, awoke in the middle of the night shaking, inconsolable, anxiously walking back and forth. "An elf," he cried, "an elf is trying to eat my heart." I carried him to my bed, and he stared at the ceiling, his body rigid. He was comforted knowing I was right next to him, but he was terrified to close his eyes. The elf could come back for a second visit, and I had no way of telling Jared for certain that he wouldn't.

Although this section begins like a second-rate science fiction novel, my point is that you never stop learning as a parent. My investigation into nightmares became ever richer because of this experience.

What Are Dreams?

Before we can understand a nightmare, we first need to understand what a dream is. Unfortunately, my definition of a dream is going to be as ambivalent as my definition of a nightmare. No one knows for certain what dreams are or why people have them. Some scientists tell us that even animals have dreams and that they are simply nonreactive purposeless brain activity. We cannot turn our brains off when we go to sleep, so we have dreams. In contrast, some psychiatrists believe that dreams are windows, direct lines to the psyche. The dream is seen as a metaphor, the body's voice for indicating trouble or imbalance. As I have said, earlier, I am not an absolutist. My own definition of dreams, however unscientific or unpsychoanalytical, rests somewhere between these two extremes. I do believe that everything the body does has a purpose, even if we have not determined what it is. Experts tell us that they don't yet have a clue to what 80 percent of our brain is doing. Scientists say that we simply don't use most of our brain. Somehow I suspect that one of them will discover what exactly these supposedly dormant brain areas have been doing for the past million years. And then, people will complain that the problem with the human race is that we use *too much* of our brains. This, of course, is my conjecture.

It is unfortunate that contemporary western cultures, unlike many others in history, seem to ignore the integrative or even possibly prophetic nature of children's dreams. The anthropologist K. Stewart (1983) described how wisely the Senoi, a Malaysian tribe, react to their children's dreams of falling, flying, or climbing. They comment to their child, "What a wonderful dream! It is one of the best you can have! What did you fall into? Where did you fly?" Remember everything I have said regarding the self-fulfilling prophecy. If the child is told he is having wonderful dreams, chances are he may indeed have them.

My interpretation of the current research on dreams is that, although dreams may be random brain activity, they serve a purpose nonetheless. Dreams can communicate to us on an unconscious level, giving us affirmations, rehearsals, or preparations for things to come. They sometimes bring us warnings and let us know how we feel when we don't seem to know the extent of our feelings. The images a dream brings may be a more exact description of our feelings than our words can express, especially regarding the complex nuances of feelings. Yet dreams don't always indicate disturbance or imbalance, as some psychoanalytical literature may lead us to believe.

There is also some interesting research that indicates dreams can be redreamt and reenacted. I found this information extremely enlightening as I have had many dreams I'd like to reexperience or redo. This reenacting of the dream on the unconscious level appears to have a parallel effect on the conscious. What we redo in our dreams, we can, in theory, redo in our lives. Dreams are, in effect, *unconscious problem solving*.

It is not my intent here to educate a new generation of dream interpreters; the use of dreams as a psychotherapeutic tool is to be undertaken only by licensed professionals. Yet parents need to know how to help their children when they do have nightmares. We do know that if the nightmare is not handled well, it can occur again, sometimes with increasing intensity. My goal here is to help parents know what to do so that children can learn to take control of their nightmares.

How Do We Dream?

We may not know why we dream but scientists have told us how. Adults sleep and dream within ninety-minute cycles throughout the night, spending 20 percent of the night in the "fast" REM (rapid-eye-movement) sleep that produces dreams. By contrast, children have been observed to spend about 50 percent of their sleep time in the company of dreams. As any parent who has watched a slumbering child knows, children's sleep is very deep but restless. Because young children spend so much time in REM sleep, they have many more nightmares than older children or adults.

Nightmares and Fear

There are specific physiological reactions to fear, which I cited earlier. When your child has a nightmare, you must respect these reactions and assume that it will take a little time for Sallie's body to resume its normal functioning.

Nightmare fears are difficult. Very young children may not even understand that they have dreamed, for they may find no distinction between the dream image and reality. They are often convinced that a dream image is quite real, and no amount of searching the bedroom will make them feel safe enough to go back to sleep.

Older children can better differentiate between dream images and reality but may be just as frightened by the power of the dream, their feeling of helplessness, and the nightmare's emotional impact. Some researchers believe that we have not fully explored our capacity to feel as human beings. Dreams, then, may be an introduction to a new dimension of feeling.

Being Alone

Carolyn seemed so different now. On one hand, she was anxious to take showers, style her hair, and coordinate clothes. On the other hand, when I wanted to go to the corner delicatessen, she always wanted to join me. She just didn't want to be alone in the house, she said.

Somewhere around age ten or eleven, your otherwise independent child may begin to fear such things as being alone in the house for a short time or being alone in her room at bedtime. This phase often represents missing the earlier security she knew as a child.

As adolescence begins, a complex chemical change occurs in your child, and a budding adolescence merging with the final vestiges of childhood creates a curious new creature. Carolyn now fears the dark and being by herself. A psychoanalyst might say her real fear is growing up.

Carolyn manifests many contradictions now, all of which may confuse you. The child who will no longer tolerate a baby-sitter jumps at the noises in the night. She locks the windows and doors to her room.

Like nightmares, this very common developmental fear is a function of the contest between *reality* and *fantasy*. The ten-year-old is quite aware of what there is to be afraid of in the world. Some fairly sensational yet quite typical fears of this age group include physical injury, injections, kidnapping, terrorist attacks, and car and plane crashes.

The feelings Carolyn has regarding being left alone are very similar to the ones she had when you left her at school on that first day or when you insisted she sleep in her own bed by herself. In addition to Carolyn's fear, there is also a long-buried feeling of *loss*. Carolyn is sitting on that precarious fence between childhood and adolescence. This fence is wobbly and very painful to sit on. Childhood is warmth and security; adolescence is excitement and privilege. Which does she choose? Both.

The whisperings of adolescence are seen in much grown-up behavior. The fear of being alone grounds her in childhood and keeps her close to those she loves and unconsciously knows she must eventually leave.

Trying Something New

Everyone fears novelty and yet is thrilled by it to some degree.

The new as an unknown is always frightening. The new as curiosity is always exciting. All experiences are new the first time one attempts them. What can encourage children to try rather than retreat?

Childhood is a time synonymous with the newness of everything. We learn to tie our shoes, to ride a bike, to swim, to read. Every day, the young child is faced with the challenge of new undertakings. Some children seem ripe and ready; others, hesitant and uncertain.

This issue of *approach* and *avoidance,* as they are clinically termed, has been explored widely by sociologists and psychologists. Although the final votes are far from in, the current consensus reveals that the phenomenon of trying is largely stylistic.

Some children are downright *impulsive*. They see something novel and literally can't keep their hands off it. They are driven toward novelty, jumping in head first, eyes closed. Their impulsivity follows them throughout life. They like flying by the seat of their pants, helicopter skiing, motorcycle riding, car racing, mountain climbing, late nights, early mornings, and whirlwind romances. They do and like doing the very things that most people only dream about, and often consciously avoid. Fear and the rush of adrenaline that tempers most and paralyzes some seems to energize these people. Ordinary life experiences aren't enough for them.

At the other end of the continuum is the more tentative, *reflective* type. These look at people and objects carefully before approaching. They stick a toe in and slowly advance, ankles, knees, belly button. They may retreat several times before they are wholly immersed. The ordinary for them may be frightening, even imposing.

Most children fit somewhere between these two temperamental styles, impulsive and reflective; yet they demonstrate distinct preferences for one style. Some researchers suggest that these temperamental differences may be evident at birth, indicating a genetic factor at play. Temperament does indicate a child's readiness for social interaction and the optimal amount and type of contact to be provided by parents. Yet, being the nonabsolutist I am, I have to say that all developmental styles respond to conditioning, to experience.

The gentle yet reassuring parent can lead a reflective Eva to the gymnastic mat. With parental support, Eva will attempt that fearful somersault or two that she wouldn't on her own. The wrong approach with Eva may also result in her never going near that mat again! The firm yet tender parent can help an impulsive Terrence look at the lovingly stacked block tower without needing to knock it to the floor each and every time. Knowledge of children's temperament coupled with wisdom about the optimal kinds of interactions needed to nurture them can help parents ensure that their children will attempt healthy developmental experiences and avoid destructive ones.

Real Fears

Robert told me he was worried, worried about growing up— about whether he'd have a job. "It's so hard," he said, "to get money. What if those people in the street don't get any money, any food?" He was so upset. I thought to myself, "Should a six-year-old be worrying about this?" And then I thought, "Why wouldn't he?"

Sex, nuclear war, drugs—the very words cause distress when used in sentences containing the names of our children. Yet one amazing fact seems to escape parents. Children know about distressing topics because we want them to. Today many parents equate ignorance—more specifically innocence—with danger. Childhood is no longer a sheltered time when so many young people are dying of AIDS, when so many abused children are filling our newscasts, when so many destitute people are living in our railway and bus stations. Perhaps protecting our children is no longer a rational goal for parents. If we cannot protect them, we must prepare them.

This early preparation for the ills of society has caused a great deal of concern among researchers, child psychologists, and, of course, parents. Children are perceived as being robbed of childhood by their too early exposure to the emotional territory of adulthood. Parents have been accused by some professionals of treating their middle-school children as personal confidants, asking their children to solve the problems of their difficult adult lives. Professionals are also concerned that children are not seeing adults as strong and certain. The media often present adults as mercenary, cruel, and corrupt. These adult images, although real in some instances, cannot support children's emotional development. Children need to know there is someone they can lean on, someone all-knowing, loving, and trusting. Our children are afraid of, or at least anxious about, the "world" because parents and society are asking them not to be children anymore, to grow up too fast, too soon.

I do agree. Children are bombarded with concepts far too difficult for them to integrate. Some psychologists suggest that there was a time in the very recent past when children learned difficult concepts in stages, in an easier way for them to assimilate. Perhaps. Yet burying your head in the sand has never proved an effective way of dealing with anything. Children are not isolated. If children or childhood has changed, it is because the world has.

Very early in this book, I alluded to the idea that childhood has not ever been the precious, idyllic time it is perceived to be. At the turn of the century, four-year-olds worked in factories; sixteen-year-olds were married, with several children. Children have always handled a great deal more than we have given them credit for. I don't believe it is the content of what we say to children that makes them anxious or afraid today; it is *how* it is said to them. Children may feel bombarded by the world because much of what is communicated to them is done through the impersonal nature of the media, often without discussion and much-needed adult interpretation and insight.

There are gentle yet instructive ways to talk to children, even the very young, about kidnapping, child abuse, AIDS, drugs, sex, nuclear holocaust, and pollution. The point is that *parents* need to do the talking, not MTV.

Children are afraid of many things. Our job as parents is to help them sort out what they need to be afraid of and what they don't. Careful guidance by parents is the key to assisting children in overcoming their unrealistic fears and confronting the real ones.

7

Fear

Strategies and Solutions

Everyone is afraid of something.

> *There I was at the top of the Twin Towers. My two children were yards across from me, literally hanging over the glass-enclosed observation platforms. I stood next to the elevator clutching a gray pole. My hands were sweating. My heart was pounding. I was so frightened, I couldn't bear to take them to the gift shop. I just couldn't wait to get downstairs, so I could breathe normally again.*

It is important for you to remember your own fears when you attempt to deal with your child's.

Fear is powerful and painful. It is important to remember just *how powerful.* Fear produces many strange behaviors. Surely, the mother quoted above would never benefit from the standard smug remark: "There's nothing to be afraid of." True, there may be nothing for the smug person to be afraid of, at least at the moment, but the fearful person will never be comforted by being told that there is nothing to fear, when her entire being is telling her otherwise.

Not all fears are inevitable. Although we cannot eliminate fear—and shouldn't even try—parents can diminish it. Parents can create a sense of security for children by

- being consistent in their behavior and comforting routines.
- making children aware of changes before they happen.
- supporting and validating fears, even if you don't understand them.
- providing children with many opportunities for fantasy play

via dressup clothes, miniature figures of people and animals, dollhouses, toy garages, and so on. Here your children can stage their own fears and, in effect, take control of them (see also "Guided Fantasy," in this chapter).
- reading children's literature that deals with fearful events that children overcome (see "Using Fairy Tales" in this chapter).
- giving your child many opportunities to be in control, and autonomous. Remember, children are afraid because they feel weak. When you are in control, you are strong.

Remember also that your child's fear may be a projection of your own. A child who is afraid to go into the water often has a parent who was frightened by water at some time. There are many Mommy-and-me swim classes in which it is Mommy who must get comfortable in the water.

Fantastic Fears

It was Halloween. Mom had bought Dierdre a wonderful Red Riding Hood costume. Dierdre was ecstatic. She couldn't wait to go trick or treating with Evelyn, her big sister, that evening. Once outside, holding Evelyn's hand, Dierdre had a very different experience. All these strange faces moved and spoke like people she knew. But she had never seen these faces before. She ran onto the porch and into the house. Halloween was not fun; it was frightening and disturbing.

Most of what I term the *fantastic fears* of early childhood are provoked by lack of understanding. Young children misread certain environmental cues and conclude much that is totally irrational, for example, "Water runs down the drain. Will I run down the drain?"

There are some fairly standard procedures that parents can follow when their child exhibits the common childhood fears of dogs, water, masks, and so on. Never make the child do something he is terrified of, no matter how irrational his fear sounds to you. If, for example, the child is afraid of petting a stuffed dog, you can reassure him: "OK, I know the big dog is frightening. You can hold my hand. You can look. No one will make you touch." Most professionals agree that to help a child overcome a fear of this nature, we should allow the child to "get used to it" slowly. For example, you can help a child overcome a fear of masks by using the following steps, moving onto the next step only when she feels comfortable:

1. Sit down together and handle the mask. Look at it inside and out. Feel it, smell it, explore it.
2. Give the child one or two more masks. Explore all three masks together.
3. Sit by a mirror.
4. Have the child try the mask on and look in the mirror. She may want to put the mask on and take it off several times before she is comfortable.
5. Once she is comfortable with one mask, introduce the others.
6. Have the child try one of the masks on you. She may want you to put the mask on and take it off several times.
7. Offer to try the other masks on, if she wishes.

Be aware that children move through these steps at very different paces. Some may not need every step to be successful, and others may need much smaller steps. Whatever the case, make certain the child is in control, for example, "Let me know when you want to put the masks away" or "You can take my hand whenever you need it."

Guided Fantasy

As confounding as the following may sound, there is much evidence to support the idea that fantasy, which can produce or accelerate children's fears, can also relieve them. Guided fantasies are planned experiences in which someone uses his imagination to create mental images. The use of guided fantasy with young children is gaining popularity among teachers and therapists who realize that fantasy is a useful resource for many children. Professionals use guided fantasy to help children reduce anxiety, to relax, to become aware of feelings, and to explore ideas mentally. Some experts believe that children gain a sense of control over what happens to them by using this technique.

To use guided fantasy:

1. Say something like the following: "We are going to take a trip by making pictures in our heads. This trip will be a lot like pretending, and all the pictures will be like movies in your head. You can use your imagination to make anything you like."

2. Find a place where you can relax without touching anyone. The two of you may lie down or just sit someplace where you both can be quiet. Close your eyes and let your bodies and your thinking rest. Take in a nice slow breath and let it out. See if you can relax a little bit more and be very, very still.

3. You, as the parent, then guide your child through several carefully selected mental images. Guided fantasies that focus on the senses are particularly useful in the early stages of this process. At first, some children have difficulty keeping their eyes closed, but once they become familiar with the process, many look forward to relaxing and creating their own fantasies. It is sometimes helpful to have music playing in the background. Music is soothing to children and usually helps them to quiet down and relax. Ask your child to imagine something familiar, such as a toy, a special food, or a pet. Encourage your child to think about how the object feels, whether it is hard or soft, whether it has a smell, whether it has color or taste.

4. Once your child is familiar with imagining something familiar, you can introduce a fantasy like the following:

   You are at the beach. The sun is warm and the waves are tickling your feet as you walk on the shore. Look up at the blue sky and hear the sounds the seagulls are making. Now picture something lying in the sand right in front of you. Walk over to this object and pick it up. How does it feel? Is it heavy or light? Does it move or is it still? Think very carefully about this special treasure you have discovered. You don't have to open your eyes yet, but keep a special picture in your head so you can tell me about this object when you do open your eyes. Let your imagination become quiet. When you feel ready, shake your head a little, stretch your feet, and open your eyes. Do you want to tell me about your special treasure?

There is no limit to the content or scope of guided fantasies. You can take trips to the zoo, the mountains, another galaxy. The parent will need to be the guide until the child has an idea of how the process works. Then he can be the guide and you can take the journey.

Guided fantasy teaches your child that she has control over her own imagination. In this way, those pictures in her head become her lifelong friends.

Using Fairy Tales

> That crazy Jack in the Beanstalk!
> I don't care if he was big and mean.
> I'd be mean, too, if someone stole my
> treasure. That's what Jack did.
> Those things weren't his.

In my graduate course in children's literature, there is always a heated debate regarding reading or telling fairy tales to children. One side sees fairy stories as sick, sadistic tales of severe human cruelty; the other as great literature, the unconscious human morality. I generally kindle this discussion by opening the session with a rendering of the original edition of Snow White by the Brothers Grimm, replete with boiling entrails and iron slippers. There are no jolly little men and singing maidens here. Why? Today we may view fairy tales as primarily children's literature, yet they were never meant for children. They were meant for adults. Until collectors, like the Brothers Grimm, began to publish these European folktales, they had never been written down. People told these tales orally, passing them down from one generation to the next.

How these tales became the dominion of childhood is not clear. It may be that because of the sophistication of publishing during the nineteenth century, the content of fairy tales, with all of their witches and dragons, began to be viewed as too immature a subject for most adults, particularly the upper class, who were the main consumers of books.

Although I would never encourage the reading of all fairy tales to all children, as many contain severely disturbing psychic elements, like the Grimm Brothers' Snow White, I do feel that many offer a service to the young. This service is best performed by fairy tales. Because fairy tales were written by ordinary people—the "folk" in folktale—they often depict ordinary people confronting extraordinary problems and overcoming them. The struggle against severe human difficulty is part of human existence. If Jack does not shy away from the giant but meets the challenge of the unexpected, he may and does emerge victorious.

Another significant characteristic of fairy tales is that they tend to take life's most existential problems and treat them straightforwardly. Life is complex; fairy tales are pointed. The questions of life and death, good and evil, the child's most essential fears, are presented in a no-nonsense format that the child comprehends immediately. Although real-life witches and fairy godmothers may be hard to discover, the child has no difficulty recognizing these beings in the context of the fairy tale. The good are beautiful and strong; the evil are ugly and mean.

What most concerns me is that many of today's children have had little or no exposure to fairy tales. If they have, it is often because they've seen them on television and not because someone has read these stories aloud to them. Television fairy tales—television, period—cannot engage children's imagination the way oral reading can. Like nursery rhymes and jump-rope jingles, fairy tales seem to be obsolete. Yet fairy tales are one of the best tools I know for speaking directly to the child's unconscious mind, providing much needed comfort and encouragement in confronting one's fears.

There is no magic formula for reading fairy tales to children, but here are a few helpful hints:

- Read the story slowly and with expression.
- Be prepared to stop when your child has questions.
- When you finish a story, always have at least a brief discussion. Ask open ended questions like: What's another good ending for this story? Who was your favorite character? Why? What was the scariest part?

Discussions at the end of fairy tales help children further develop their problem-solving skills.

Nightmare Monsters

I'm gonna take that lion-pig and put him in a cage. Then he is going to listen to me. When I am finished talking, I will let him out. I can't talk to him when he is running around scaring everyone. But when he's in his cage, he listens.

The next time your child is awakened by a bad dream, give the support and comfort you usually do, lots of hugging and reassurance. When some degree of calm has been achieved, instead of taking the standard "It was only a dream" approach, try acknowledging the lion, the dragon, the big bad monster. Tell your child to tell the monster to please not visit anymore tonight. Everyone needs some sleep. Together you will talk about the monster in the morning or whenever there is a good time. During that special time together, give your child some paper and markers or crayons. Tell Mary she is going to draw her dream. As she draws, you may ask her questions similar to the following:

- How do you feel about drawing this scary dream?
- If this dream is too scary, do you want to keep yourself out of this picture?
- How could you protect yourself in this dream?

Children can be particularly gifted when they use drawings to empower themselves against their fears:

- They become invisible.
- They make the monster very small.
- They create an army of friends.
- They draw special escape devices like parachutes and tunnels.

Although many children will want to kill their monster, ask Mary to consider the option of talking to it. Her monster may have something important to tell her. Ask Mary to ask the monster what it wants and why it came. When a child communicates with her monster, the monster almost always becomes more human. By the time it is invited to say what it wants and why it feels like attacking, the dreamer may begin to recognize her own complaints or anger. The monster's anger is often a reflection of the dreamer's own rage, frustration, or fear of unacceptable emotions that she feels she must repress.

When you, as the parent, play the part of guide in this dreamplay process, do not diminish fear and do not give Mary answers or solutions. When Mary confronts her monster, she learns she doesn't need to be afraid. She is in control. Ask Mary to find her own answers. Try several options, such as "*I talked to the monster,* and

- "I told him to stop chasing me."
- "I asked him why he growled so much. He said it was because no one ever let him talk."
- "I told him to take off that silly costume. He was really just a yellow duck."

See which one *feels* right to her.

Children are literal, and that is the best approach to take with them and their dreams. Avoid hidden meanings unless they recognize these immediately and make the connection.

Being Alone

I was at Margaret's house, working on a report, I really thought that this planning was going to be effective. There were so many interruptions at home, and this simply had to be done! Emily called nine times. Nine times! Next time I'll stay at home.

As living organisms, we must constantly respond to demands for inner and outer adaptation. Things, good and bad, can be stressful. As Emily becomes an adolescent, she is confounded by the so-called stress of freedom. All through the years, she has pressured you into allowing her to do things by herself, on her own, to leave her alone. When she is finally granted this longed-for privilege, like the adult who dreams of a promotion and obsesses over it when it is received, she is not so certain she wants it.

Freedom has that frightening price tag of responsibility. Freedom is great as long as we don't have to be responsible for it. Riding on a bus by yourself or going into a strange store and asking for something can produce tremendous anxiety for the preadolescent. They have got used to relying on their parents for so many things. Whenever they need to go somewhere, they don't have to think. Joey asks Dad to take him. Dad does.

A perfectly capable child who was eager a short time ago to ask for a specific kind of sandwich from the deli man, now wants you to ask. He wants you to choose from the restaurant menu and lay out his clothes every evening. This behavior can be very perplexing.

The preadolescent is ambivalent. Ambivalence creates anxiety and fear. We also know that in times of stress, regression is very likely to occur. Younger children will resort to previously relinquished habits like thumb-sucking and bed-wetting. These big boys and girls still love you very much. They want to be grown up, and yet they still want to be taken care of. The whole world is telling them they must leave you very, very soon. This fear will cause them to cling to you strongly, as long as they can. There are a number of things you can do to make this difficult process a little easier.

First, this is no time to remind your child how grown up he is. He wants to be babied. Baby him. Let him know that even though he is getting older and is accepting more responsibility, you love him just as much as ever. This is a good time to take out the old photo album and reminisce about "when he was little." Plan a few special outings for just the two of you. Go to dinner or a show. Sit up late and watch some films.

Most people who are able to explore options in life find they need an emotional centering. The family unit, the spouse, or a special friend performs this function. The explorer knows that whatever changes occur in her life, there is at least one thing that will never change. Knowing that this stability exists is what allows her to move.

Preadolescents need this centering, as do many other people. They need to know that, as they relegate their childhood baggage to the attic and redecorate their lives anew, you are, as you always have been, there for them.

If Tammy is anxious about being alone, it may be important to speak with her about how you can make this experience more comfortable for her. What exactly is Tammy concerned about? Remember, Tammy's fears are to be anticipated. The world is not safe, and unexpected things happen all the time. Respect her concerns. Once you know what she is afraid of, you can address these fears directly. Here are some suggestions for when you leave Tammy alone. First, limit her time alone to an hour or two. Then, give her the basic safety information:

- Give her a phone number where you can be reached. If you cannot be reached, give her a specific time when you will call. Call at that time.

- Leave one or even two emergency numbers—just in case.
- Tell her what to say on the phone when someone calls, for example, take a message and say something like "Mom's busy right now. She'll get back to you as soon as she can," or use your answering machine.
- Show her how to lock and unlock all the doors. Practice a couple of times.

As with everything else, Tammy will become comfortable being alone the more she practices. She will become comfortable making phone calls and answering phone calls, and she will know what to expect. Emphasize her coping skills in alternate areas, which you know she will develop here. The familiar is always easier than the unknown.

The Big Stuff

Listen I know you can get AIDS without ever taking drugs. OK! Now I want to know how exactly you can get it.

Kids don't have easy questions today—not that they ever did. Specific fears are prompted by the times in which we live. The questions in big cities is no longer "Have you been mugged?" but "How many times?" Today, parents feel pressure to answer tough questions accurately and clinically. Often, parents aren't shocked by questions, as perhaps they once were; yet they do feel inadequate and uninformed about many subjects. Parents feel that if their child comes to them with a difficult question, they should be able to answer it.

Yet parents can't know everything. Believe it or not, most children can understand and empathize with this predicament. Children aren't always asking for answers as much as they are looking for listeners. Another problem is that parents often attempt to answer difficult questions without really listening. The classic example:

Ted: Mom, where did Joshie come from?

Mom: Well . . . (*Mom launches into a detailed discussion of conception, reproduction, and birth.*)

Ted: Oh, I thought he came from Michigan.

When children pose questions, parents need to *answer* the questions that are asked, not to interpret them.

Children want to see the world as a beautiful, enjoyable place. However, there is much in the world to confound that perception. Everywhere they turn there are very frightening things happening to strangers, to people they know, maybe even to members of their own family. How can you help your children to be cautious without making them apprehensive of life in general?

It is not my purpose here to highlight the content of specific social ills—what you should say to children about poverty, about drugs, about pollution, about strangers, about war. There are many fine books that discuss each of these topics in detail. Children are anxious about social problems and need this information. These are real fears as opposed to the fantastic ones discussed earlier. Here are a few considerations:

SAFETY

1. Show your child how to use the 911 emergency telephone number.
2. Emphasize that children's usual behavior toward adults is not expected toward strangers. Children should learn to ignore questions, to say no, to walk away, to refuse to do a task, and to cry or make a scene if someone is following or pestering them. All offers of rides, money, kittens, canaries, toys, and so on should be refused. Remind your child that normal adults do not ask children, particularly young ones, for either directions or the time.
3. Do some role plays, for example, "If a man comes up to you and asks you to help him find his lost money, what do you do? What do you say?"

SEXUAL ABUSE

1. Provide your child with proper sex education, using the correct terms for all body parts.

2. Remember that a warning against strangers is not helpful in this instance. Most sexual abuse does not result from an isolated incident or from violent attack by a dangerous stranger. Sexual offenses are almost always committed by *people the child knows, gradually and repeatedly,* and *subtly* rather than by explicit force.

3. Tell your child about "body zones," that certain parts of our bodies are off limits except for *older* people who truly love each other, like Mommy and Daddy, and for medical exams by doctors or nurses.

4. Teach your child that, he can say, "No," "Stop," and very effective, "I'm going to tell."

5. Teach your child that he can run away without explanation. These people do not deserve answers to questions, thanks for any help they may have given (in exchange), or whatever respect a child usually renders an adult.

WAR

1. Let your child know that no one wants a war, that every country seeks to protect its children.

2. Stress that the prospect of war is one more area of life that everyone must face despite numerous fears, both real and unreal.

3. Politically motivated parents have the option to get involved in various ways and have the right to educate their children on these issues. The challenge here is how to achieve this without further frightening or worrying children. Ideally, the example of a politically active parent encourages a youngster's optimism about the future and faith in individual and collective effort.

No matter what the content of the tough question, the process of answering is the same:

1. *Listen:* Don't assume you know the answer before you know the question.

2. *Listen:* Once you've heard the question, make sure you know what is really being asked.
3. *Listen:* Hear your child's responses to their own questions. Many of these tough questions don't have answers. Your child's options are just as valid as any adult's in this instance.

If it is any comfort, safety has long been an issue for humankind: "Fear is the foundation of safety" (Tertullian, c. 220 A.D.).

8

Transition

"I Like Things the Way They Are.
Why Are They Changing?"

There is nothing worse than change. I hate it. I like to know where everything is, who everybody is. Some people like meeting new people. I don't. I like being with my friends. I guess if nothing ever changed, I'd be pretty bored. But when everything changes—just everything—I don't want to get out of bed.

This expression of ten-year-old June sums up this chapter in a nutshell. In the previous chapters, I've discussed several issues that had transition as a component: going to school, being alone, trying new things. Yet there remain the two larger issues of transition in our three- to twelve-year-old society: moving and puberty.

Although change is an aspect of the issues presented earlier, it is the central aspect of moving and puberty. All of us must deal with change everyday—unless, of course, like our friend June, we make a deliberate decision to stay in bed. Yet no one is truly safe from change even in bed: Suppose there is a leak in the ceiling, drenching our sheets? Change, like loving and losing, success and failure, reality and fantasy, is pretty unavoidable in our present culture. We can diminish change by pretending to avoid it, yet avoiding change can be more taxing than simply learning to face it head-on.

Many day-to-day transitions are manageable because, although an aspect of change is present, not everything changes. Jay loses his math homework. OK, something like this has happened before. Jay can cope with this. He knows his math teacher. He can speak with him. He has a free period during which he can redo his math homework. Or Alicia has just had a big blowup with Cori. Alicia does have other friends. She can confide in them until she figures out a way to patch up things with Cori. When these day-to-day transitions occur, children can usually cope because the change is imbedded in an overall consistency.

Major life transitions present children with the need of a wider array of coping skills than they normally use. When a child moves or reaches puberty, her whole life changes dramatically. The overall consistency disappears and is often replaced by dire panic or depression. Children, particularly young children, rely on the familiar, the comfortable, in order to continue learning and communicating. When the environment becomes overwhelmingly unfamiliar, as in the case of moving to a new home, young children may become disoriented and frightened—just as adults do. Older children reaching that all-important transition period, puberty, exhibit all sorts of new behavior to compensate for the strangeness they feel in their minds as well as in their bodies.

In one sense, all change should reflect growth. Yet too much change, too soon, can inhibit it. The best kind of change occurs through a process known as *integration*. In the social realm, integration occurs by learning (1) how experiences are different from one another and (2) how they are alike.

During early childhood, Karen must have many different experiences and register exactly how these experiences are different. If she is successful in this differentiation process, she will gradually be able to see how these very different experiences are indeed alike. Our brains perceive differences before similarities. This is why our friend Jay, in losing his math homework, or Alicia, in losing her friend, can see these experiences, although unusual, as following distinguishable patterns. These children are able to *see differences as similarities*. This is actually a good definition of the highly complex integration process: looking at the different, the new, and seeing these new experiences as familiar.

Because of his more limited experiences, the young child has more difficulty with this integration process than the older child. It is interesting, however, that the extreme changes of puberty seem to make integration a difficult process to maintain during later childhood as well.

A child who is not an effective integrator approaches new experiences with the idea that the entire experience is new and thus every step of the experience must be completely learned. The effective integrator does not view new experiences this way but looks at the experience with the idea that she already knows at least part of it. The integrator can find comfort in experiences, new and old, because of the mental stance she takes. The child who has difficulty integrating cannot make the previously described connection and thus often creates additional stress for herself.

Both moving and puberty require heightened levels of integration. The better your child is at integration, the more smooth the experience will be.

Moving

Everyone automatically identifies with the trauma of moving. I just mention that we're moving, and everyone rolls their eyes and groans. I don't know, you watch those old westerns— moving, traveling, adventure. Andrew seemed excited enough packing his bags. I guess it hadn't hit him yet! He woke up three times last night, though. It's not going to be easy.

Certainly the physical exhaustion of moving would be enough, but it is the emotional exhaustion of change that makes moving so difficult for children—and adults. The degree of planning involved in a cross-country move and in one across town, or the move that involves a so-called culture shock, like a move from an expansive rural community to an intense urban one, will vary. The bigger the change, the more the planning involved. Children of all ages react to moving both as individuals and as members of distinct developmental groups. As it is impossible to enumerate all the individual differences that may emerge, I will use the developmental framework.

Three- to Five-Year-Olds

Early childhood is marked by growth in specific cognitive skills, particularly language that is used to communicate ideas. The task of moving presents the young child with a great many cognitive tasks to assimilate, many of which relate to highly abstract notions, like time and space. These concepts are advanced and will not be fully integrated by Janet until she is close to seven years old. Much of her distress during this difficult period will be a result of her lack of understanding:

> *"How far is far away?" asked Tommie. Far away to him was a thirty-minute ride. How could I explain to him that far away now meant thousands of miles? No more one-two-three trips to Grandma's.*

There are ways to communicate abstract ideas concretely. If parents take the time to plan and talk to their young children, certainly moving will not be a breeze, but it will be met with less frustration and confusion.

Six- to Eight-Year-Olds

Six- to eight-year-olds have a great deal more understanding than younger children. They can understand distance and time and are apt to be the group most responsive to the idea of moving. Cheryl understands the concept of lost friendship and is extremely distressed by it. Yet she is also a member of the group who most easily reconciles themselves to this social predicament and, as a result, begin the task of making new friends sooner than their older counterparts.

Cheryl will have a great many questions about the impending move. The pleasure with this child is that you can give many straightforward answers to these questions and be comforted in knowing that your responses will be understood.

Sometimes Cheryl is so cooperative and apparently jubilant about the move that her parents may not expect the unavoidable trauma to emerge. When the inevitable crying and confusion occur, her parents may be unprepared and somewhat shocked. Cheryl was singing and looking at travel guides two days earlier. Where did all this emotion swell from?

Nine- to Twelve-Year-Olds

As your child approaches puberty, nothing becomes easy (read "Maturing," in this chapter). If nothing traumatic happens, trauma happens nonetheless. The older child has built a deliberate social framework for himself. Jesse has spent a great deal of time organizing his life, which, in every real sense, *is* his friends. A move represents disruption in this very delicate framework. Enthusiasm should not be expected.

When children approach adolescence, their whole life changes. Their bodies grow, their mental development matures, and their emotions go haywire. Throw in the additional stress factor of moving, and you have one very upset person.

The older child is so emotionally tied to his friends that he truly cannot envision what life would be like without them. The separation here resembles that of the first day of school, when the child felt literally wrenched from his parents; now the child feels wrenched from his friends.

No matter how you cut it, moving is never an easy transition, Even so, parents can prepare their children for this difficult time with understanding and sensitivity.

Maturing

Worry that there is a right way to neck and you don't know it.

Worry that your date will be able to tell that you don't know it.

If you are a girl, worry that your breasts are too round. Worry that your breasts are too pointed. Worry that your nipples are the wrong color. Worry that your breasts point in different directions.

If you are a boy, worry you will get breasts.

Worry that your nose is too fat. Worry that your nose is too long. Worry that your neck is too fat. Worry that your ears stick out. Worry that your eyes are too close together.

If you are a boy, worry that you will never be able to grow a moustache.

If you are a girl, worry that you have a moustache.

Worry that you will eat too much food at other people's houses.

Worry that when you go to the bathroom people will hear.

Worry that the lock on the door doesn't work and someone will come in.

Worry that everyone hates you.

Worry that everyone thinks you are stupid.

Worry that you have ugly toes.

—(Ephron, 1981, pp. 115–116)

Puberty is probably one of the most difficult life experiences through which one must pass. It combines the drives and urgent needs of adulthood with the naïveté and vulnerability of childhood, the struggle to spring away from parental authority with the still desperate need to cling for comfort. The young adult world is one of uncharted landscape, navigated tenuously at some points and carelessly at others.

In order to become a complete person, Keith must create an identity of his own. This task is extremely complex in Western society. There are few remaining rites of passage through which he can see concretely, "Childhood is over. Adult life has begun."

It is certainly not my objective here to present all the nuances of early adolescence. There are many wonderful books that discuss adolescent development in depth and that provide fine recommendations. What I will do is discuss early adolescence as it relates to the issue of transition and the concept of change versus staying the same. There are three developmental pathways that parents need to see clearly: physical changes, cognitive changes, and socioemotional changes.

Although all of these changes are independent of one another from a theoretical point of view, each single developmental area has a very specific impact on the other two. So although we can discuss each area independently and distinctly; in reality they are all part and parcel of the self-same thing: human development.

I also integrate gender from the vantage point of transition. Although adolescence—and human development in general—has traditionally been described within a male framework, the most current research, specifically that of Carol Gilligan of Harvard University, indicates that girls are very different from boys. Not that we didn't suspect this without the supporting research, but now we can describe female development not as *different* from that of males (the male being typical and the female atypical), but as unique. Girls and boys develop distinctively, each having strengths and weaknesses.

Physical Changes

That first day of gym and I had no pubic hair. It was the first time I'd actually prayed I would turn into my sister. Girls don't shower in public. God! who invented these communal baths anyway!

The physical changes associated with puberty begin roughly at age ten and may end as late as age eighteen. These include rapid changes in height, weight, distribution of body fat, appearance of body hair, and development of the organs of reproduction.

Until nine or ten, there is little difference between boys and girls in terms of height, weight, or physical strength. They have each reached approximately four fifths of their adult height and more than half their adult weight. The onset of puberty, however, brings with it a virtual explosion of physical changes.

GIRLS. Ninety-five percent of all girls demonstrate at least one sign of puberty between the ages of nine and eleven. Their height spurt begins at approximately age ten, most girls achieving their adult height by age fourteen. Although previous generations of girls were self-conscious about being "too tall," the newest data indicate that 56 percent of young girls are worried that they will be "too short." Obviously, society's relatively recent adoration of the six-foot high-fashion glamour girl has contributed to this reverse of anxiety.

Before puberty, beginning at age seven, both boys and girls accumulate body fat that they will lose during puberty. Girls lose less of this body fat than boys do. Females, in general, enter adulthood with a higher percentage of body fat than males. Males enter adulthood with more muscle tissue. Extra body fat beneath the skin gives females a more rounded shape than males. This extra body fat has also contributed to young women's obsession with weight, food, and dieting.

Breasts

> *I had this whole routine. I actually took adhesive tape and wrapped it around my chest. Then, I put on a T-shirt, then my regular shirt—until my mom caught me and accused me of cutting off my circulation. I just couldn't stand it. "Boobers," they called me. "Boobers!" I was eleven and a half.*

Breast development begins around age eight or nine and is most normally completed by age fifteen. Breast development is usually the first sign of puberty for girls. Breasts develop in stages:

1. elevation of the nipple and the surrounding area
2. enlargement of the entire breast and deepened pigmentation and widening of the areola
3. formation of the final breast contour

Again, perhaps because of society's; that is, males' adoration of the female breast, no young girl, no woman, believes her breasts to be exactly the right size. Young girls worry that they will be "flat as a board" or "enormous," subject to the stares and teasing of their peers.

Another important piece of information is that one breast generally develops more quickly than the other one. This is perfectly normal. The smaller breast soon catches up with the bigger one. Young girls can be saved a great deal of distress once they realize they will not be permanently lopsided.

Menstruation

> *As I belong to a family of contemporary culture, it figured I would be at work when Jane got her first period. Al called me from home hysterical. He had just been to the local drugstore with her. "Oh, my God!" he said, "I never imagined there would be so much stuff. You'd think they'd have something called 'first time.'"*

Perhaps the most notable phenomenon of female puberty is the menarche, the initial menstruation. In more tribal communities, it is a public event. In traditional Western culture, it is private and, until a decade ago, surrounded in mystery and superstition. In contrast, today's young girls, more anxious than ever to become adults, eagerly await menarche's arrival and are often traumatized when they don't get "it" when all their friends do.

Menarche occurs approximately two to three years after the onset of breast development, but again, it may occur as early as nine years or as late as eighteen. Once a girl begins to menstruate, she will be irregular until ovulation is fully established. Because of this irregularity, young females are *theoretically infertile* for at least a few years after ovulation begins. Even so, pregnancy is always a possibility once menstruation begins.

BOYS. A most prevalent concern for young men continues to be height. The growth spurt in boys may begin as early as ten and end as late as their twentieth year. Ninety-eight percent of all boys achieve their full adult height by age sixteen.

Boys worry about their height more than girls do, particularly if they are short. Being short has never been considered a manly trait, even though Napoleon himself was an imposing five feet! (Hence, the term *Napoleonic complex.*) Tallness in males is extremely valued in most societies. The boy who is tall is complemented often. The boy who is short is often self-conscious.

Between the ages of ten and thirteen, the boys' testes begin to enlarge gradually. This enlargement continues for three or more years and may end as late as age eighteen. Pubic hair appears around the same time that the testes enlarge, the hair becoming darker, coarser, and curlier than other body hair.

Boys' greatest concern is the growth and the relative size of their penis. This organ grows rapidly, beginning approximately one year after the testes begin to enlarge. Growth continues until between thirteen and sixteen years of age. In its flaccid state, the average penis is approximately four to six inches in length. Differences in size diminish in its erect state, the average erect penis being six inches.

There are as many myths surrounding men's penises as there are about women's breasts. The scientific facts remain. The size of a boy's penis has absolutely nothing to do with his virility, strength, or ability to sire children. It does not grow with use or atrophy with disuse. Straightforward information like this can ease confusion and undue concern.

Although the physical changes are the changes most associated with puberty, young adolescents would be in a state of transition during this period even if they remained essentially the same physiologically. Less documented are the fluctuations in thinking and socioemotional development.

Cognitive Changes

"You know you really shouldn't be eating meat or animal products of any kind! Animals are high on the food chain and destroying them contributes to the destruction of our planet! Don't you even care!?" This was Jeffrey talking—the kid who hadn't eaten anything but burgers for ten years.

Because adults are so attuned to the physiological changes of early adolescence, they tend to attribute all distress to this onslaught of physical growth. In reality, the greatest transition of this period is not physical, but mental. As uncomfortable and inept as young teenagers feel about the growth of their bodies, they are even more uncomfortable and inept in using their new thinking processes.

Jean Piaget (1952) identified a *second* age of reason, one observed much later than the one previously identified centuries earlier by the Jesuits. The onset of formal operations between ages ten and twelve allows children to think in abstract terms, "to be not so concrete;" to modify time and space; to predict; to realize that words have double meanings. Their new ability to reorganize reality explains their colorful and sometimes irritating reinvention of language.

CRITICISM. Because Matt has this new-found ability to abstract, he is able to envision life outside his immediate family. He can see the perfect world, the perfect city, the perfect family, the perfect parent. Matt now sees his family, his parents—once omnipotent—as seriously flawed when measured against these new, more perfect visions.

This new criticalness on the part of our once-adoring children may be very abrupt, emerging, it seems, without reasonable cause. Here we are doing it just as we're used to doing it, and now there are discerning eyes all around us, quick to point out our faults: We are never on time. We are always too early. We talk too loudly. We never say anything. We wear stupid clothes. We wear expensive clothes. We don't love them. We don't love ourselves. We don't love the world.

> *I had been dyeing my hair for twelve years. One morning, Angela gets out of bed and says, "You know, that's the worst color for you," as if she had never seen me before.*

ARGUING

> *Who are you to talk to me! You filled the world with garbage, drugs, and disgusting music, like the Doors. You—you hippie!*

All parents would like to prevent the horror of early adolescence. Most of us have strained memories of the severe entanglements we experienced with our own parents. Our own parents were not "hip," "cool," or with-it." They had antiquated ideas regarding sex, war, and money. They didn't let us hang out with the people we wanted to hang out with. They didn't let us stay out all night. Our generation of parents was going to be different: sensitive, aware, all-caring, all-knowing.

It may be quite a jolt to our egos to realize that perhaps many parents over the centuries have felt this same way. Why wouldn't parents want to have healthy relationships with their children? Why wouldn't they want to listen to them and give advice when it is needed? Most parents do love their children. Why wouldn't they want to do what is best for them?

However, the reality of this stage of development is, sadly, that no matter what you do, your child is going to confront you. As the young child practices reading or tying his shoes, the older one practices arguing. The young adolescent has finally realized that, mentally, she has the power to think distinct thoughts. Her parents are not the only people who think. Their ideas may be very different from those she has heard elsewhere. In order to form her own opinions, the young adolescent argues to see what opinions there are to choose from. Although a heated discussion may emanate from a formerly innocent television program, this exhausting debate is actually healthy from a cognitive point of view. This is Allison's attempt to extract, from the vast body of information surrounding her, just what she is going to believe about how the world works and how the people in it work.

Socioemotional Changes

> *You don't get it, Mom. It doesn't matter if it's cool and all the models in the magazines are wearing it. It's only cool if everyone you know is wearing it.*

When we think of puberty, we often think of emotional turmoil right alongside the physiological turmoil, the physical changes being responsible for the severe emotional uproar. Although there is more than a grain of truth in this (there is nothing more stressful than hormones running amok), hormones do not alone produce the emotional "craziness" of early adolescence. In fact, the cognitive changes previously described are *just as* responsible, if not *more* responsible. Because the child is able to see things from a new intellectual perspective, things once black and white are now horribly gray. He now realizes there are many important questions to which there are, sadly, no answers. This confusion produces the peculiar logic of this age, followed closely by the equally peculiar emotional life.

SEXUAL INTEREST

Why is it so important for you to know who it was? It was a guy, OK? No one you know.

Beginning at around age ten, girls, in particular, demonstrate a renewed interest in the members of the opposite sex. From about age six or seven until now, both boys and girls have remained fairly homogeneous. Boys operate in social networks distinct from those of girls. There are many theories proposing why this occurs, from "innate tribal instinct" to "deliberate segregation." Again, I am not one to take sides. The facts are simple and observable in most cultural groups. Children emerge from early childhood having had somewhat equivalent experiences with members of each sex. Roughly around age six, a division appears, and children make many more same-sex than opposite-sex friends. During early adolescence, there is another shift, and children are drawn to one another with not friendship but sexual attraction as the motive.

Interestingly, young teenagers often wonder if there will be enough love to go around. If Eliot loves Dawn, doesn't that mean taking away some of the love he has always given to Mom and Dad? On one hand, Eliot is a very concrete reasoner. Love is finite. Everyone has a certain amount. If you give some to a new person, you must take some away from someone else. Why children raise this question about their feelings for those to whom they are sexually attracted and don't deal with their friendship feelings in this way is unclear. It may be that the intensity of the love relationship between parent and child is rekindled only during sexual relationships. Friendship is not felt with this same intensity, so it may not be viewed as threatening.

On the other hand, Eliot has learned to think from a multidimensional point of view. Conflicts emerge because he feels guilty giving this love to a strange new someone when he knows and feels that his parents deserve it. Although his logic is still bound to the concreteness of childhood, he does possess a new ability to consider the feelings and motivations of others. Eliot is not as egocentric and self-involved as he might have you believe. It's not cool to love your parents, so overt manifestations of this love are buried. Inside, however, Eliot is extremely confused.

One way to resolve this internal conflict is to find fault with the parent. After all, if the parent is unworthy of Eliot's love, it becomes perfectly legitimate to withdraw it and give it to this more worthy someone.

EVERYONE IS STARING AT ME

Here I am. I am in the railroad car. I have made a special effort to go to the bathroom in the station. It never fails: The minute the train starts to move, I have to go. I stand up and head to rear of the car. Every eyeball is fastened to me. I get to the toilet and slam the door shut. I am forty-four years old. This is how I remember being eleven years old.

Young adolescents can "think about thinking," a process known as *metacognition*. They think about what they are thinking, and they think about what everybody else is thinking.

Even as adults, we continue to perform for an audience. This is why we shower, dress appropriately, style our hair, and spray ourselves with assorted deodorizers. True, we might engage in these activities even if there were no observers, but most of us certainly alter our behavior when others are about, particularly unknown others.

It is at the dawning of early adolescence that children, too, begin to view themselves with this second mirror. The child who never bathed and would wear the same underwear three days in a row if permitted now has laid camp in the bathroom, spending hours to look just right.

This second mirror is formidable when it first presents itself. Although with maturity we can choose whether or not to pay attention to the mirror, Joyce does not have enough experience of the world to make these decisions. She is certain that everyone is devoting as much exhausting energy to her new skirt as she is. The reality, of course, is that most young teenagers are often so excruciatingly self-absorbed that they barely notice what is going on around them—which can also explain the flipside of this perception: "No one ever pays attention to me."

CHOICES

> *With all of the choices out there, it's just safer to have a kind of uniform—jeans, a denim shirt, sneakers—each day. Yet I would croak if I had a real uniform like the one some of those kids at Osborne wear.*

It is interesting that this group, so outspoken regarding choices, in reality prefers not to make them. It's important to look as if you do have a choice, but it is safer to conform. A great deal of decision making is avoided in early adolescence because of the fear of being different: Before you agree to anything, make sure everyone else agrees to it.

Although teenagers like to be considered trend setters, if carefully examined they are the most routinized group of all: same clothes, same hair, same language, same food. Whatever they do may be truly outlandish, but no one does the unexpected alone—no one cool, that is.

This fear of being different and its emotional turmoil is rooted strongly in parallel cognitive developments. Young children think serially, one thought and then the next. Their comprehension problems occur because they lack the ability to fully integrate or synthesize information. Young teenagers' problem of understanding is the reverse. They have so many ideas floating around in their heads that they have difficulty picking one out or focusing on one idea. Their temporary solution to this dilemma is simply to avoid the decision, to go along with the crowd.

Gender

There has been some serious investigation, of late, into the individual ways that boys and girls develop. Girls do pass through the pubertal transition earlier than do boys. Physiological changes peak earlier and hence are resolved earlier. This information should come as no great surprise. Most of us are aware of the female's earlier physical development.

What we have not been explicitly aware of, although many of us can attest to an intuition, is that girls think and feel differently from boys. Although these differences may be distinguished early in development, they become strikingly apparent during this transition period. Carol Gilligan (1982) of Harvard University has spent many years researching female development. Although her book is far from closed on this issue, she has made some intriguing contributions. During the 1970s, most research was directed at how similar boys and girls were, and although they certainly are, there remain fundamental differences.

Girls tend to think globally, and boys tend to think serially. Girls think about the big picture, boys the individual puzzle pieces. Although it is easy to be straightforward here on paper, how these behaviors manifest themselves may not be so easy to distinguish. Girls make decisions based on emotional comfort. Girls do not like to see people being hurt and often sacrifice their own gain to stand by a friend. Although that prized team spirit is certainly an issue for boys, boys deal with the issue of connectedness in a very different way. When a fight breaks out during a team activity, it is often resolved very quickly. Even if there has been a fistfight, Peter and Joel can speak to one another the very next day. Girls, on the other hand, do not resolve disputes quickly or easily. If a fight breaks out while they are at play, the play ends. In "girl culture," hurting another is simply not permissible.

Girls tend to communicate one to one, using many nonverbal and hidden signals. Boys hang out in groups and are less receptive to nonverbal communication. Whether these behaviors are innate or conditioned by society is not clear. It is most likely a combination of the two. What is clear is that boys and girls require different kinds of support to pass through this transition period calmly and effectively.

Although the physical signs of puberty create great anxiety for the young teenagers who must cope with them, it is the cognitive and emotional changes that make this period particularly stressful. Knowing what Marla is thinking and feeling is as important as knowing how her body is changing.

9

Transition

Solutions and Strategies

If I didn't know he'd reached puberty, I'd think he was schizo-phrenic. Talk about mood swings. One minute, he's running twelve miles, the next he can't get out of bed. I thought infancy was rough. This is insane!

Transitions are very tough. No one adapts eagerly, easily, or readily. The way a parent handles transitions such as moving will vary according to the age and flexibility of the child. Children who are prepared appropriately will be less anxious about the actual move and more fearless when dealing with difficult circumstances in the future.

Although early adolescence is a tug of war no matter how you slice it, all is relative. When young teenagers feel your support, they do appreciate it, no matter how ambivalent their behavior. Reciprocal interactions now pave the road for healthy relations.

Moving

Three- to Five-Year-Olds

Judy looked so helpless standing there. She stared at the packed cartons as if her whole world had just come apart. She was holding her stuffed rabbit, Tillie, by one arm. He dangled to the floor, listless.

As the young child's major problem with moving involves understanding, parents should do all they can to ease confusion. The more concrete the experience of moving, the easier it will be for Judy to comprehend.

The following activities can help young children understand the concepts of time and space and consequently prepare them for moving:

1. *Teach Judy her new address, including the town or city.* If you know what your new telephone number will be, teach her this, too, by helping her dial it on the phone.

2. *If you have pictures of the new house, discuss them with her.* If you are fortunate enough to have several pictures, have Judy mount them on construction paper. Using these photos as a guide, Judy can begin to draw her own pictures of the house along with you.

3. *Make a picture journal.* Approximately one month before the move, help Judy make a simple construction-paper booklet. A composition book is also good. Every day, Judy puts something in her journal. One day, she may draw a picture of her kitchen or backyard. The next, she may take a Polaroid walk of the old house, shooting a picture of each room. Every day, she says something, and every day, Mom or Dad writes whatever Judy says in her special book. The day of the big move, Judy can draw a picture of the moving truck and take a picture of the moving man. When the moving book is finished, it actually becomes a keepsake, reminding not only your child, but you, of where you've been and how far you've come, literally and figuratively.

4. *Hang a calendar and mark off the days.* If I've said this once, I've certainly said it one thousand times: Children are concrete reasoners. One of the big questions Judy has will definitely be *when*. Give her a way of knowing. Hang a big calendar on the refrigerator, and carefully tick off the days in bright colors. When Judy asks, "How many more days?" you can say, "Well, let's go to our calendar and count. Twenty more. That means you will have to go to sleep in your bed and wake up twenty times before it's time to go"; "Two more days. That means you will go to sleep in your bed and wake up two more times."

5. *Let Judy pack.* Of course, young children don't have the organizational skills to pack in the sense that they are "really packing." The benefit of packing for Judy is cognitive and emotional. The act

of packing one's things and taking them to another place establishes for Judy the concept of space. Have her pack her most intimate things in a specially decorated box marked something like "Judy's Treasure." Make sure this box is easily available right off the moving truck. Have Judy pack another bag or box with other small items. She will take this bag or box with her during the move.

6. *Let Judy know how you are going to get to the new house.* If you are all going to drive in the family car, this is not necessarily an issue. However, if you are going by alternate transportation that Judy is not accustomed to, you will want to prepare her. Drawing pictures of airplanes and buses is helpful; so is visiting an airport or a bus station.

7. *Friends.* Certainly three- to five-year-olds have friends, but as I discussed earlier, very young children don't formulate friendships the way older children do. The final days at the old house may be spent in the company of friends, whose addresses and phone numbers may be taken by the adults. However, it is important for adults to realize that these attachments are very likely to fade when Judy arrives at the new house. The phone number, the letter, and the photo are abstractions far too difficult for Judy to grasp. Who is this voice on the phone? This flat photo isn't a real person. For children this age, friendships require real flesh-and-blood people. As Judy plays with her newly found friends in her new neighborhood, she will forget her old friends very easily.

8. *Setting up.* As you allowed Judy to pack, allow her to unpack and organize her new room. You might encourage her to set things up in a way similar to the arrangement of her old room—just for security's sake. As with the packing, you must recognize Judy's lack of organizational skills. This is normal. It is the emotional experience of unpacking that's important for Judy, not her ability to decorate.

9. *Child care.* Any new child care arrangements will take a period of adjustment (see also "Starting School," in chapters 2 and 3). You may feel as if you are beginning at square one all over again. Separation anxiety is to be expected. Judy's life is topsy-turvy at the moment. A new school and new baby-sitters are all strange to Judy. She doesn't know where she fits in. As it will take time for her to adjust to her new home, it will take time to adjust to any new child care arrangement.

10. *Regression.* Because moving may be so traumatic for the young child, regressive behaviors may emerge. There may be thumb-sucking, bed-wetting, and recurrent nightmares. Remember, change requires adjustment. When we exert ourselves, something has to be relinquished. With the young child, this letting go often involves a loss of control. Reassure Judy of your confidence in her. If these bouts of regression are handled with sensitivity, they are most often temporary.

Six- to Eight-Year-Olds

I felt great. It was the first time I'd been on a plane. I couldn't wait to see the new house, my new school. Then I started to think about things, like: What was I going to do on the school bus? Who would I sit next to?

The six- to eight-year-old is your best moving helper. As a group, six- to eight-year-olds are truly adventuresome. A move, at least its initial presentation, has all the excitement of Disney World. Still, you must be careful with Max. He appears to be coping, but he will crash eventually, and you'll need to know what to do.

Most of the tips for three- to five-year-old Judy will apply to six- to eight-year-old Max:

• Practice the new address and telephone.
• Take plenty of pictures.
• Hang a calendar.
• Let him pack and unpack.
• Expect some school phobia and regression.

Because Max is able to handle more sophisticated ideas, try the following:

1. *The journal.* Max should be able to write simple sentences. You can help, but his journal should have pictures and words of his own construction.

2. *Maps.* If your journey will be a long one, use a globe to focus on your departure and destination points. Lay out some colorful maps and do the same. If your destination is more local, there are community maps available.

3. *Friends.* Forming friendships is the developmental behavior that is most different from the behavior of younger children. Max does have relationships that approximate those of slightly older children. He will miss his friends, unlike his younger sister, Judy, who embodies the "out-of-sight–out-of-mind" theory; yet he probably won't feel just how much he misses them until the move is complete (see also "Losing Friends," in chapters 2, and "Lost Friendships," in chapter 3). Max needs to know that it's OK to miss his friends and to be eager to make new ones. He will be able to maintain his old friendships through phone calls and photos, which younger children cannot do. Yet this adjustment will take time. Extracurricular activities will help ease Max's introduction to new friends, along with inviting neighborhood children to the house. Children Max's age are activity and play-oriented. Although, Max may miss his old friends, what he tends to miss more is the diversion that his old friends offered him. Once he is immersed in school and social life, he will be less lonely for his old friends, although he will still want to keep in touch with them.

4. *Make a videotape.* The last days before the move are a great time to make a videotape of friends and of the old neighborhood. Take pictures of shopkeepers, laundromats, secret hideaways, and the schoolyard. Again, like Judy's picture journal, Max's video will become a family keepsake, to be watched time and time again in the years to come.

5. *Have a party.* Humans have traditionally marked milestones with celebrations of some kind. Max will be very responsive to having a good-bye or bon voyage party. From a cognitive point of view, the celebration will help Max bring closure to this time in his life.

Nine- to Twelve-Year-Olds

Well, how exactly am I supposed to feel? My life is over! I just started to hang out with the right kids and got a spot on the gymnastics team, and we're moving in a few months!

OK, Margo doesn't feel too chipper, and living with her these next few months isn't going to be a hayride for you either. As much as young teenagers insist that they are advocates of change, the reality is that they hate it! So much of their time and energy are spent trying to fit in that the last thing they want to hear is that they'll have to start fitting in all over again.

The problems in this stage of development are many and varied. In the case of moving, the concern is not cognitive. Although Margo's basic geography skills may be lacking, she does have a good sense of how far away she will be going and how long it will take. Margo may enjoy perusing a few maps or going through an atlas, but these activities are not going to relieve her essential anxiety: being alone and friendless. This is the young teenager's worst fear. Margo's sense of herself is currently under siege, and she is uncertain whether she is fit for the arduous task of friend making that awaits her. Margo's relationships with her current friends have deepened, one close friend playing the role of confidant. Without Kathy, whom will Margo turn to? At one end, the prospect of having to make new friends looms on a foreboding horizon; at the other is the sadness of saying good-bye to treasured old friends.

Margo's relationships are not very different from our own. We know how torn we can feel as adults when the prospect of moving presents itself. Our concern, like Margo's, is often emotional. Do we have the stuff to make it in this new place? And how do we say good-bye? Only time will give us these answers.

Most of the suggestions I've related for younger children can apply to Margo. She needs all the practical where-and-when information. She needs to pack, unpack, have parties, take photos, and make videos. The difference here is that Margo will remember her friends with intensity and miss them terribly. She will want to write to them, talk to them on the phone, and be offered reasonable opportunities to visit. All of these options can be discussed and mutual decisions made, particularly with regard to telephoning and visits, which are time-consuming and costly.

As the young child needs to understand the idea of moving, the older one needs to understand the feeling. The following suggestions may be helpful when you are speaking with Margo about the move:

1. *Ask Margo what she is most concerned about.* None of us has a crystal ball. We may think Margo is concerned about what her new teacher will think of her report card from the old school when what is causing her the greatest anguish is who is going to sit

with her at lunch. Listen carefully. Be empathic. The very best question you can ask is "What do you think we could do about that?"

2. *Be honest.* Again, I've said this many times in previous chapters. This is no time for frothy, sugar-coated stories of new friends and exciting adventures. Margo will be upset, even depressed. No parent and no amount of emotional bolstering is going to be able to extinguish these feelings. (See also "Losing Friends," in chapter 2, and "Lost Friendship," in chapter 3.) Let Margo know you appreciate her feelings. You don't expect her to be sunny and jubilant. If she asks, let her know that long-distance friendships are often difficult to maintain. True, there is the adage "Distance makes the heart grow fonder." But there is also "Out of sight, out of mind." Remember, Margo is relying on you to give her the facts. If you don't, she won't learn to trust her instincts, and she won't trust yours either. It will be up to her to make her friendships last.

3. *Give her as much information about her new community as you can.* If you are moving to a large city, certainly there are brochures and travelogues, featuring hotels and assorted points of interest. Even smaller towns and some rural communities have attractions. True, this diversion will not relieve her mental turmoil, but it will give Margo "something to look forward to." Anticipation can be very uplifting.

Another word of advice: Take your time. Keeping people together is more important than unpacking boxes. Expect the unexpected. Be inventive. Have some picnics in the new living room or in the backyard. Pitch a tent outside, and all huddle together in sleeping bags while you barbecue. Get friendly with the new pizza place. When you do unpack, do it together, each person offering commentary on the enclosed items. One night, buy tickets to the circus. True, this all may sound a little crazy, but laughter and camaraderie do ease tension, and this will be a tense time for everyone.

Maturing

"OK, what is that you have inside your shirt!" This is what Brad, Lauren's father, my husband, was saying to Lauren. I thought I was witnessing a scene from Neanderthals I. Of

course, I chimed right in. "Nothing," I said. "Nothing, She is inside her shirt." At which point, Lauren removed herself from the table. I glared at Brad. "Yes," I said. "Your daughter has breasts."

As nothing can prepare children for early adolescence, nothing can prepare their parents for it. It's as if parents develop a kind of amnesia. Don't we remember or don't we *want* to remember our own "teenagerhood"?

- Did we like our bodies?
- Did we like the rules our parents made?
- Did we feel popular?
- Did we feel confident about our friendships?
- Did we say the right things?
- Did we wear the right clothes?
- Were we "cool," "groovy," "hip?"

No? Then, how can we expect our children to feel wonderful? Many contemporary parents want their children to see them as they see themselves, as aware, "with-it" people who have exceptional taste in music. The problems we had with our own parents were the fault of our parents. Our own parents were not cool. They didn't know anything. The reality is that no young teenager, no matter how extraordinary the parent, ever feels her parents are cool. Having cool parents is not a normal perception. Normal is for parents and their teenagers to fight and bicker. Parents say their children are uncontrollable, and children say their parents are uncool. This is the first rule of teenage parenthood. The quicker you learn it, the easier the whole experience will become.

The second rule will be somewhat easier to digest. Even though you are uncool, your children do know that you love them more than anyone else does. Don't forget this. This is an especially healing piece of information when Carl starts shouting, "I hate you! I hate you!"

Physical Changes

There we were, Mark and I, staring at every acne product in creation. God, I thought, did everybody go through this— Einstein, Margaret Mead, Christopher Columbus?

Remember, long ago in chapter 1, when I asked you to see problems the way your child sees them? You might think it's ridiculous to keep looking for hair on your face or agonizing over the size of your feet, but shift your perspective for a moment. Many contemporary adults are concerned—even obsessed—with their physical appearance. Diet books are still the best-selling form of nonfiction in this country—along with cook books, interestingly enough. Gymnasiums and health spas are experiencing an all-time boom in membership. People jog, bike, walk, roller-skate, swim, play tennis, "circuit-train," "cross-train." Just take a look at the variety of sneakers there are available for purchase. Surely, the concept of health is imbedded in this fervor for exercise, but people also do want to look better. The cosmetic industry continues to be a billion-dollar enterprise. The more obsessed adult opts for hair transplants and voluntary plastic surgery, which are also flourishing businesses. My point is that teenagers' physical obsession is borrowed from the culture that instituted it. If Audrey were not concerned about her appearance, it would be unusual, not the reverse.

Try to imagine your body totally out of control. Within a year, you are six inches taller and have hair all over your body, and your face is covered with pimples. Or all of a sudden, you have enormous breasts, and people, particularly men, are looking very differently at you. Now, some of these changes you might find welcome, and as a mature adult, you would certainly be able to cope better than your child. Yet changes in body image are very distressing both to children and to adults.

Most people in the Western world define who they are by how they look. Psychologists have known for a long time that people who pay no attention to their appearance tend not to have healthy self-images. At the other end of the spectrum are people who pay an inordinate amount of attention to themselves. These people also have distorted self-concepts. Very young children's mental functioning is still to immature to appreciate their rapidly changing physiques. In contrast, young teenagers have reached a point in development where they are mentally very aware of the physical changes in their bodies but are still unprepared emotionally to accept and appreciate these changes. Adults experience emotional stress related to body image when they lose or gain weight; they become ill; and they grow older. This is also true of women when they become pregnant.

People who experience this body-image stress do not feel that they are in control of their bodies any longer. Someone or something else is controlling their bodies, and they are completely at its mercy. This is exactly how the young teenager feels, with one exception: Most adults have had the experience of being in control of their bodies. Audrey has not had this experience. She is not sure whether she will be able to muster the bodily control she feels she needs. This may explain the high incidence of anorexia in teenage girls and the increasing use of steroids in young boys. Uncertain they will ever have appropriate control over their developing bodies, they overcontrol.

There are ways you can help your child deal with the physical anxiety that puberty brings:

1. *Give Audrey the correct information about the physical dimensions of puberty.* Whatever she wants to know, make sure you give accurate information. If you don't know the answer, say so, You can then research the question together. Contrary to the common belief that the truth about physical development may cause anxiety, it is really the myths surrounding puberty that cause the greatest distress.

2. *Give Peter privacy.* The child who once waltzed about the dining room stark naked will now gasp as you enter his room. He might be dressing, after all! He bolts the bathroom and wears several layers of clothing. Let Peter know that you respect his privacy. Yes, you did give him his baths and change his diapers not very long ago, but now he is maturing and needs the kind of space an adult needs. Knock on his door *always.* If you do walk in on him, mistakenly, in the bathroom, for example, excuse yourself, just as you would if you walked in on an adult. These actions let Peter *know that you know* he is reaching maturity. You respect him. He respects himself.

3. *Don't make light of Audrey's physical concerns.* Try to remember the last time you gained five pounds, noticed a gray hair, or felt a balding spot on the back of your head. Physical change is upsetting no matter how "perfectly normal" it is! Let Audrey know that there isn't anything any one of us can do about the physical

changes of puberty. All of us have to come to grips with the way we look. All of us have physical strengths and weaknesses. Ask her what she thinks her own strengths and weaknesses are. You can offer to share yours. This kind of talk allows Audrey to know that physical perfection is never a realistic goal—no matter what the media promote.

4. *Help teenagers take care of their bodies.* Young teenagers have many questions, about vitamins, deodorants, toothpastes, exercise programs. Provide as much information as you can, but let them make the final choice. They will vacillate, eating tons of alfalfa sprouts one week, doughnuts the next. This ambivalence is to be expected. The health habits they form now will provide the foundation for the habits they will have as an adult. Help them make sound judgments regarding nutrition, exercise, and hygiene.

Because the physical changes associated with puberty are so concrete, children focus a great deal of time and energy on them, totally unaware of their even more dramatic mental development. Parents need to remember that no matter how intense the physical changes are, young teenagers' perception of them is truly due to their developing minds, not their developing bodies.

Cognitive Changes

I had to be born in a family of idiots—that's it. Do the three of you share one brain—is that it? "No," I said. "We're too mean and miserable to share anything!"

I remember not very long ago asking a colleague of mine why he was working so many hours. "Are you kidding?" he replied. "I love it here. The chaos here is nothing like the chaos at home." The criticism and arguing in the household with a child in the heat of puberty can be quite disconcerting. You've made some perfectly innocent remark and bang! You have a door slammed in your face—literally. You don't see Allen very much anymore. He comes home, has a snack, and marches straight to his room. He never comes out. It used to be punishment for him to stay in his room. When there are interactions between the two of you, they are explosive. Parents often feel that they are being unfairly criticized, that arguments are being deliberately staged to cause turmoil.

There are some rules in the criticism and arguing arena that can help parents and children keep the channels of communication open:

1. *Help Allen put his own criticisms into perspective.* Let Allen know you accept his criticisms of you. You realize you are not perfect. There are many things you must continually work on. Sometimes you will agree with his criticisms; sometimes you won't. Accepting criticism is not the same as agreeing with it. In your household, all persons have the right to express their opinions about other people's behavior. What concerns you is that sometimes when Allen criticizes you, he hurts your feelings. Has he thoughts about that? There are ways to criticize others, or perhaps *offer advice,* that preserve people's feelings. Allen has the right to offer criticism or advice to you at any time. He does not have the right to hurt yours or anyone else's feelings.

2. *Help Allen to take responsibility for his arguments.* If you listen to most arguments, they have the characteristic of blame, for example, "Look what you did!" "You made me forget!" "You made me late!" Rather than spend time deciding at whom to point the finger, help your child and yourself talk about feelings. When you were late (or lost or ignored), talk together about how you felt. For example, "When I was late for work the other day because I waited for you to find your books, I felt angry. I don't like making excuses to my boss. If you need help getting ready in the morning, please ask for it." or "Mom, please don't talk to me when I am on the phone. I can't hear you, and then I forget to ask you what you've said. I feel stupid later on when you ask me where something is when I never really heard what you said in the first place." This is good practice in the art of argument for both adults and children. (See also "Sibling Rivalry," in chapter 2, and "How to Keep the Kids from Quarreling," in chapter 3.) Discuss how you feel, and tell the other person exactly how you would prefer he respond.

Criticism and argument need not destroy relations between parents and their children. If parents take the lead in helping their children discover constructive avenues for these emotional expressions, peace may not be attained, but certainly understanding will.

Social-Emotional Changes

I told Maggie she could take ballet, skating, gymnastics; they even had air ballooning. Maggie said she just couldn't decide. She wouldn't take anything.

Right alongside these stressful physical and cognitive changes are the ever-familiar social-emotional ones. Although Paul's new sexual interest, self-consciousness, and inability to make choices can drive you crazy, they are all, in reality, very legitimate responses to his developing maturity.

SEXUAL INTEREST. If it is any comfort at all, the eleven-year-old sweetheart you've found smoking in your bathroom is very unlikely to be your daughter-in-law. Children on the brink of puberty are experimenting with their feelings. True, a few are experimenting with their bodies as well, and for this reason, Paul should be given accurate information regarding reproduction. It is difficult to make a case for abstinence in this day and age. The incidence of eleven-year-old girls' delivering full-term infants in major cities, and in isolated rural communities, is increasing at a disturbing pace. Nonetheless, no eleven- or twelve-year-old in this culture has any business being sexually active. Eleven-year-olds are not given drivers' licenses, permitted to buy tobacco or alcohol, allowed entry to an R-rated movie without an adult, or given the privilege of voting for the candidate of their choice. Why? Because they are not physically or emotionally prepared to exercise these rights. Any adult who knowingly gives reproductive information to a child without the appropriate "don't" is not acting responsibly.

Paul will have all kinds of questions regarding his new sexual interest. He may be embarrassed to ask straightforward questions. You can provide the opening by stating simply and directly, "Paul, if you have any questions about sex, you can ask me. I may not know the answer but I will always help you find information."

This approach may not ensure that Paul will come to you all the time, but it keeps the door open.

Here are a few suggestions:

1. *Don't be too critical of Paul's new female friends.* In true Romeo and Juliet fashion, disapproval may, in fact, have the opposite of the desired effect. The minute Paul discovers you are not crazy about Marie, the more he will rally to defend her.

2. *Do set ground rules for the behavior in your home.* Of course, in Paul's view, everyone else's home is more liberal than yours. At least, this is what Paul will have you believe. Don't believe it! Paul and Marie need to abide by the rules in your house when they are there.

3. *If you like Marie, let Paul know, but be careful.* Don't be too adoring. Remember, Paul is hypercritical of you at this time. Announce your love of Marie, and you are likely to see less of her.

SELF-CONSCIOUSNESS. With young teenagers, it is not always the behavior but the degree of the behavior that is disturbing. As I discussed earlier, all humans are concerned about their second mirror, the audience of persons "out there," theoretically judging and remarking on our every move. It is Jane's intensity of concern regarding this jury of anonymous persons, who have, interestingly, no final verdict (that is, one minute they see Jane as marvelous, the next as socially borderline), that can make her life and ours difficult. It is the process of metacognition, this incessant thinking about thinking, that, on one side, is responsible for Jane's higher abstract thought, and that also allows this invisible audience to dominate her behavior.

The best approach here is some reality orientation:

1. *Ask Jane what she thinks about most of the time.* If she is like most people, she thinks about herself. It is natural and productive for humans to be somewhat self-absorbed. Again, it is a matter of the degree of the absorption. Point out that people are not all that different from one another. If she is thinking about herself, then that is exactly what everyone else is doing: thinking about himself. No one really has enough time to immerse himself in the minuscule study of another. She doesn't have to worry about others' dwelling on her because the truth is that other people dwell on their own concerns, not hers. This concept will take some time to sink in, but the point is a good one to make.

2. *Help her continue her development of a strong self-concept* (see also chapters 2 through 5). The more confident the child, the less concerned she will be about what she supposes others are thinking. Remember that successful people learn to handle rejection and failure and still keep going.

CHOICES. No on is a born decision maker. Good decision making is learned, as are almost all of the skills described in this book. There isn't a moment in the day when we are not making a decision. Even a decision *not* to choose is still a decision.

There are choices to make in life that have a far weightier toll than others, such as the choice to marry, to go to college, to accept a job, or to move to another state. The outcome in these cases has a far greater effect on our overall well-being than choosing what shoes to wear. Yet being able to choose our shoes, our lunch, and our hair style, as young adolescents, does lay the groundwork for making the more involved decisions later on.

In general, children do tend to be shortsighted. They think day-to-day, moment-to-moment. In some respects, it is healthy to look at life this way. Many self-help groups, like Alcoholics Anonymous, choose to focus people on life day-to-day. The alcoholic knows she needs to stay sober for only twenty-four hours at a time. Each morning she renews this commitment. When one encapsulates time in this way, anxiety is reduced. This reduction of anxiety is probably one of the reasons why young teenagers choose to make short-range rather than long-range decisions. And this type of short-term planning is fine within certain contexts, like habit breaking for instance. When you are attempting to diminish a well-ingrained habit, it is sometimes easier to focus on "not-doing" something for a few hours rather than for a lifetime.

Other types of decision making require long-range time management skills. Even though Cindy may have a good deal on her mind, the sooner she learns to cope with her mental clutter, the more directed and less anxiety-ridden she will be.

1. *Have Cindy purchase a desk diary.* By the age of ten, most children can learn to manipulate the abstractions of time and space. It is never too early to learn to plan. A desk diary can make Cindy feel very grown up. A good time to purchase one is at the beginning of the school year.

2. *Have Cindy conduct her own time management assessment.* How much time does she really spend doing various things during the average week: homework, talking on the phone, reading, exercising, watching TV, showering, doing her hair, and so on. This kind of assessment is often an eye-opener. There is nothing like

hard data to make a point. If Cindy has difficulty turning her school reports in on time, it may be that she is on the phone for too long. When she is finished with her time assessment, have her make a goal to redistribute her time and then assess her use of time again within the next month. Assessments like this can give her information on how long it actually takes her to do a school report or prepare a class assignment.

3. *Help Cindy establish priorities.* One can never establish priorities for someone else, but you can help Cindy begin to examine what is important in her life. In order to succeed in life, Cindy needs to learn to forgo immediate gratification. You might begin by asking her, "What do you think are the three most important things in life?" Help Cindy be exact and realistic. She may answer this question with "world peace" or in "eliminating world hunger." But what can she actually do about these world conditions? Is she willing to focus her complete attention on these issues? Most young teenagers are not truly ready to make such enormous commitments, even though they think they are. More realistic and achievable goals are raising my science grade, making the track team, learning photography, and calling Sylvia once a week. When Cindy is leafing through magazines for an hour, you can gently remind her of *her* priorities: half an hour for magazines and half an hour studying science; or half an hour for magazines and half an hour running.

All people need to learn the process of *integration* (discussed in chapter 8) pretty much by trial and error, that is, life experience. Parents can help ease this process by providing guidance, making sound suggestions, and avoiding demands. Remember that teaching children to obey your demands does not teach them to make their own decisions. Rather, it teaches Cindy to rely on others to do her thinking.

Gender

I could never do justice to the topic of gender in this short section. There are many others who have spent decades investigating this provocative area of research (see the appendix and the selected bibliography for a listing of resources). What I will say is that the women's revolution that began legitimately more than a century ago has spurred an examination resulting in discoveries not of how the genders are alike, but of how they are truly very different. These differences are observable very early in development, and it is still unclear how much both biology and conditioning contribute to the thinking processes of boys and girls. The bottom line is that boys may need different mental handling from girls.

There are a few suggestions:

1. *Because boys tend to be analytic, reinforce this process while introducing more global thinking,* for example, "This is a terrific report on eagles, Bruce. You have a lot of information here. I do have a few questions for you. How are eagles different from and yet similar to other birds? Why do you think eagles are here on earth? What do you think their function is?" Boys tend to isolate information rather than provide the necessary threads between ideas. Questions like these help boys see the big picture more clearly.

2. *Because girls tend to be gestalt (global) in their thinking, reinforce this holistic thinking while helping them use analytic processes,* for example, "Nancy, you talked a little about the golden eagle here, but I think readers might like to know more. What about looking at two or three types of eagles in detail rather than skimming over the many species?" Nancy feels safer than Bruce does with the big picture. Nancy may need more attention to detail to bring her reports alive.

3. *Encourage Bruce and Nancy to be friends.* As Nancy enters more sports and as Bruce enters more cooking classes, there may be more opportunities for boys and girls to share experiences formerly relegated to just one gender. Although Bruce and Nancy are quite naturally professing a sexual interest in one another, it is perhaps even more important for them to remain friends. There is some current research that may indicate that the key to bridging the gender gap lies in each sex's being able to see the other as people and friends, and not simply as objects of sexual attraction. Although some say friendship between the sexes is impossible because sexual tension looms in the most platonic relationship, this attitude may be the result of boys' and girls' not having enough shared social experiences throughout childhood.

When we teach our children the process of change, we teach them a most valuable lifetime survival skill. The only thing consistent about life is change.

10

Inappropriate Behavior

"I'm Not Getting What I Need Easily.
This Is What I Must Do."

The scene is so typical, I wonder if it's been rehearsed:

Jodi goes over to Tamara and grabs her "ring-thing." She starts to cry and hit. Jodi starts to run. There I am. I want to take the toy and throw it out the window.

Even though when we speak of children "behaving themselves," we actually mean "*good* behavior," a behavior itself, or *what* a *person does,* is neutral. A behavior becomes "good" or "bad" when it is judged against a backdrop of circumstance or context. Lying is a good example of the neutrality of behavior. Although we generally consider lying "bad," how often do we tell the truth? People ask us each day "How are you?" How often do we respond truthfully? Most of us respond routinely, "Fine, thanks. How are you?"

Or you are having dinner at some close friends' home. They are serving a cauliflower casserole dish. You hate cauliflower. You can't remember a single instance in which you've enjoyed it. Your dear friend, Molly, urges you, "This is wonderful, Emily, you must have some." You reluctantly spoon a portion onto your plate. Everyone is ooh-ing and ah-ing, What a superb casserole!" Everyone simply must have this recipe. You have sampled your portion. It is exactly as you had anticipated: absolutely awful. Now what are you going to do? Stand your ground, demand integrity, state crisply and straightforwardly you can't stand the food you've been served? No. Unless you are emotionally distressed or mentally disordered, you will take your fork, move the cauliflower strategically from one side of your plate to the other, and smile appreciatively. Why? Because to state the truth in this context would be blatantly inappropriate. Lying, as objectionable as this behavior would be in an alternate context, is the appropriate response here.

Getting back to my original point, all isolated behavior or behavior without context is neutral. Behavior is not "good" or "bad," but "appropriate" or "inappropriate" to the context in which it occurs. All parents must remember this when they choose to judge any child's behavior. The question to be asked is *not* "Is Wendy behaving herself?" but "Is Wendy's behavior appropriate to the context?

Once parents come to see behavior as directly linked to context or circumstance, they need to understand a second, although no less significant issue: All of Wendy's behavior makes sense—to Wendy. Remember that a long time ago, back in chapter 1, I told you to see the world with your child's eye? No one, including children, behaves inappropriately just for the heck of it. Inappropriate behavior is exhibited because children feel compelled to perform that way. I am certainly not saying that if Wendy is stealing money from your purse, it is because you or someone or something else has provoked this. Theoretically, no one is responsible for anyone else's behavior other than her own. What I am saying is that if Wendy is stealing, she generally feels one of two things: She must steal, or stealing is permissible. Wendy can think only with the mind she has. She acts or reacts to a given situation based on the way *she* sees this circumstance, not on the way you see it. You cannot help Wendy shape her behavior so that both you and she are comfortable until you understand why she acts the way she does.

Yes, there is a third issue. Many parents believe children should behave themselves. One never speaks of adults' misbehaving, although certainly many adults do. When adults describe children as behaving themselves, the image painted is of quiet, complacent, doll-like creatures—in other words, not real live people. An adult who sat quietly smiling and nodding attentively for several hours would be considered seriously, if not profoundly, impaired. Yet this type of mindless complacency is often the good behavior we have in mind for our children.

Children's behavior is communicative. It has meaning, just like our own behavior. If a child takes his fist and slams it firmly down on the dinner table, this behavior should be seen as a meaningful communication of some kind. If Uncle Bill came to dinner and slammed his fist firmly down on the dinner table, we would certainly take his gesture seriously. This is not to say that Uncle Bill's behavior is appropriate. It may not be. But we would never say that Uncle Bill was *misbehaving* at the table, or that he was *behaving badly*. Even if Uncle Bill's behavior is deemed inappropriate, adults assume that other adults have "good reason" to behave the way they do. Children are not ordinarily given this consideration. Their behavior is often deemed arbitrary; meaningless. It is important for parents to understand that Elaine's behavior is an expression of the way she thinks and feels in a given moment. All behavior is reasonable and communicative at some level, even if we, the observers, don't know the reason or perceive the communication.

Again, there are many issues related to children's behavior that could have been discussed here. As always, those selected most reflect concerns that are of enduring impact: tantrumming, aggressive behavior, TV and video obsession, lying, and stealing.

Tantrumming

I had learned to steer clear of the cookie aisle whenever Peter was with me grocery shopping, but he seemed to know exactly where the cookies were. As we strolled casually past the Mallowmars, it would happen. Peter would fling himself on the floor and screech. I would attempt to maneuver him back into an upright position, but he had developed a defense for this tactic as well. He would hang like a thread of spaghetti, with me holding one limp wrist, the dead weight of this small body throwing my own equilibrium completely off center. One of us was bound to surrender, and it wasn't going to be Peter. The Mallowmars were purchased. It took me an awful long time to realize that I had been conditioning Peter to think that tantrumming is the way one asks to have Mallowmars.

This mother's story is very telling, not only in terms of tantrumming, but in terms of how inappropriate behaviors develop and resist change. Her story also supports the idea that all behavior is purposeful and communicative. As far as Peter is concerned, the equation is simple: Have tantrum = get Mallowmars. The more the tantrumming is reinforced with cookies, the more difficult it will be for Peter to learn an alternative to tantrumming.

Another concept supported by Peter's example is the idea that behavior is contextual, meaningful within a given circumstance. No child tantrums for the sake of tantrumming. Tantrumming communicates.

So what is Peter trying to say? Obviously he wants Mallowmars. What is Peter's mom trying to say? Perhaps she's trying to tell Peter she doesn't want to buy Mallowmars because she doesn't feel they are nutritious. But she is not communicating this message. Her behavior tells Peter, "Tantrum long enough, and you will have Mallowmars." Given this insight, it is somewhat surprising that parents continue to be puzzled by the consistency and persistence of their children's tantrumming.

The second piece of information important here is that tantrumming is a tensional outlet for Peter. Some tensional outlets are better and less destructive than others. For example, some adults smoke. Smoking is a tensional outlet, but a destructive one. Tennis is also a tensional outlet. Tennis can hardly be considered the same kind of tensional outlet as smoking. Yet both serve a similar purpose. They relieve tension. All human beings need to drain tension in one way or another.

The young child is not sophisticated enough mentally, emotionally, or socially to make choices regarding the way he drains tension. Remember that the very young child does not have a cohesive sense of time and space. He cannot plan. Peter lives moment-to-moment. He does not choose. He reacts. He does not select tantrumming as a tensional outlet the way an adult might select tennis. In one sense—the developmental one—the tantrumming chooses Peter.

Let me explain what I mean. We expect Peter to tantrum between the ages of two-and-a-half and three-and-a-half. The tantrumming two-year-old is a classic, if not totally stereotypical, representation of early childhood. Most children relinquish this behavior by the time they are four years old. They don't need it anymore. They can ask, using words, for what they want. Tantrumming, no matter how annoying and deliberate it may seem to a parent, is initially a device that helps Peter cope with tension and frustration. Tantrumming is a normally developing tensional outlet for two- and three-year-olds. However, if Peter learns that he will be rewarded for this behavior, he will definitely use it to this end. The first time Peter tantrums, he does so out of frustration. If cookies arrive on this first occasion, the second or third time he tantrums he may be doing so to test his equation: tantrumming = getting Mallowmars.

Tantrumming may also appear spontaneously, seemingly unprovoked. This kind of spontaneous tantrumming often appears at the end of the day, after nursery school, or before dinner. Peter is tired and hungry, and tantrumming is his most available tensional outlet. Remember that however blissful the world of a three-year-old may seem to us, it is not blissful for Peter. For Peter, the world is a very big, confusing place. People say things he doesn't understand. When he wants something, he doesn't always know how to ask for it. He doesn't have enough experience in life to predict what will comes next. Imagine yourself alone in a foreign country. You don't understand the language. You can't communicate your needs. You are unfamiliar with the customs. It shouldn't be surprising that Peter is frustrated at the end of his incomprehensible day. Although his tantrumming may seem arbitrary to us, it is, in reality, very understandable under the circumstances. This is not to say there aren't viable measures parents can take to diminish the frequency and/or duration of these episodes. What is important for parents to remember is that Peter's tantrumming is *purposeful* and *communicative;* and not some mysterious or manipulative behavior developed by an irrational preschooler. Understanding tantrumming for what it is, a tensional outlet, changes both our attitudes about this behavior and our strategies for dealing with it.

Aggressive Behavior

Kevin came home with a bloody nose. I got hysterical, as usual. When I asked him why had been he fighting, he said, "You see, I had to hit this kid. I just had to!" And that was that.

Everything that has been said about tantrumming applies to a discussion of aggressive behavior. When viewed in context, aggressive can be seen as *purposeful* and *communicative*. It is exhibited for the same two reasons that all inappropriate behavior occurs: Children feel they *must* use this behavior to get what they want, and this behavior is permitted. Yet aggressive behavior is different from tantrumming. First, when you use aggression, another person is hurt. Tantrumming, although it is disturbing to others, doesn't hurt anyone. Second, aggressive behavior doesn't subside with maturity. In fact, if a child is allowed to be aggressive, the behavior often increases with age.

There are many ways children can be aggressive toward both adults and each other: biting, hitting, kicking, pulling hair, and pinching. The goal is simple. The child who is attacked has interfered, deliberately or not, with the other child's wants or needs. Charlie uses aggressive behavior to get what he wants. If getting what he wants means biting Henry, then that is what Charlie will do. Aggression is power. When a child uses aggressive behavior he takes power away from someone else. Using power makes him feel powerful.

Aggressive behavior is also a tensional outlet. Children do fight with each other to let off steam. Like tantrumming, fighting out of frustration is most normally seen when children are fatigued or hungry.

Young children who use aggressive behavior to get what they want often do so because they are unaware of the more appropriate alternatives to this behavior. These children feel they *must* bite or kick. They feel there is no other action or set of actions that will get them what they want. In contrast, older children who use aggressive behavior are usually aware, at some level, of alternatives. They use aggressive behavior because it has worked for them. They may have tried alternatives. Yet, as far as they are concerned, aggression works better and faster than anything else they've tried. The use of aggressive behavior in older children can be very serious because, depending on the physical strength of the children involved, they can be permanently impaired.

It is not my objective in this section to address children with serious behavior disorders, that is, extremely aggressive, dangerous, hostile children. Surely these children exist and warrant extensive intervention and counseling (see the appendix for resources). In a majority of instances, however, parents can teach alternatives to physical aggression when children are young. As children mature, they see these alternatives working effectively. They have no need to continue to act aggressively. Older children occasionally have the typical schoolyard fight. Yet, if children know how to behave in these situations ahead of time, they will use direct physical aggression *only* as a final resort to protect themselves or another. Remember, aggression, like fear, is functional. If a child finds himself in a physically dangerous situation, he needs to know how to recognize this situation as dangerous, and how to escape.

Although physical aggression is most damaging, there are other forms of aggression that have a serious psychological impact. One is the use of profanity. It is interesting that almost all cultures have given certain words an unusual power. Defined, these words indicate a specific sexual act, the process of elimination or its product, a private part of the human body (normally, one connected with reproduction or elimination), or persons of a questionable moral persuasion. There are synonyms for these proverbial "curse words," yet none of these has the power of "bad language." Again remember that aggression is power.

It is important for parents to understand that no child comes into the world knowing profanity. Children learn profanity not because the words are meaningful to them but because of the power or impact the words seem to have. Most young children have no idea what they are saying when they use profanity. They do know that when they say these words, immediate attention is directed toward them either by adults or by other children.

Where do children hear these words? It may be more appropriate to ask where they don't hear them. There are few adults who can say they have never, ever used profanity within earshot of children. Even if parents have never used this language themselves, how can they control the behavior of neighbors, children at school, or actors on rented video movies? Profanity is rampant in our culture. Older siblings are notorious for goading younger children into using this "bathroom talk." Four-year-old Philip can be guaranteed to shock anybody except the most seasoned nursery-school teacher. He beings a litany of rhyming patterns which include *the* words, accompanying these with laughter and side glances to indicate his knowledge of the inappropriateness of this behavior. Yet this use of profanity, however inappropriate and however we wish to diminish it, is not aggressive, that is, its goal is not to hurt anyone.

Most young children use profanity for one of the following reason:

- To gain attention from either adults or peers.
- To feel powerful, that is, adults seem to get so agitated by its use that the young child feels she can exert control by using profanity.
- To act and sound like an adult.

Most older children use profanity for these same reasons. Yet some children use profanity as a form of aggression, to hurt. The young child, although she has little knowledge of the meaning of the words, may observe adults using profanity in moments of anger. She also observes that the words have an additional power, other than attention getting. Profanity can hurt a person the way a slap in the face can. Profanity is perceived as an alternative to hitting, kicking, and biting, particularly when it is used with adults, who seem to react so violently to it.

Older children can use profanity more deliberately than young children can. For the most part, they understand the meaning of the words and carefully select the ones they use. They use the words consciously to hurt peers who understand the threatening and demeaning nature of profanity.

Profanity is only one form of nonphysical aggression. There are many other more subtle behaviors that, if examined, are indeed aggressive. Name calling and excluding children from play are intended to hurt others. Children who use this form of aggression feel the same sense of power as children who use more direct physical forms of aggression.

Regardless of the aggressive behavior they use, children who feel they must take power away from or, for the lack of a better term, must disempower another do not feel empowered themselves. Like many other issues addressed in former chapters, feeling empowered is the result of a healthy self-image or self-concept (see also chapters 1 and 2).

TV and Video Obsession

Maybe TV really is an underground form of mind control. There they are—like zombies—planted in front of that set.

Their entire bodies fall relaxed, their faces motionless, expressionless, as if they have been entered by alien beings.

Every generation needs a scapegoat, and in this generation, television and the media in general have taken their place right alongside the schools. When examined objectively, the current attack on children's media is not a new phenomenon. Every new technological advance has traditionally been received with a suspicion that includes the undermining of youth. MTV and Nintendo have been subjected to such extensive scrutiny.

Children in our culture do spend a great amount of their leisure time watching television and playing video games, an astounding three to four hours per day! Such extended viewing has been charged with the development of both violent behavior and illiteracy in children. As Mark Twain once said, "There are lies; there are damn lies; and then there are statistics."

Any person who wants to can find a feasible argument for anything—if he finds the right statistics to support his allegations. Research on the correlation between violent behavior or illiteracy and watching television or playing video games is still largely inconclusive. This is not to say that television and videos are never responsible for distressing behavior in children. A child who is in a difficult home situation and consistently watches sadistic, violent programming will certainly be affected by this viewing. Yet this child has problems before she watches television. Violent television programming and videos are only *one* factor in developing violent behavior in this child. This child represents the exception to the rule, not the rule.

Researchers have also predicted that the so-called Sesame Street Generation would far surpass the intellectual performance of previous generations. The reality is that this privileged generation has done no better and no worse than any other.

Like all behavior and other phenomena, television and video viewing is neutral, benign outside a given context. Problems occur when one of two things happen: Television and videos usurp time from children that they could legitimately use for other viable activities, and their parents don't give enough input to them regarding TV programs and video games.

It takes time to watch television, time that could be better used studying, practicing a new skill, or playing with friends. No child should be encouraged or permitted to spend all of her free time in front of a television screen. No pun intended, the screen does not give anyone a complete picture of what is available in life. Children need to be exposed to alternative leisure activity.

Although overall television viewing may not have a direct thread to violent behavior, parents need to help their children make appropriate selections nonetheless. Parents know their children and what information their children are able to handle. Just because a program is on television or a video game is available in the local store does not mean that all children should have access to it. There are some programs and videos that no child should be permitted to see. Parents are responsible for monitoring their children's viewing and making recommendations. Children cannot be expected to make these judgments themselves. If parents don't monitor, no one will.

The last issue is the amount of TV viewing a child does or the intensity with which he views or plays video games. Excessive or intensive viewing makes this behavior inappropriate, not the isolated television watching or playing of video games. The TV- or video-obsessed child has in effect made a life for himself in front of the screen. Joey sits and watches TV or plays games for hours and is distressed by recommendations of other activities. He may forgo eating and friends and seems hypnotized by television, being totally unresponsive to requests or conversation generated by others. Joey may develop this kind of behavior for two reasons:

1. This may be Joey's primary tension outlet. He uses his TV and video time to escape from frustrations.
2. Joey feels out of control for some reason. The TV or video offers him an opportunity to be completely in control of something.

Most TV or video obsessions are not serious. They emerge most often when Joey is feeling stress from school or from home. Joey will generally tire of this absorption once he discovers more suitable outlets. Again, TV or video obsession is a power issue. Once Joey feels empowered, he will no longer rely on the medium to fill his time.

It is also important for parents to recognize that, like schools and the telephone, television and video games are probably here to stay.

It may be that we have spent too much time trying to figure out how to get rid of them. What we should be doing is finding ways to make them a more valuable resource for children.

Lying

It was not simple. Adrian said he had forgotten the night's homework, which could legitimately happen. Yet somehow I couldn't trust him; he had pulled this forgetting business before. He wanted me to write a note to his teacher absolving him from everything. I just couldn't do it!

Children lie, and adults lie, either to avoid the consequences of their behavior or to preserve feelings when they feel telling the truth would be compromising and hurtful to another. All people lie, and as an isolated behavior, lying may be fairly benign. Like all behavior, lying is inappropriate only in a specific context.

Young children lie because they "don't know any better." In order for one to tell the truth, one needs to know exactly what the truth is. Tammy can't possibly know the truth; she doesn't know what color the sky is yet. Everyone tells Tammy, "The *sky is blue,* Tammy. The sky is blue." But the sky doesn't look blue to Tammy, not always. Sometimes, it looks gray, or blue *and* white. But it's not always just blue. All information presented to Tammy is extremely confusing and disorienting to her. Children cannot begin to tell the truth until they can see the difference between reality and fantasy and some of the ambiguities of these concepts. In addition, because young children do think so differently from adults, in most instances they do not see lying as doing something wrong or immoral. They believe it is acceptable to lie if it prevents them or a friend from being punished. As a result, moral lectures will not change their behavior. They don't see what was wrong with what they were doing in the first place. Your reprimands will be meaningless until Tammy understands why you are upset with her. After all, she was only telling a story.

Compulsive lying, or lying that happens frequently and consistently, is a sign that the child is not happy with himself; that is, he has not developed that all-important *good* self-concept. He has the need to build himself up and to be seen as always good and right, in order to protect his weak sense of himself from further damage.

When older children lie, they generally have a concept of "what the truth is." They choose not to tell this truth for one of two reasons: They want to protect themselves from the consequences of this truth (lying is, after all, a kind of survival mechanism, protecting one from a perceived danger), or they want to manipulate another's behavior.

As with many other behaviors described before, children lie because it works. They haven't been rewarded for telling the truth. In fact, they often are punished. In order for children to want to tell the truth, they must feel comfortable telling it. Remember that telling the truth *is* a behavior. If Kathi has broken an expensive lamp and tells you she did indeed do this, and you punish her for it, think about the message you are sending. Now think of the converse situation; Kathi breaks the lamp and tells you she didn't break it. She doesn't get punished. Parents must decide what behavior is more important to reinforce in the long run: telling the truth or avoiding lamp breakage.

This is not to say that older children should not be responsible for their actions. Yet being responsible for your actions is not the same as being punished for them. If you yourself break a valuable item, you are surely upset with yourself—but you are not ashamed or humiliated. If we want our children to tell the truth, we must make this "truth learning" an esteem-building process.

Stealing

I looked into my purse. Only a few dollars were missing. Cori must have been hurting very badly to do this. I didn't want to make a fuss. But I just couldn't stay silent. This was the third time. Frankly, I didn't know what to do.

Stealing is different from lying in a number of ways. For the most part, you take something concrete when you steal. Because of the concrete nature of stealing, children tend to understand this concept earlier than they do lying. The smallest child will approach you and ask, "May I keep this?" or "Is this mine?"

The concept of "yours and mine" has been reinforced throughout early childhood alongside the concepts of sharing and "please and thank you." Lying, because it is basically an abstraction, is understood as a developmental behavior, that is, most children lie quite normally until they have a more sophisticated understanding of the truth. Because children understand the concept of "don't take something that isn't yours," very early in development, young children don't steal with the frequency that they lie.

Although young children may lie with little intent and almost no cause, stealing usually indicates that the child is distressed. People steal because they feel deprived, the key word being *feel.* Toby may come from a wonderful, warm home yet still *feel* deprived, Or as is often the case, Toby may want something very badly that he feels incapable of requesting. The classic example is your coming home with him from a friend's house and finding his pockets crammed with caramel candy. Toby just didn't feel comfortable asking for the candy in a group of strangers—so he took it.

The important thing to remember is that no child wants to steal. Again, most children are driven to this behavior because they believe they have no alternatives. Also, the things children steal are not what they feel is missing. Most children do not feel deprived of things. They feel deprived of people.

Inappropriate Behavior

Strategies and Solutions

*What ever happened to discipline? Do you discipline badly be-
haved children? Is that it? I know, there are times I am not
behaving appropriately, and I'm an adult! I certainly wouldn't
appreciate someone disciplining me. Maybe the word* discipline, *maybe the word* behavior, *just has a bad connotation.*

Inappropriate behavior is disturbing, annoying, and distracting. It
is a tensional outlet for the child that can create a great deal of
tension and stress for adults. This is why adults are so focused on
"how to get rid of these nasty little habits." Yet, as for every other
problem mentioned in these chapters, there is no magic solution
available. The most important rule for adults to remember when
dealing with inappropriate behavior is, rather than focusing on the
"bad" behavior, teach instead the correct behavior and provide
meaningful consequences. Here are a few suggestions:

1. Avoid rewards and punishments. Using mechanisms like toys
and "being sent to your room" too often do not give children an
internalized sense of control. Reinforcements, both positive and
negative ones, are tempting to use because they can change behavior very quickly, but they give all the control to adults. Set as your
goal Liz's getting satisfaction or dissatisfaction from her own actions.

2. Make your expectations clear and reasonable. Set a few rules
and enforce these few consistently. If Liz breaks one of the rules
five times and finds a consequence only once, she is confused, not
apologetic. It is better to truly enforce *two rules* religiously than to
be inconsistent in enforcing *ten.*

3. Remember, a consequence is *not* a punishment. It is a direct, meaningful result of the inappropriate behavior. If Liz spills her milk, she cleans the spill and pours herself another glass. If she smacks her brother Joey, she does not retain the privilege of sitting next to him at the table.

4. Stay calm. In some cases, it may be appropriate to demonstrate anger. However, it is important to remember that Liz may behave inappropriately because she is intrigued by the big response her behavior gets from adults. Liz may learn to thrive on the attention, excitement, anger, or confusion she senses she has the power to create.

Tantrumming

Every morning it was the same thing. I would drive Michael to nursery school. Once I parked the car, the screaming and kicking would begin. There he was lying in the back seat. I was so exhausted getting him into school that I felt my day's work was done. Who had the energy for anything else?

One of the most important things we can do for children experiencing the classic temper tantrum is to find out what things, or what kinds of situations, provoke these outbursts. Finding the reason is always more helpful than waiting until the tantrum occurs to treat it.

Temper tantrums occur most often when Barry is tired or frustrated. Adults are prone to outbursts when they are fatigued or overwrought. Why wouldn't children feel the same? Some frustration in life is inevitable and necessary if the child is to develop appropriate coping skills. However, tantrums are most likely to be a result of this frustration when Barry is tired.

If you take the time to record *when* Barry is having his tantrums, you will find they occur at the time of the day when he is most fatigued or distressed. His tolerance is low. The same refusals handled earlier in the day will result in a tantrum just before dinner, for example. If you examine your own behavior, you may discover a similar pattern. Think about how you react to a disheveled, toy-strewn living room in the morning when you are refreshed as opposed to when you arrive home after an exhausting day of work.

The bicycle you maneuvered skillfully earlier in the day is now a major obstacle.

Fatigue is not the only factor that contributes to tantrumming. Sometimes a specific circumstance will bring it on. Children, like adults, find specific situations more difficult than others. Barry likes to sit in his red chair at dinner. He doesn't want his sister Lois sitting there. One night Lois chooses to sit in Barry's red chair. Well, that just drives Barry crazy! Lo and behold! We have a tantrum. Now, sitting in the red chair may seem pretty ridiculous. But it is not ridiculous to Barry. Remember that all child behavior is meaningful.

Let's examine adult behavior again. Each one of us has a host of idiosyncratic behaviors. This is not to say that everyone is neurotic. Yet individualized behavior is what makes each one of us uniquely human. We must sleep on the left side of the bed. We wear only cotton socks. We must have a window open. We can't leave dishes in the sink. All of these behaviors seem perfectly reasonable to the adult who has them. They also seem perfectly unreasonable to the adult who doesn't.

In order for adults to be accepting of one another, they must be mutually accepting of each other's idiosyncratic behaviors. If an adult chooses to violate one of these behaviors and purchase wool socks for the cotton-sock-wearing person, the cotton-sock-lover may become very distressed and angry at the purchaser. Certainly, this incident seems trivial, yet it is exactly this type of argument that causes difficulties in most marriages, and in almost any adult partnership. This argument is not about socks, and Barry isn't really upset about red chairs. This kind of frustration stems from the issue of acceptance. Barry's implicit message to his family is this: "These little things make me happy and comfortable in the world. When you don't give me these little things, how can you really care about *me*?"

Barry certainly isn't conscious of his need to have these specific desires met. Many adults aren't aware of these issues either. Barry's feeling is much more primitive: "I want that red chair! Why aren't you giving it to me? If you don't give it to me, I'll have a fit—until you do!"

Now, of course, in situations like this, Lois will inevitably want a red chair, too. So, you may have to buy a few more red chairs.

My point is that children should be allowed their own peculiarities, within reason. No one can have absolutely everything she wants. But as members of the human race, we are all entitled to a few little quirks. If Barry wants to wear a Batman T-shirt to bed each night, make sure you have a good supply. If he wants to keep a box of Nabisco Honey Grahams on the *bottom* shelf of the refrigerator, so be it. Permit Barry a few consistent indulgences and he won't *demand* many. He will be happy and comfortable with those he has—and you will see less tantrumming.

To prevent tantrums:

1. Provide many outlets for Barry to express his feelings.
2. Set reasonable expectations for him.
3. Observe Barry carefully. When he appears frustrated, step in and begin problem solving with him. Do only enough for him to gain skill and to become self-sufficient.

When a tantrum occurs:

1. Ignore Barry except to ensure his physical safety. Giving any attention generally results in an increase in the number of tantrums because you are reinforcing Barry's behavior.

2. If Barry is causing a disruption, move him to a quiet place away from other people. Let Barry know that although it is OK for him to be frustrated, it is not OK for him to disturb other people.

3. Watch Barry to observe when his tantrums occur. Make adjustments in Barry's schedule so he feels more comfortable, for example, have a nutritious snack available for him and read him a favorite story immediately after school. If you can help it, don't rush off to do food shopping or to the dentist at Barry's difficult time of day. Remember, you can manage changes in your schedule far easier than can Barry.

4. Help Barry find a way to calm himself down without resorting to tantrumming. It is important for him to make his own contributions to this end, but you can certainly make some standard "calming" suggestions: looking at favorite books, listening to quiet music, or watching a video.

5. When Barry is quiet, sit with him and try to determine how he can deal with the problems that make him angry and frustrated. For example, if Lois wants to sit in his red chair, how might he ask

her to have his chair returned? Help him practice words and actions to get his needs met without having to resort to tantrumming.

Please note that if Barry has repeated temper tantrums and is beyond three-and-a-half years old, there is a chance that he may be developmentally or language delayed, or under a great deal of emotional stress. In any case, he may need professional help. Remember that temper tantrums may also be the result of Barry's inability to express his thoughts or feelings. A child like this can be terribly frustrated.

Aggressive Behavior

I'm waiting outside to pick Tommie up after his softball game. Right in front of me, he goes over to this other kid and smacks him. Of course, this kid's mother is standing right next to me. She doesn't know who to yell at, Tommie or me! There I am. I can't move. I simply can't believe it!

Aggression is perhaps the greatest behavior concern of parents. Although adults can rationalize many actions, aggression, except in instances of life and death, does not seem to be one of them. Physically aggressive behavior is dangerous and emotionally demeaning. Physical aggression is the child's plea for power. Although aggressive people may seem powerful, in fact they feel very powerless.

To prevent problems:

1. Let Carrie find what the alternatives to *aggressive* power feel like. Give her special responsibilities at home. Let her be a *leader,* instead of an aggressor.
2. Role-play. Stage scenarios with other family members to give Carrie an idea of what acceptable and unacceptable behavior are, for example, "If Tony grabs your toy (and it is not acceptable to hit him), what could you do, Carrie?"
3. Give clear directions: "Carrie, you must tell other children what you want. If they won't listen to you, then you must ask an adult for help."

Remember that the redirection of physically aggressive behavior is best accomplished when Carrie is young. As Carrie learns to use words to make her needs known, she will be less likely to use aggressive action.

The useful parental responses to diminish profanity are very similar to the ones useful in diminishing aggression:

1. Teach the appropriate behavior. Help Eric use alternative phrases: "I'm angry"; "I'm frustrated"; "I'm hurt"; "I'm embarrassed." There are acceptable ways to discuss negative feelings without resorting to profanity.
2. When Eric does use appropriate phrases, talk to him about it, for example, "I heard you *tell* Danny you were angry. What happened? Do you think this worked well." Remind him that you appreciate his using these words because they let others know how he is feeling yet don't hurt other people.

TV and Video Obsession

No wonder kids can't listen! Did you ever walk into the typical home with two, three, kids and two, three, four television sets? Sometimes, it's not even the kids! The parents are so absorbed in the TV, you can't talk to them. There are fifty channels on the cable. Dad is flipping vigorously through these, two or three remote controls directly in front of him. And these parents are concerned about the amount of television their children are watching. Who are they kidding?

Again, the problem here, as discussed in the previous chapter is not the actual television watching. The problem is limiting television watching, counteracting of the sometimes counterproductive messages that television promotes, and helping children understand what they see. Here are a few suggestions:

1. Share at least some of Paula's television viewing with her. Watch her favorite shows and videos to gain insight into their appeal.
2. Limit viewing by creating alternatives. If Paula's week is filled without overscheduling, friends, homework, after-school activities, lessons, it should logically follow that there will not be many empty hours for her to fill.

3. Be an example. Try to demonstrate through your own selectivity that television viewing is not automatic. If the television in your house is almost always on, the message that there are options to viewing is not communicated to Paula. Paula should see you reading, exercising, engaged in conversation, and listening to music. If your leisure time is spent productively, the message communicated is that television is an option for leisure time, but not the only or even the most desired one.

4. Limit your purchase of mass-produced TV-character figures and assorted paraphernalia. These toys may create a need for unwarranted television watching. Create alternative outlets for dramatic play, using generic items such as fire hats, hospital supplies, briefcases, and costume jewelry. Have your children act out their fantasies using more creative items than those that are commercially produced.

5. When you watch television with Paula, ask thought-provoking questions: "Is that reasonable?" "Do people really act that way?" "How do people act?" "What would you do if . . . ?" In this way, television can be used for probing and problem-solving. Often discussions not normally initiated during ordinary conversation emerge during a television program.

Lying

I would put Chris's cereal in front of him, and then I would go in to do my hair. I would come out of the bathroom. The cereal would be gone. Later I would find the cereal in the garbage. Chris insisted he loved this cereal. He cried when I offered to buy something else.

As discussed in chapter 10, all children lie occasionally. Most lying is innocent, not maliciously intended. Even so, parents must take steps to ensure their children's understanding of the importance of telling the truth in the appropriate contexts. Here are a few suggestions:

1. Whenever the opportunity arises, help Linda learn the differences between reality and fantasy, asking, for example, "Are monsters real, Linda?" Explain that many people create monsters in

their minds—just as Linda does. These monster makers draw monsters, write stories about them, and make movies. It would be very exciting if monsters were real, and very scary! But monsters are all make-believe.

2. Don't put Linda in a situation where she feels she must lie. For example, rather than asking, "Linda, did you leave your toys in the living room?" say "Linda, could you help me find out how all these toys got into the living room? Why don't we start picking them up together while you tell me about this?" Help Linda to learn effective problem solving rather than to feel she needs to protect herself by lying. Create consequences only when Linda's lying persists after several problem-solving sessions.

3. As always, self-esteem is the key. Help Linda toward responsible behavior by offering your assistance and praise while she is learning new skills. For example, help Linda prepare her schoolwork, clean her room, and finish her chores adequately. Leave her on her own only when she feels comfortable and capable. Don't expect Linda to handle responsibilities until she is ready. If you do, you may find Linda lying to escape consequences.

4. Be attentive. Lying may be an attention-getting behavior. Make certain Linda gets the much-deserved attention she needs and craves.

When Linda does lie:

1. Realize that young children are especially apt to tell stories of the tall-tale variety. Linda may make up an outlandish story about another child and insist that it's true. If Linda's lying falls into this category, support her imagination. After all, she finds this kind of mental stimulation fulfilling, and if this talent is channeled correctly, it will be a tremendous source of self-esteem. Rather than asking if the story is true (this may place Linda in the position of having to lie), tell her, "Gee, Linda what a great story. I'd love to be able to tell one like that!" In this way, Linda is given a completely positive message and is told at the same that you know her story is a construction.

2. Lying compulsively, is usually a sign that a child doesn't feel good about herself. No one is perfect, yet Linda may feel she must be. She lies to hide her shortcomings. Again, help Linda reinforce

her self-image by pointing out her strengths and focusing her attention on these rather than becoming absorbed in her weaknesses.

3. If Linda lies directly to you, do *not* confront her. First, try to determine the purpose of her lie. If you can determine this purpose, the lie becomes a springboard for problem solving. Suppose Linda tells you that Joshua took her lunch money from her. You suspect otherwise. You might ask Linda, "If you lose your lunch money, Linda, what kinds of things can you do?" If you and Linda problem-solve together, Linda will not feel compelled to lie to you. She will be compelled to problem-solve.

4. If Linda lies to conceal a wrongdoing, again confrontation is not recommended. After you determine Linda's purpose for lying, talk to her. Tell her you know she is a good person. Everybody makes mistakes. There are options to lying when Linda makes a mistake. You and Linda should talk about these. If Linda knows what the options to lying are, she can choose to exercise them.

Stealing

I was cleaning Janey's room. I found a shopping bag in the back of her closet. There were pencil sharpeners and stickers, pieces of candy, all sorts of things. I couldn't imagine why she was hiding these. Yet I knew she didn't have the allowance to purchase all these little items herself, and I couldn't imagine other children giving her these things.

Children steal because they feel deprived. It is never easy for caring parents to cope with a child who is hurting in this way. Yet warm, generous intervention is absolutely necessary for Carl to give up this behavior. Carl must feel that there are options to stealing, as there are to lying. He must not feel the need to steal nor that he is a *bad* person for having stolen.

Prevention and Intervention

1. Make certain Carl's needs are being met. We may think Carl has everything, and to the outsider, he may well indeed. Often children give significance to items that parents are completely unaware of. Carl may be hoarding construction paper from school because

the last three times he's asked you for it, you've been completely absorbed in something else. Message: "Carl, you can't have construction paper." The advice given in chapter 1 still applies here: *Listen. Listen. Listen.*

2. If you catch Carl stealing, ask him calmly to put the item back: "Carl, put that money back in my purse. I need that to buy a workbook for Susie later. Is there something you need? I can get that for you also." Let Carl know that he can *ask* for what he needs.

3. If Carl desperately wants something he absolutely cannot have, talk with him about it. Explain that there are options for this desire. The two of you can then decide together what kinds of things you can substitute for that ten-speed bike, or for the fact that you have had to leave so early for work that you haven't had breakfast with him for two months.

Appendix I

Resource Information

The following organizations may be helpful in assisting you with information regarding crises intervention:

Adoptee-Birthparent Support Network   (301) 464-5755
Post Office Box 23674, L'Enfant Plaza Station, Washington, D.C. 20026

Adoptees in Search   (301) 656-8555
Bethesda, Maryland 20814

Alcoholics Anonymous World Services   (212) 686-1100
Post Office Box 459, Grand Central Station, New York, New York 10017

Alcoholism Center for Women   (213) 381-7805
11475 Alvarado Street, Los Angeles, California 90006

Amend-Network   (303) 220-1707
777 Grant Street, Suite 600, Denver, Colorado 80202

Association for Children with Learning Disabilities (*Down's Syndrome*)   (516) 221-4700
2616 Martin Avenue, Bellmore, New York 11710

Association for Children with Retarded Mental Development
(212) 741-0100
162 Fifth Avenue, 11th Floor, New York, New York 10010

Association for the Behavioral Treatment of Sexual Abusers
(503) 494-8144
Post Office Box 66028, Portland, Oregon 97266

Association for the Care of Children's Health   (301) 654-6549

7910 Woodmont Avenue, Suite 300, Bethesda, Maryland 20814

Batterers Anonymous (*Domestic Violence*) (714) 355–1100
1269 North East Street, San Bernadino, California 92405

Division of Family Psychology(c/o Alan Entin, Ph.D.) (804) 359–01019
1805 Monument Avenue, Suite 510, Richmond, Virginia 23220–7088

Division on Career Development of the Council for Exceptional Children (703) 620–3660
1920 Association Drive, Reston, Virginia 22091

Emerge—A Men's Counseling Service on Domestic Violence (617) 547–9870
18 Hurley Street, Suite 2, Cambridge, Massachusetts 02139

International Association of Counseling Services (703) 823–9840
5999 Stevenson Avenue, 3rd Floor, Alexandria, Virginia 22304

International Society for Prevention of Child Abuse and Neglect (303) 321–3963
1205 Oneida Street, Denver, Colorado 80220

National Association on Drug Abuse Problems (212) 986–1170
355 Lexington Avenue, New York, New York 10017

National Cancer Care Foundation (212) 221–3300
1180 Avenue of the Americas, New York, New York 10036

National Cancer Center (516) 349–0610
88 Sunnyside Boulevard, Plainview, New York 11803

National Center for Learning Disabilities (212) 687–7211
99 Park Avenue, 6th Floor, New York, New York 10016

National Center for Missing and Exploited Children (703) 235–3900
2101 Wilson Boulevard, Suite 550, Arlington, Virginia 22201

National Foundation for Depressive Illness (212) 620–7637
Post Office Box 2257, New York, New York 10116

National Runaway Switchboard   (800) 621–4000
3080 North Lincoln Avenue, Chicago, Illinois 10657

Siblings of Disabled Children   (408) 288–5010
535 Race Street, Suite 220, San Jose, California 95126

Stepfamily Association of America   (402) 477–7837
215 Centennial MallSouth, Suite 212, Lincoln, Nebraska 68508

Appendix II

Children's Literature

In addition to the general guidelines outlined in *Life's Little Miseries,* parents and teachers should select literature that reflects the life experiences and immediate concerns of children. Books that describe typical situations, and characters who are struggling with issues children relate to, are a source of comfort to many children. This is the major reason care must be taken in selecting good children's literature.

Self Concept

Arkin, A., *Tony's Hard Work Day*
Barrett, J., *I Hate to Take a Bath*
Bottner, B., *Messy*
Clifton, L., *The Boy Who Didn't Believe in Spring*
Cohen, M., *When Will I Read?*
Cole, B., *No More Baths*
DePaola, T., *Oliver Button Is a Sissy*
Ets, M., *Just Me*
Freeman, D., *Corduroy*
            Dandelion
Hutchins, P., *Titch*
Isadora, R., *Max*
Krasilovsky, P., *The Shy Little Girl*
Kraus, Robert, *Leo, the Late Bloomer*
            The Littlest Rabbit
            Owliver
Kraus, Ruth, *The Carrot Seed*

First Experiences

Alexander, M., *I'll Protect You from the Jungle Beasts*
            Sabrina

Anderson, K., *What's the Matter, Sylvie, Can't You Ride?*
Bate, L., *Little Rabbit's Loose Tooth*
Bright, R., *Georgie and the Noisy Ghost*
Brown, M.W., *The Runaway Bunny*
Cohen, M., *Tough Jim*
         Lost in the Museum
Crary, E., *I'm Lost*
         Mommy Don't Go
Degroat, D., *Alligator's Toothache*
Delaney, N., *Two Strikes Four Eyes*
Fisher, A., *My Mother and I*
Jensen, V., *Sara and the Door*
Kraus, R., *The Bundle Book*
Ungerer, T., *The Three Robbers*
Waber, B., *Ira Sleeps Over*
Watanabe, S., *How Do I Put It On?*
Whitney, A., *Leave Herbert Alone*

Starting/Going to School

Berenstain, S., *Berenstain Bears Go to School*
Bram, E., *I Don't Want to Go to School*
Breinburg, P., *Shawn Goes to School*
Chapman, C., *Herbie's Troubles*
Cohen, M., *First Grade Takes a Test*
         The New Teacher
         Will I Have a Friend?
Hurd, E., *Come with Me to Nursery School*
Kantrowitz, M., *Willie Bear*
Reif, P., *The First Day of School*
Stanek, M., *Starting School*
Wolde, G., *Betsey's First Day at Nursery School*

Bedtime/Nightime

Bother, B., *There Was Nobody There*
Brown, M., *Goodnight Moon*
Ginsburg, M., *The Sun's Asleep Behind the Hill*
Hoban, R., *Bedtime for Frances*
Jewell, N., *Calf, Goodnight*

Johnston, J., *Edie Changes Her Mind*
Ormerod, J., *Moonlight*
Steverson, J., *We Can't Sleep*
Zemach, H., *Mommy Buy Me a China Doll*

Fears/Nightmares

Babbit, N., *Something*
Buckley, H., *Michael is Brave*
Crowe, R., *Clyde Monster*
Dragonwagon, C., *Will It Be Okay?*
Mayer, M., *There's a Nightmare in My Closet*
Sendak, M., *Where the Wild Things Are*
Zolotow, C., *The Storm Book*

Hospitalization/Illness

Bemelmans, L., *Madeline*
Brandenberg, F., *I Wish I Was Sick Too*
Collier, J., *Danny Goes to the Hospital*
DePaola, J., *Now One Foot, Now the Other*
Mack, N., *Tracy*
Marino, B., *Eric Needs Stitches*
Reit, S., *Jenny's in the Hospital*
Rey, H. & M., *Curious George Goes to the Hospital*
Rockwell, R., *My Doctor*
　　　　　　 My Dentist
Rockwell, R. & A., *The Emergency Room*
Sharmat, M., *I Want Mama*
Stein, S., *A Hospital Story*
Vigna, J., *Gregory's Stitches*
Whitney, A., *Just Awful*

Brothers and Sisters

Alexander, M., *I'll Be the Horse If You'll Play with Me*
Hazen, B., *Why Couldn't I Be an Only Kid Like You, Tigger?*
Kellog, S., *Much Bigger than Martin*
Lasker, J., *He's My Brother*
Pearson, S., *Mommie Hates Lydia*

Viorst, J., *I'll Fix Anthony*
Zolotow, C., *Big Sister and Little Sister*
        Big Brother
        If It Weren't for You

New Baby

Alexander, M., *Nobody Asked Me if I Wanted a Baby Sister*
Greenfield E., *She Come Bringing Me That Little Baby Girl*
Hoban, R., *A Baby Sister for Frances*
Keats, E.J., *Peter's Chair*
Lindgren, A., *I Want a Brother or a Sister*
Relf, P., *That New Baby*
Scott, A., *On Mother's Lap*
Winthrop, E., *I Think He Likes Me*

Adoption

Caines, J., *Abby*
Lapsley, S., *I Am Adopted*
Wasson, V., *The Chosen Baby*

Love/Cooperation

Cohen, M., *Be My Valentine*
Ets, M., *Play with Me*
Flack, M., *Ask Mr Bear*
Keats, E., *A Letter to Amy*
Leodhas, S., *Always Room for One More*
Minarik, E., *The Little Bear*
Schenk de Regniers, B., *May I Bring a Friend?*
Silberstein, S., *The Giving Tree*
Ward, L., *The Biggest Bear*
Zinael, P., *I Love My Mother*
Zolotow, C., *Hold My Hand*

Friendship

Anglund, J., *A Friend Is Someone Who Likes You*
Beim, L., *Two Is a Team*
Burningham, J., *The Friend*

Carle, E., *Do You Want to Be My Friend?*
Charlip, R., *Harlequin and the Gift of Many Colors*
Cohen, M., *Best Friends*
Delaney, N., *Bert and Barney*
Delton, J., *Two Good Friends*
Flack, M., *Angus and the Cat*
Hogan, R., *Best Friends for Frances*
Hoff, S., *Lengthy*
Kafka, S., *I Need a Friend*
Kellogg, S., *Can I Keep Him?*
Mannheim, G., *The Two Friends*
Sharmat, M., *I'm Not Oscar's Friend Anymore*
Sherman, I., *I Do Not Like It When My Friend Comes to Visit*
Sloboklkin, L., *One Is Good, But Two Are Better*
Snyder, Z., *Come On, Patsy*
Steig, W., *Amos and Boris*
Turkle, B., *Thy Friend, Obadiah*
Wells, R., *Benjamin and Tulip*
Zolotow, C., *My Friend John*
               New Friend

Anger/Jealousy

Bennett, R. & Preston, E., *The Temper Tantrum Book*
Hitte, K., *Boy Was I Mad*
Minarik, E., *No Fighting, No Biting*
Simon, N., *I Was So Mad*
Terris, S., *Amanda the Panda*
               The Redhead
Udry, J., *Let's Be Enemies*
Viorst, J., *Alexander and the Terrible, Horrible, No Good, Very Bad Day*
Waber, B., *But Names Will Never Hurt Me*
Wells, R., *Noisy Nora*
Zolotow, C., *The Hating Book*
               It's Not Fair
               The Quarreling Book
               The Unfriendly Book

Moving

Berenstain, S., *Berenstain Bear's Moving Day*
Hickman, M., *I'm Moving*
               My Friend William Moved Away
Hughes, S., *Moving Molly*
Jones, P., *I'm Not Moving*
Sharmat, M., *Gila Monsters Meet You At the Airport*
Tobias, T., *Moving Day*
Zolotow, C., *Janey*

Divorce/Separation/Single Parents

Adams, F., *Mushy Eggs*
Badgehala, B., *Daddy Doesn't Live Here Anymore*
Caines, J., *Daddy*
Clifton, L., *Everett Anderson's Year*
             Some of the Days of Everett Anderson
Goff, B., *Where Is Daddy?*
Hazen, B., *Two Homes to Live In*
Kindred, W., *Lucky Wilma*
Lexau, J., *Benjie*
            Emily and the Klunky Baby
            The Next Door Dog
Lindsay, J., *Do I Have a Daddy?*
Mann, P., *My Dad Lives in a Downtown Hotel*
Perry, P., & Lynch, M., *Mommy and Daddy Are Divorced*
Schuchman, J., *Two Places to Sleep*
Simon, N., *All Kinds of Families*
Steptoe, J., *My Special Best Words*
Vigna, J., *She's Not My Real Mother*
Zolotow, C., *A Father Like That*

Grandparents/Old Age

Aliki, *The Two of Them*
Borack, B., *Grandpa*
Brandenburg, F., *A Secret for Grandmother's Birthday*
Buckley, H., *Grandfather and I*
            Grandmother and I

Burningham, J., *Grandpa*
DePaolo, T., *Watch Out for the Chicken Feet in Your Soup.*
Douglass, B., *Good As New*
Flourney, V., *The Patchwork Quilt*
Gauch, P., *Grandpa and Me*
Goldman, S., *Grandma is Someone Special*
Hein, L., *My Very Special Friend*
Henkes, K., *Grandpa and Bo*
Kirk, B., *Grandpa, Me and Our House in the Tree*
Skorpen, L., *Mandy's Grandmother*
Sonneborn, R., *I Love Gran*
Udry, J., *Mary Jo's Grandmother*
Williams, B., *Kevin's Grandma*

Death

Abbott, S., *The Old Dog*
Alike, *Go Tell Aunt Rhody*
Bartoli, J., *Nonna*
Brown, M., *The Dead Bird*
Carrick, C., *The Accident*
Clifton, L., *Everett Anderson's Goodbye*
DePaolo, T., *Nana Upstairs and Nana Downstairs*
Fassler, J., *My Grandpa Died Today*
Freschet, B., *The Old Bullfrog*
Hurd, E., *The Black Dog Who Went into the Woods*
Kantrowitz, M., *When Violet Died*
Stein, S., *About Dying: An Open Family Book for Parents and Children Together*
Tresselt, A., *The Dead Tree*
Viorst, J., *The Tenth Good Thing About Barney*
Wilhelm, H., *I'll Always Love You*
Zolotow, C., *My Grandson Lew*

Handicaps

Clifton, L., *My Friend Janet*
Cohen, M., *See You Tomorrow, Charles*
Fassler, J., *The Boy with the Problem*
            Don't Worry Dear

Howie Helps Himself
One Little Girl
Keats, E.J., *Apt. 3*
Larsen, H., *Don't Forget Tom*
Lasker, J., *He's My Brother*
Levine, E., *Lisa and Her Soundless World*
Peterson, J.W., *I Have a Sister, My Sister is Deaf*
Rosenberg, M., *My Friend Leslie*
Shelley, J. & Cairo, T., *Our Brother Had Down's Syndrome*
Stein, S., *About Handicaps*
White, P., *Janet at School*
Wolf, B., *Anna's Silent World*
Don't Feel Sorry for Paul

Multicultural

Aardema, V., *Why Mosquitoes Buzz in People's Ears*
Baylor, B., *When Clay Sings*
Hawk, I'm Your Brother
They Put on Masks
Bishop, C., *The Five Chinese Brothers*
Breinburg, P., *Doctor Shawn*
Brenner, B., *Barto Takes the Subway*
Ets, M., *Gilberto and the Wind*
Nine Days to Christmas
Feelings, M., *Jambo Means Hello*
Moja Means One
Flack, M., *The Story About Ping*
Gray, G., *Send Wendell*
Greenberg, P., *Lord, I Wish I Was a Buzzard*
Keats, E.J., *Goggles*
My Dog Is Lost
The Snowy Day
Whistle for Willie
Politi, L., *Song of the Swallows*
Three Stalks of Corn
Scott, A., *Sam*
Sonneborn, R., *Friday Night Is Papa Night*
Surat, M., *Angel Child*
Dragon Child

Uchida, Y., *The Rooster Who Understood Japanese*
Udry, J., *What Mary Jo Shared*
Zemach, M., *It Could Always Be Worse*

Nonsexist

Alexander, M., *I'll Protect You From the Jungle Beasts*
Burton, V., *Katy and the Big Snow*
 Mike Mulligan and the Steam Shovel
Byers, B., *Go and Hush the Baby*
Kellogg, S., *Can I Keep Him?*
Lasker, J., *Mothers Can Do Anything*
McCloskey, R., *One Morning In Maine*
 Blueberries for Sal
Rothman, J., *I Can Be Anything You Can Be*
Segal, L., *Tell Me a Mitzi*
Zolotow, C., *William's Doll*

Miscellaneous

Alexander, M., *And My Mean Old Mother Will Be Sorry, Blackboard Bear* (Running Away)
Blaine, M., *The Terrible Thing That Happened at Our House* (Working Mothers)
Boyd, S., *The How* (Embarrassment)
Delton, J., *My Mother Lost Her Job Today*
Dickinson, M., *Alex's Bed* (Messiness)
Gackenback, D., *Binky Gets a Car* (Responsibility)
 Claude and Pepper (Running Away)
Hazen, B., *Very Shy*
Merriam, E., *Mommies At Work*
Ness, F., *Sam, Bangs, and Moonshine* (Honesty)
Sharmat, M., *A Big, Fat, Enormous Lie* (Honesty)
 Say Hello, Vanessa (Shyness)
Wells, R., *Unfortunately, Harriet* (Running Away)

This list is intended as a sampling of good children's books. There are many others. Parents and teachers should select those titles which best reflect the interests and concerns of their children.

Selected Bibliography

Ainsworth, M. X. (1989). Attachments beyond infancy. *American Psychologist, 44*(4), 709–716.

Alger, H. A. (1984). Transitions: Alternatives to manipulative management. *Young Children, 39*(6), 16–25.

Allen, J. P. (1989). Social impact of age mixing and age segregation in school: A context sensitive investigation. *Journal of Educational Psychology, 81*(3), 408–416.

Ames, C. (1984). Competitive, cooperative, and individualistic goal structures: A cognitive motivational analysis. In R. James & C. Ames (Eds.), *Student motivation.* New York: Academic Press.

Ames, R., & Ames, C. (1984). *Student motivation.* New York: Academic Press.

Anderson, E. (1984). *Self-esteem for tots to teens.* Deephaven, MN: Meadowbrook.

Anderson, H. (1949). Teaching the art of listening. *School Review, 57,* 63–67.

Anderson, S. M., & Pnawat, R. S. (1983). Responsibility in the classroom: A synthesis of research on teaching self control. *Educational Leadership, 40*(7), 62–66.

Armstrong, T. (1987). *In their own way.* Los Angeles: J. P. Taucher.

Bagley, M. T., & Hess, K. K. (1982). *200 ways of using imagery in the classroom.* Woodcliff Lake: NJ: New Dimensions of the 80's.

Bank, S. P. (1987). Favoritism. *Journal of Children in Contemporary Society, 19*(3), 3–4.

Bar-Tal, D., Kfir, D., Bar-Zonar, Y., & Chem, M. (1980). The relationship between locus of control and academic achievement, anxiety, and level of aspiration. *British Journal of Educational Psychology, 50,* 53–60.

Basch, M. F. (1983). Empathetic understanding: a review of the concept and some theoretical considerations. *Journal of the American Psychoanalytic Association, 31*(1), 101–126.

Bedell, S. (1982). Junior knows best: TV's view of children today. *New York Times,* September 19.

Berndt, T. J., et al. (1988). Friends' and classmates' interactions on academic tasks. *Journal of Educational Psychology, 80*(4), 506–513.

Berne, P., & Savary, L. (1981). *Building self-esteem in children.* New York: Continuum Publishing.

Bloom, B. (1982). The role of gifts and markers in the development of talent. *Exceptional Children, 48*(6), 510–522.

Borg, M. G., & Falzon, J. M. (1990). Teachers' perception of primary school children's undesirable behaviors: The effects of teaching experience, pupil's age, sex and ability stream. *British Journal of Educational Psychology, 60,* 220–226.

Borman, K. M. (1982). *The social life of children in a changing society.* Hillsdale, NJ: Erlbaum.

Bowlby, J. (1973). *Attachment and loss: Vol. 2. Separation anxiety and anger.* New York: Basic Books.

Briggs, D. C. (1975). *Your child's self-esteem.* New York: Doubleday.

Brody, G. H., & Stoneman, Z. (1987). Sibling conflict: Contributions of the siblings themselves, the parent-sibling relationship, and the broader family system. *Journal of Children in Contemporary Society, 19*(3–4), 39–53.

Bruner, J. S. (1985). *Child's talk: Learning to use language.* New York: Norton.

Bryant, B. K., & Litman, C. (1987). Siblings as teachers and therapists. *Journal of Children in Contemporary Society, 19*(3–4), 185–205.

Butler, R., & Kedar, A. (1990). Effects of intergroup competition and school philosophy on student perceptions, group processes, and performance. *Contemporary Educational Psychology, 15*(4), 301–318.

Buzan, T. (1983). *Use both sides of your brain.* New York: Dutton.

Carey, S. (1987). *Conceptual change in childhood.* Cambridge, MA: MIT Press.

Carrier, C. A., & Williams, M. D. (1988). A test of one learner control strategy with students of differing levels of task persistence. *American Educational Research Journal, 25*(2), 285–306.

Cherry, E. (1983). *Please don't sit on the kids: Alternatives to punitive discipline.* Belmont, CA: David S. Lake.

Clemes, H., & Bean, R. (1980). *How to teach responsibility to children.* San Jose, CA: Enrich.

Cooper, D. H., & Farran, D. C. (1988). Behavioral risk factors in kindergarten. *Early Childhood Research Quarterly, 3*(1), 1–19.

Doris, J. et al. (1971). *Separation anxiety in preschool children.* Paper presented at the 79th Annual Convention of the American Psychological Association, Washington D.C., 9:3–7.

Dunn, J., & Kendrick, C. (1982). *Siblings: Love, envy and understanding.* Cambridge: Harvard University Press.

Ephron, D. (1981). *Teenage romance.* New York: Ballantine.

Erickson, A. (1985). Listening leads to reading. *Reading Today, 2,* 13–15.

Field, T. (1984). Separation stress of young children transferring to new schools. *Developmental Psychology, 20*(5), 786–792.

Flavell, J. H. (1985). *Cognitive development.* Englewood Cliffs, NJ: Prentice-Hall.

Ford, M. (1989). Student's perceptions of affective issues impacting the social emotional development and school performance of gifted/talented youngsters. *Roeper Review, 11*(3), 131–134.

Freud, A. (1966). *Writings of Anna Freud:* Vol. 6. *Normality and Pathology in Childhood: Assessments and Development* New York: International Universities Press.

Freud, S. (1962). *Three essays on the theory of sexuality.* New York: Basic Books.

Gardner, H. (1983). *Frames of mind.* New York: Basic Books.

Garofolo, J., et al. (1989). Some observations of seventh graders solving problems. *Arithmetic Teacher, 37*(2), 20–21.

Gatto, J. T. (1990). True knowledge, true education. *The Christian Science Monitor,* September 10.

Gilligan C. (1982). *In a different voice.* Cambridge: Harvard University Press.

Gittelman-Klein, R. (1985). Childhood anxiety disorders: Correlates and outcomes. In *Anxiety disorders of childhood.* New York: Guilford Press.

Goldberg, P. (1983). *The intuitive edge.* Los Angeles: J. P. Tarcher.

Gordon, J. (1988). Separation anxiety how to ask a family to leave your center. *Child Care Information Exchange, 59,* 13–15.

Harris, T. (1969). *I'm OK, You're OK.* New York: Harper & Row.

Hart, L. (1983). *Human brain and human learning.* New York: Longman.

Hatch, J. A. (1989). Alone in a crowd: Analysis of secondary adjustments in a kindergarten. *Early Child Development and Care, 44,* 39–49.

Hess, A. (1981). *Teenage sexuality.* New York: Ballantine.

Hignett, W. F. (1988). Infant-toddler day care: yes: but we'd better make it good. *Young Children, 44*(1), 32–33.

Holt, J. (1964). *How children fail.* New York: Dell.

Howes, C. (1990). Can the age of entry into child care and the quality of child care predict adjustment in kindergarten? *Developmental Psychology, 26*(2), 292–303.

Jones, G. P., & Dembo, M. H. (1989). Age and sex role differences in intimate friendships during childhood and adolescence. *Merrill-Palmer Quarterly, 35*(4), 445–462.

Kagan, D. M. (1988). Divergent thinking and social cognition among fifth and sixth graders. *Early Child Development and Care, 37,* 133–146.

Kagan, J. (1986). *Nature of the child.* New York: Basic Books.

Katchadourian, H. (1977). *The biology of adolescence.* San Francisco: Freeman.

Keeshan, R. (1989). *Captain Kangaroo tells yesterday's children how to nurture their own.* New York: Doubleday.

Keller, M., & Wood, P. (1989). Development of friendship reasoning: A study of interindividual differences in intraindividual change. *Developmental Psychology, 25*(5), 820–826.

Kleckner, K. A., & Engel, R. E. (1988). A child begins school: Relieving anxiety with books. *Young Children, 43*(5), 14–18.

Knoblach, R., & Chambliss, C. (1989). Teenagers whose moms worked: Did it make a difference? Paper presented at the Annual Eastern Symposium on Building Family Strengths. (3rd, University Park, PA, March 23–25, 1987).

Ladd, G. W., & Price, J. M. (1987). Predicting children's social and school adjustment following the transition from preschool to kindergarten. *Child Development, 58*(5), 1168–1189.

Laing, R. D. (1972). *Knots.* New York: Pantheon Books.

Lay-Dopyera, M., & Dopyera, J. (1990). *Becoming a teacher of young children.* New York: McGraw-Hill.

Levy, J. (1980). Cerebral asymmetry and the psychology of man. In M. Wittrock (Ed.), *The brain and psychology.* New York: Harper & Row.

Lossis, S. P. (1990). Effects of maternal behavior on toddler behavior during separation. *Child Development, 61*(1), 99–103.

Matthews, D. B., & Burnett, D. D. (1989). Anxiety: An achievement component. *Journal of Humanistic Education and Development, 27*(3), 122–131.

McBride, S. L. (1990). Maternal moderators of child care: the role of maternal separation anxiety. *New Directions for Child Development, 49,* 53–70.

Meisel, C. J., & Blumberg, C. J. (1990). The social comparison choices of elementary and secondary school students: The influence of gender, race, and friendship. *Contemporary Educational Psychology, 15*(2), 170–182.

Miller, G. P., & Oskam, B. O. (1984). *Teaching your child to make decisions.* New York: Harper & Row.

Myers-Walls, J. A., & Fry-Miller, K. M. (1984). Helping children overcome fears. *Young Children, 39*(4), 27–32.

Norman, J., & Harris, M. (1981). *The private life of the American teenager.* New York: Rawson Wade.

Ollendick, T. H. (1985). Fears in children and adolescents: normative data. *Behavioral Research Therapy, 23*(4), 405–407.

Park, A. K., & Waters, E. (1989). Security of attachment and preschool friendships. *Child Development, 60,* 1076–1081.

Piaget, J. (1952). *The Origins of Intelligence in Children.* New York: International Universities Press.

Postman, N. (1981). *The disappearance of childhood.* New York: Delacorte.

Purkey, W. W. (1970). *Self concept and school achievement.* Englewood, NJ: Prentice-Hall.

Ravitch, D. (1983). *The troubled crusade.* New York: Basic Books.

Richardson, R. A., et al. (1986). Parent-child relationships in early adolescence: Effects of family structure. *Journal of Marriage and the Family. 48*(4), 805.

Rogers, C. (1980). *A way of being.* Boston: Houghton-Mifflin.

Rogers, D. L., & Ross, D. D. (1986). Encouraging positive social interaction among young children. *Young Children, 41*(3), 12–17.

Rosenberg, E. (1985). *Getting closer: Discover and understand your child's secret feelings about growing up.* New York: Berkley.

Ross, C. (1988). *How to really know your child.* Wheaton, IL: Victor Books.

Rotenberg, K. J., et. al. (1989). Children's use of a verbal-nonverbal consistency principle to infer truth and lying. *Child Development, 60*(2), 309–322.

Sabato, G. (1989). Cooperation and competition unleash creative potential. *Social Studies Review, 28*(3), 103–109.

Samuels, S. C. (1977). *Enhancing self-concept in early childhood. New York: Human Sciences Press.*

Segal, M., & Adcock, D. (1981). *Feelings.* Atlanta: Humanics Limited.

Slough, N. M., & Greenberg, M. T. (1990). Five-year-olds' representations of separation from parents: Responses from the perspective of self and other. *New Directions for Child Development, 48,* 67–84.

Spock, B. (1988). *Dr. Spock speaks about parenting.* New York: Simon & Schuster.

Stern, D. (1985). *The interpersonal world of the infant.* New York: Basic Books.

Stewart, K. (1983). *God Made Me Special.* John's Island, SC: Happy Days Press.

Stone, C., et. al. (1989). Procedures for assessing children's social behavior: Dyadic tasks. *Moral Education Forum, 14*(1), 12–21.

Tannen, D. (1990). Gender differences in topical coherence: Creating involvement in best friends' talk. *Discourse Processes, 13*(1), 73–90.

Thorkildsen, T. A. (1988). Theories of education among academically able adolescents. *Contemporary Educational Psychology, 13*(4), 323–330.

Travick-Smith, J. (1988). Let's say you're the baby, OK? Play leadership and following behavior in young children. *Young Children, 43*(5), 51–59.

Trelease, J. (1979). *The Read-Aloud Handbook.* New York: Penguin Books.

Tuchsherer, P. (1988). *TV interactive toys: The new high tech threat to children.* Bend, OR: Pinaroo Publishing.

Vough, S., & Lancelotta, G. X. (1990). Teaching interpersonal skills to poorly accepted students: Peer pairing versus non-peer pairing. *Journal of School Psychology, 28*(3), 181–188.

Webb, P. K. (1988). *The emerging child.* New York: Macmillan.

Wigfield, A. (1988). Children's attributions for success and failure: Effects of age and attentional focus. *Journal of Educational Psychology, 80*(1), 76–81.

Wilkerson, R. M., & White, K. P. (1988). Effects of the 4MAT system of instruction on students' achievement, retention, and attitudes. *Elementary School Journal, 88*(4), 357–368.

Winfield, E. T. (1989). Books that focus on family. *PTA Today, 14*(5), 16–17.

Wolman, B. (1978). *Children's fears.* New York: Grosset & Dunlap.

Yamamoto, K. (1971). *The child and his image.* Boston: Houghton Mifflin.

Ziegler, P. (1985). Saying goodbye to preschool. *Young Children, 40*(3), 11–15.

Acknowledgments

*It is not often that someone comes along
who is a true friend and a good writer.*

E. B. White, *Charlotte's Web*

Of all the books I have written during the past ten years, *Life's Little Miseries,* represents the longest and most expansive journey for me, literally and figuratively. I planted seeds for thought in the hearts of many generous people. Some gave their intellect; some their time; some their support. All gave themselves. Thanks are due to Skye and Jared, my children, for their unending joy; to Drs. Zarif Bacilious, Christine Radziewicz, William Sanders, and Ellenmorris Tiegerman, my colleagues and friends; to Margaret Zusky and Sarah Zobel, my editors, for their sincere encouragement; to Jacqueline Ilardi and Janet Tammero, for their concerned effort in typing the original manuscript; to Eileen Infurna, Lissette Mesiano, Sheila Moran, and Christine Russo, my graduate assistants, for their research; to Dr. Stephen Cavallo, Elaine Cohen, Amy Feldman, Sherry Gaines, Tanya Linzalone, Virginia Rizzo, Bonnie Soman, Joyce Steinmetz, and Kathleen Theo, my staff at the School for Language Evaluation and Treatment Center, for their patience; to Grandmas Mary and Frances and Grandpas Jim and Joe, just for being there; and to the countless parents who answered my litany of questions and, as a result, helped me to gain insights other than my own about the realities of contemporary parenthood.
Thank you all very, very much.

—Dr. Di

Index

About the Author

Diane Lynch-Fraser, Ed.D., is assistant professor of child development at Saint John's University, Jamaica, New York, and assistant director of the School for Language and Communication Development, North Bellmore, New York. In addition, she is a consultant to the New York City Board of Education, and a frequent lecturer, television guest, and contributor to parenting magazines. Dr. Lynch-Fraser received her doctorate from Columbia University, where she specialized in Early Childhood Education, and also holds New York State Teaching Certificates in Early Childhood N-6, Special Education, and Supervision and Administration. She is the author of six previous books, including *Playdancing: Discovering and Developing Creativity in Young Children, Baby Signals: How Understanding the Language of Babies Can Make You a Better Parent*, and *Danceplay: Creative Movement for Very Young Children*. Dr. Lynch-Fraser lives in Manhattan with her husband and two children.